A WOMAN UNKNOWN

A
WOMAN
UNKNOWN

Voices from a Spanish Life

Lucia Graves

COUNTERPOINT
WASHINGTON, D.C.

First U.S. edition published in 2000 by Counterpoint

First published in Great Britain in 1999 by Virago Press,
a division of Little, Brown and Company UK

Grateful acknowledgement is made to the following publishers for permission to
reprint copyrighted material: Flamingo, an imprint of HarperCollins Publishers
UK, for lines from 'The Betrayal', by Brian Patten, from his book *Armada* (copyright © 1996 by Brian Patten); Carcanet Press Ltd, for lines from 'Instructions
to the Orphic Adept' and 'To Lucia at Birth', by Robert Graves, from his
Complete Poems Volume 2, edited by Beryl Graves and Dunstan Ward (copyright ©
1997 by the Trustees of the Robert Graves Copyright Trust); Hill & Wang, Inc.,
for an excerpt from *Black Sea*, by Neal Ascherson (copyright © 1995 by Neal
Ascherson), and Harcourt, Inc., for permission to reprint lines from 'East
Coker', by T. S. Eliot, from his *Four Quartets* (copyright © 1943 by T. S. Eliot,
renewed 1971 by Esme Valerie Eliot). All rights reserved.

Library of Congress Cataloging-in-Publication Data
Graves, Lucia.
A woman unknown : voices from a Spanish life / Lucia Graves.
p.   cm.
ISBN 1-58243-097-7 (acid-free paper)
1. Graves, Lucia.   2. Graves, Robert, 1895–.   3.   Spain—Biography.
4. Spain—Social life and customs.   I. Title.

CT1358.G69 A3 2000
946.08'082—dc21   00-055512

Printed in the United States of America on acid-free paper that meets the
American National Standards Institute Z39–48 Standard

Counterpoint
P.O. Box 65793
Washington, D.C. 20035–5793

Counterpoint is a member of the Perseus Books Group.

00 01 02 03 / 10 9 8 7 6 5 4 3 2 1

For Frank

Contents

There was so much I ought to have recorded,
So many lives that have vanished —
Families, neighbours; people whose pockets
Were worn thin by hope. They were
The loose change history spent without caring.
Now they have become the air I breathe,
Not to have marked their passing seems such a betrayal.

Brian Patten

Author's Note

The people who appear in these pages mark some of the most important encounters of my life. Many of the names have been changed for the purpose of telling this story; some, incidentally, are spelt in Spanish, others in Catalan.

London, July 1998

A WOMAN UNKNOWN

I

Arrival

26 September 1996

6.30 a.m. Daylight is filtering through the russet curtains of
the eye hospital, revealing the details of the weave: the dark
vertical lines where the threads are dense, the lighter, almost
threadbare patches and the small silky knots that have managed to escape the sharp needles of the combing machine. I
stretch out my arm to part the curtains an inch or two. The
sky is cloudless and pale, and the air seems heavy with its own
stillness. A slender black cat hurries past the lily pond, without even glancing at the dark water, the shiny lily pads or the
goldfish. It heads straight for the low, red-brick wall at the far
end of the terrace and disappears into the greenery of the
neighbouring gardens, of which only the tops of a few trees
are visible from this window. Beyond them stands a tall block
of flats – its wooden blinds still down.

I let go of the curtains and look around the room, at my
mother still asleep in the shiny metal bed; at the books, newspapers and plastic bottles of water on the black wooden shelf
that runs along the wall at the foot of my couch; at yesterday's

clothes piled on the armchair. The only decorative element is a frieze with birds, gazelles and human figures, stretching across the wall behind my mother's bed. It looks Egyptian, like the large alabaster cats in the hall, and like the hospital's logo of the Wedjat eye, an amulet used in ancient Egypt to ensure good eyesight and to avert the evil eye. You see it everywhere in this hospital, on the large doorknob of the main entrance, on the stationery, even embroidered on the pockets of the doctors' coats – a blue, almond-shaped left eye, with the Vulture-goddess Nekhbet standing on one side, her wings extended protectively, and on the other, the Serpent-goddess Wadjit.

I'm in Barcelona, however, not Cairo or Alexandria – even though the world outside the hospital seems remote and irrelevant as I lie here cocooned by the early morning silence – and I think that there is something refreshingly Catalan about this choice of a logo, this subtle way of avoiding the Catholic imagery that traditionally dominates all hospitals in Spain. It is a clever way of proclaiming the hospital's ideological independence and its policy of welcoming people from all over the world; all the more striking when one considers that the symbol dates back to 1941, the year the hospital was built, when the country was still smouldering and shaking after the Spanish Civil War, and the power of the Catholic Church – working hand in hand with the state to unify all Spaniards and eliminate any trace of independent thought – was absolute. I had almost forgotten this element of the Catalan character, this serene sense of purpose and pragmatism – they call it *seny* – that is so much a part of everything here, and the originality that often emerges from it; but since my return a few days ago I have been reminded of it again and again, just by walking through the immense Gothic nave of Santa Maria del Mar, and feeling once more the strength that emanates from the simple lines of its vaults and columns, or by watching a group of schoolchildren with their teacher drawing pictures in bold colours of the boats in the port, or by looking at the beautiful displays of fish and vegetables in the covered markets.

A wave of memories and sensations is engulfing me; things that at one time were central to my life are now slowly returning to my mind, and I can look at them, perhaps for the first time, with all the attention and appreciation they deserve. Yet when I boarded the flight at Heathrow I had felt apprehensive about returning to Barcelona. I was not sure what I would feel after an absence of five years, and as I flew over France and then the Pyrenees and finally saw the city and its semicircle of hills from the air, my anxiety increased. For five years I had been trying to put all that part of my life behind me, concentrating only on what lay ahead, like the cat crossing the terrace to jump down into the garden. I had not felt the need or the desire to return to this corner of the Mediterranean that had been my home for twenty years. Those twenty years of marriage and family life had come to an end with my divorce and belonged to the photograph albums that had been packed away in crates and stored in the attic – or so I thought.

Arrangements for my mother's eye operation in Barcelona made me put all those feelings to one side. I was the obvious person to go over and stay with her until she was well enough to return to Majorca, where she lives, and now I am glad that circumstances have forced me to come, even if the occasion is not a happy one. I know the time is right, and that by coming here with my mother, for her sake, not for mine, I have found the perfect framework from which to look back on my past. Both in the little hotel where we spent the weekend – the Hotel Suizo, on the edge of the Gothic quarter – and in this hospital, high up in Carrer Muntaner, which has been our residence for two days, I have felt invisible and anonymous, one more person in the motley crowd – and what better way to observe my old world than to do so unobserved, like the masked gatecrasher at a fancy-dress party?

I must admit that at first everything looked so different that I felt like a stranger, a tourist, even. The city had been completely transformed by the hosting of the 1992 Olympics. A new airport – all glass and indoor palm trees and luxurious marble floors – new motorways, colourful street sculptures, and a port that looks like a modern opera set. Next to the port, a brand-new seafront of pale, clean sand and the new buildings of the Olympic village, where in my time the battered warehouses stood, and the makeshift fish restaurants, and the gypsy camps, and the old railway, where Republican Catalans had been taken and shot at dawn at the end of the Spanish Civil War and the grim years that followed. All those ghosts had now disappeared, together with the rusty wagons and roofless ruins of factories. In their place there were children flying coloured kites, while their parents ambled up and down the seaside promenades, and everything seemed to look to the future, as the leaflet I had picked up at the airport unequivocally proclaimed: 'Catalonia, leader of Spain's economy' and 'New Catalonia, new visions of the future'. I had expected some changes, but never imagined they would make me feel as if I was in a completely different city. Then I remembered these two lines from a poem by Marta Pessarrodona – a poem about returning to Barcelona –

> Si retornes, no trobaràs cap petjada,
> cap racó que fossis tu, alguna vegada.

> If you return, you will find no footstep,
> no corner that once was you.

and I began to understand what she meant, because even when I walked around the centre of town, and suddenly found myself in a street that looked exactly as I remembered it – the trees in their square plots on the pavements, the little bookshop, the café on the corner and the large entrance to the car park I had so often used – I felt as if I had never been there before. The familiarity ended with the first impression, then the street took on another air and became a new place for me to discover. It soon became obvious that in these five years, while I had been away from Barcelona, the city had quite simply moved on, with that unstoppable Catalan energy, accelerated to a point of frenzy by the Olympics, and I had been left behind. Its new look influenced the atmosphere of the entire city, and when I drove out of town and into the hills on the other side of the river Llobregat, past the cement factory and the wine cellars, and arrived at the sprawling village where I had lived all those years, that too was almost unrecognisable. There were new buildings everywhere, the main road had been widened, new shops sparkled, old ones had been revamped. Only the white two-storey house that had been my home seemed unchanged as I drove past it in the early evening. But its lights were out, its life gone from it, and it stood there like an empty shell, with the lemon tree we had planted in the early seventies now towering boastfully over the garden wall – without my tending.

None of this should have taken me by surprise; I knew how enterprising Catalans could be when given the opportunity. How could I forget the excitement when it was announced that the 1992 Olympic Games would take place in Barcelona? Seconds after Mr Samaranch, himself a Catalan, had opened the white envelope in front of the television cameras, cars started hooting, flags were being waved everywhere, schools closed for the day, champagne was uncorked . . . What I was seeing now was the sequel, the work derived from all that excitement. Besides, I myself had observed profound changes during my twenty years' residence in Catalonia. With the arrival of democracy and the reinstatement of the Catalan autonomy in the late seventies, Barcelona had slowly become livelier, cleaner, more prosperous, and had absorbed social improvements faster than any other city in Spain. Later, during the eighties, the Catalans went design-mad; everything was high-tech, postmodern and minimalist, and we became bombarded by the simple Miró-style designs in primary colours that have since become a sign of the city's identity.

All of which marked a great contrast with my first memories of Barcelona – in the late forties and early fifties – when as a child I used to pass through it with my family on the way to London to visit friends and relatives. We came by boat from Majorca, where we had made our home in 1946 and lived in a large stone house built by my father in the early thirties on the proceeds of his books. He had been living on the island since 1929, and loved it, but had been forced to leave in the summer of 1936 when the Spanish Civil War erupted, after which the Second World War had kept him in England. By the time he was able to return to Majorca, in 1946, he had written many more books and started a second family, of which I was the second child and the only girl. For my father our move from England to Spain was a return to what he considered his real home; for my mother and for us children it was a new life.

In those days, the island was quiet and rural, and when the ferry entered the port of Barcelona the city that stretched out endlessly before my eyes was like one large factory with smoke rising out of its many tall, industrial chimneys. When I walked down the gangway on to the docks I was always impressed by the large, gloomy buildings in the port and all along the waterfront: the customs' offices, the post office, and the station at the far end. The only colours that come to my mind when I think of Barcelona then are the blue of the smocks worn by the dockers and the green uniforms of the *guardias civiles*, the Spanish Civil Guards with their shiny black three-cornered hats. Everything else was grey and drab, like the narrow street near the cathedral where my parents' friends lived and ran an antique shop. They were German-Hungarian Jews, who had somehow managed to make their home in Barcelona after escaping from the Nazis – curiously, although the Spanish government sympathised with German Nazism and was obsessed with the idea of Jewish-Masonic conspiracies, a number of Jews were saved from Hitler by the efforts of Spanish officials. I remember going to visit them in their small flat above the shop, where a tortoise wandered up and down a long narrow corridor, while my father talked to Mr Rosenstingl about antiques. Those are memories of a gloomy, dusty city, with cobbled streets and tramlines, full of vigilant policemen and *guardias civiles*, and people with sombre expressions – memories that are inextricably bound in my mind with the excitement of our annual journey to England, with my father dressed in smart travel clothes and my mother reassuring everyone in her calm voice as she found lost passports, counted suitcases and ordered food for me and my brothers in dimly lit restaurants near the port.

What also contributed to make me feel like a stranger, when I arrived in Barcelona the other day, was that this luminous new city was in the middle of its Festes de la Mercè, the liveliest of its public holidays, which, when I lived in Catalonia, I usually avoided like the plague, because of the crowds it attracted and the traffic jams it caused. Indeed, Our Lady of Mercy – La Mercè – was said to have saved the city of

Barcelona from a plague of locusts in 1637, and that is why she became its patroness. There was a profusion of Catalan flags everywhere, on balconies, in shops, on cakes, on book covers, on T-shirts and caps hanging outside souvenir shops, and the people of Barcelona wandered about arm in arm in their best clothes, the children ahead of the grown-ups, running and jumping and being told off by their parents, while tourists in shapeless shorts and sandals took photographs of the buildings and the flags. The atmosphere seemed to me shallow and phoney, as if the whole show was part of the marketing effort aimed at investors, bankers and Japanese tourists.

I was coming to the conclusion that both Barcelona and I had changed far too much in the last five years for there to be any real rapport between us. But then came the turning point, the moment when you suddenly recognise an old friend you have not seen for some time and rush over to embrace him. My mother and I were unpacking our overnight bags in the hotel bedroom when I heard music in the distance, the sound of pipes and drums and the wind instruments of a *cobla*. Tears started to prick my eyes. The music drew nearer, so we opened the shutters and stepped out on to the balcony to watch the procession. First came the *gegants*, the giant king and queen dressed in flowing fifteenth-century robes and gowns, made of beautiful printed satins; they rose three or four times above the men and women in the crowd and turned from side to side in time to the haunting, reedy sound of the *tenora*, a sort of oboe. Then came the *drac*, the huge green dragon with its flaming mouth, followed by smaller figures, the *nans*, men or women with large papier-mâché heads, who danced around with the rest. There was a small crowd in the square opposite the hotel, shouting and singing and waving, and all the time the sound of the pipes and drums was growing louder and awakening in me forgotten emotions, reminding me of the days when my children sang beautiful Catalan folk songs on the way back from school, piled up in the back of the car, and we were a part of all this; of the stories told by my Catalan father-in-law about the Spanish Civil War; of watching brave people struggle for linguistic and cultural freedom, for democracy; of partaking in the excitement of every victory. On the pavement opposite our balcony stood a young girl in jeans and a tight black T-shirt, watching the procession. Her face looked so familiar, so Catalan; I have seen those dark, sad eyes, and that stream of wavy hair in *modernista* paintings of the turn of the century. She became an emblem: in her half-smile, her lovely features and her resolute expression, I suddenly saw the whole story of her country as I had known it. Catalonia's new look had faded away, to reveal its inner self, its essence, and I knew I was bonded to it in ways that I had never properly fathomed until then.

Now that we have entered the closed world of the hospital, with its designer Egyptiana and its monastic timetable, everything seems conducive to reflection. All the more so since I am in the company of my mother with whom I seldom share quiet moments, as I am doing now, in this parenthesis of time and space, in this neutral atmosphere where we are both out of our contexts. The experience of my weekend's re-encounter with Barcelona has set me on a journey of remembrance into the years when I was married to a Catalan and lived here, in the village on the other side of the river Llobregat where my old home still stands like a white ghost among the living; difficult years that were punctuated by the normal events of child-rearing and family life, and by the presence of other people, especially women, whose lives touched mine in many ways. As I review the past, I can see myself fifteen or twenty years ago; I can even remember how I thought and felt, but I find it hard to reconcile the person I was then with the one I am now. Some of those thoughts and feelings concern the slow growing apart of two people who fell in love and married when they were young, and found themselves unsuited to one another as they developed and matured. Others are about my relationship with the outside world, with my Spanish background, and with myself – feelings of entrapment, of unsuitability to my surroundings, of wasted years, that were momentarily set aside the other day when I watched the procession from the hotel balcony. At that moment I felt a deep attachment to this nation and its people and a wave of melancholy and nostalgia swept over me, changing my perception of the past. Could it be, then, that I have misinterpreted those years? That perhaps they were not as aimless and empty of significance as I have tended to conclude?

Being here with my mother makes a journey into the past all the more significant: she is my beginning, my origin, the fixed point of reference for my assessment of the world, a woman whose poise has given me strength and inspiration at all stages of my life. From time to time I have been reading to her, just as she used to read to me when I was a child. We have a choice of poetry and prose between us – the latest volumes by Brian Patten and Adrian Mitchell, and *Black Sea* by Neal Ascherson – and she always listens attentively, eager for her daily dose of words and thoughts. I remember what a wonderful reader she was, never adding too much emphasis of her own, or dramatising more than necessary, but letting her voice be a vehicle for the author's words, making them come to life of their own accord. My mother is like that in everything she does: she has a way of standing back to make room for others, but without effacing herself. Years ago, I would hear the sound of her voice at night through my bedroom wall, when she read aloud to my father in bed, and that sound was like a safety net under the scary thoughts that sometimes assailed me on the brink of sleep.

We talk a lot too, in this hospital room, especially about the work she is doing, collecting and annotating all my father's poetry, everything that he ever published, for the definitive *Complete Poems of Robert Graves*. Her main concern at this moment is to be able to read again after the eye operation, so that she can get back to the computer, the first editions and the manuscripts, and finish the task she has undertaken. I know that for her this work is the end of a journey that began in 1937, when she and my father first met in London – she, a young Oxford graduate with strong socialist convictions, a sharp mind and a gentle nature, he, a man almost twice her age, living in the enchanted forest of poetry from which he never would emerge. Now, as she goes through each poem, she finds that her memories are folded in his words, in the pauses of every comma and every question mark.

Where are my memories hidden?

8.00 a.m. The nurse has come in to check my mother's blood pressure, and informed us that at nine o'clock she will be taken down to the operating theatre. So I go up to the *cafetería* on the top floor to get myself coffee and a croissant. I pass the two large cat statues that preside over the hall – Egyptian cat-goddesses made of shiny white alabaster – and when I reach the landing to call the lift, two or three men are standing there smoking, still half asleep, grunting and rubbing their arms in an effort to wake up. In the lift two dark young men wearing tunics and headgear speak to one another cheerfully in what must be Arabic, and an elderly Spanish couple stand together in silence, arm in arm. A male nurse, in a short white coat and white trousers, leads them all out of the lift when it stops on the next floor up. The Arab men smile and nod at me, and I smile back. I love my present anonymity and hope I will not bump into anyone I know while I am staying here.

When I reach the bar, the two waitresses in the coffee shop are busy tapping out used coffee from the filter, filling it again with fresh coffee, cleaning the bar with swift movements, washing up. They wear navy blue nurse's dresses with white aprons, and both have short dark hair, and smile when they serve. I sit at a table by the window and look down on Barcelona, at the mass of pale buildings spreading down towards the misty blue line of the sea. Behind the bar, the waitresses are chatting. They are not Catalan, but from central Spain, judging by their accent. Now one of them is talking to her mother on the phone, asking her to buy something for her in the market. 'Get me about ten slices, very finely cut. But if it doesn't look really good, then get me some of those small round savoury pastries, filled with anchovies and peppers . . . Yes, you do, we had them last month at Aunt Conchita's house! Oh, never mind, I prefer the ham, anyhow, so long as the quality is good – but you must make sure the slices are cut really fine . . . But I won't have time to get there, I have to pick up Santi from school, and by the time I get home . . . *Vale, vale,* don't get in such a mood, Mamá. I'll see you later.' Then she puts down the phone and turns to her friend: 'Guess what? My mother refuses to go shopping for me!'

But her friend smiles and says, 'Ah, she'll go, don't worry, she'll go, what do you bet?'

Downstairs, in the large waiting rooms where in-patients and out-patients gather to have tests and see the consultants, the atmosphere is more sombre, the conversations are brief and whispered. These are people who have come from all over the world, and from every corner of Spain, in trains, buses and planes to see the famous specialists. They are like pilgrims, full of faith and hope. My mother and I spent the whole of yesterday among these silent crowds, down on the ground floor, waiting for her name to be called out.

The main hall was packed all day, with people sitting in brown leather armchairs, or standing against the grey walls; the two or three Greek statues of beautifully athletic men looked a bit out of place among the eye patients, some of whom were wearing eye patches, dark glasses or glasses with thick lenses. At one point we saw Doña Carmen with her husband Don José, and she waved at us. They have the room next to my mother's, and he is having the same operation as she is. Doña Carmen and her husband come from Madrid, but they live in Valencia; they have no children, and as they are very old a niece has come over with them to make sure they are all right. Everyone here has an *acompañante*, or even two: a mother, a daughter, a father, a husband, a wife. The health system all over Spain depends on the help of relatives, and in hospitals relatives are expected to watch over the patients day and night, making sure the drips are in place, and carrying out all kinds of minor nursing chores. The Spanish sense of family unit is at the heart of everything, it bridges generations, it projects itself on to other families, it is ever-present in conversations. I had almost forgotten its intensity, the way it overrides all other concerns, the way it ensures that personal identity begins with one's place in a family. How I resented that pressure when it was exerted on me!

In the large hall where we sat yesterday, time was measured by the regular appearances of male nurses in their white trousers and jackets, holding sheets of paper with the names

of the patients, which they read out like a litany. Every time
they came into the hall we waited hopefully for my mother to
figure in the list, among the impressive Spanish names that
soon became familiar to us: 'Ambrosio Gómez Delgado,
Mauricia Limón del Pueyo, Pedro Ferrer Casals, Asunción
González Fecundo, Dolores Quer Ríos, Montserrat Serra
Bohigas . . .' Each consisted of a Christian name and two surnames – the first surname of the person's father followed by
the first surname of the person's mother – even in the case of
married women, since Spanish women do not take their husbands' names. There were names from all corners of the
Peninsula, names belonging to industrial families, to noble
families, to labourers, to millionaires; names that may have
been enemies in former generations. Some sets of surnames
told the story of a mixed marriage: a man of Andalusian
origin and a Catalan woman, or a Basque woman and a
Galician man, tales of journeys, displacements and chance
encounters. There were also names from other countries,
French and Italian names, Arab and German, or English, like
my mother's, which sounded just as Spanish as the rest when
pronounced 'Beryl Gravés'. For a long while we sat next to
an old Sicilian lady and her daughter. The old lady was dressed
all in black with black felt slippers and black stockings. She
told us she had spent all her savings to come here for a second
opinion – 'St Lucia is too busy for miracles,' she said, tapping
the floor with her feet.

8.45 a.m. The nurse has come in to give my mother an injec-
tion and put some drops in her eyes. There is no kindness in
her voice as she dresses her for the operation, with a green
paper cap and pinafore, and asks her to remove her necklace
and her watch. My mother obeys like a schoolgirl. A few
minutes later two orderlies come in with a hospital trolley

and lift her on to it. She raises her hand to wave goodbye to me, then lets it drop limply down by her side, already affected by the drug she has been given. Soon she will be dosed with a general anaesthetic and will fall into a deep sleep. I begin to feel anxious. I stand by the door watching her disappear down a corridor, then I go back into the room and close the door. I pick up a book, then a newspaper, but find it hard to concentrate on anything. Suddenly I feel utterly lost and alone in this strange place, where no references link me to anything, past or present, and only the absence of my mother fills the room. There is nothing left between me and my thoughts, and I feel an overwhelming need to be strong without her, to fill the room with the sounds and colours of my own life, both the vibrant and the dull – the full spectrum. Above all, I need to rescue the person I was during those twenty years of residence in Catalonia from the dangers of my own oblivion and rejection, because the present can only be fully understood and appreciated by looking at the finished pattern of the past, the pattern of cause and effect in events that have become history.

Outside, on the terrace, the large rectangular pond mirrors the morning sun and I open the window to stare at the still water, the pink and white water lilies that are already half open, and the shimmering goldfish. Every leaf, every flower, every dark patch of water seems charged with hypnotic powers, inviting me to continue on the memory voyage that began when I opened my eyes this morning and that has now become a need – to remember from the source, from the childhood my parents gave me in a land of oranges and lemons, and the years that followed my childhood, when I was away from Spain; and the time after that when it became my home again, when I came to live here in Barcelona. I see many images in the water: the face of my mother when she was young, with dark short hair, and there is my father too, wearing a straw hat and smiling; I see the faces of people who made this land what it was then and what it is now, people I have loved and people I have feared; and the faces of some exceptional women whose quiet, unnoticed lives have run parallel to my own life and enriched it. Can I take the strength I see in them and make it mine? Will they illuminate my journey? Unexpectedly, some lines from one of my father's poems come to my mind:

> To the right hand there lies a secret pool
> Alive with speckled trout and fish of gold . . .
> Run to this pool, the pool of Memory,
> Run to this pool!

and a story begins to unfold.

II

The Fisherman's Tale

It begins in the days when the summer seemed endless and it was impossible to imagine that the crickets would ever stop their singing, or that the vines that spread their bright green leaves over the patios would turn into twisted brown twigs; when an old fisherman down in the pebbled cove sat for hours on end mending his nets under the shade of dried palm branches. He sat on a low stool, with the net he was repairing curled up like a brown cat at his feet, while other nets hung like spider's webs from the weathered grey rods tied horizontally to vertical poles. Near his small stone hut stood a large metal drum filled with dark dye for the nets, like a witch's cauldron. The fisherman loved talking to children, and children loved listening to him, for his voice rolled like the waves and he infused his words with the wisdom he had acquired from years of solitary seafaring. Sometimes he told us stories. 'Once upon a time . . .' he would begin, holding the wooden netting needle between thumb and forefinger, and pushing it in and out of the net as he spoke.

'Once upon a time, a long time ago, there was a king in Majorca who had an only son called Miquelet. What Miquelet enjoyed most in life was journeying upon the sea and one day, just to please him, his father sent him to take a boatload of saffron as a gift to his friend the Moorish king. The ship was much much larger than the largest of my boats – though probably not as large as the Barcelona ferry – so Miquelet went away very happily with a dozen sailors to man the vessel. The winds blew favourably all the way, and he stood on deck smelling the sweet saffron and feeling the bracing fresh air on his cheeks.

'When he reached his destination, the Moorish king was so overwhelmed by his gift that he invited Miquelet to stay with him for seven days while he thought of an appropriate present to send back to his father. At the end of the seven days he said, "I am going to fill your boat with the finest utensils for a great banquet: dishes, cutlery, glassware and tablecloths, all made by the best craftsmen in my land. And as a present for yourself I will allow you to choose the most beautiful flower from my palace garden."

'They walked through the lovely gardens that were shaded by palm trees and freshened by crystal-clear fountains, and there Miquelet saw exquisite roses and sweet-smelling jasmine and every variety of geranium and iris imaginable, but he could not decide which flower to pick. After a while they came upon a wooden hut, almost hidden behind the lush foliage of a red bougainvillaea, and Miquelet heard a whimper coming from inside. "Who is in that hut?" he asked.

'"Oh," said the king, "a Christian maiden captured by my men who refuses to convert to my religion so that I can marry her. She will remain locked up until she changes her mind."

'Miquelet peeped through a tiny window to have a look and when he saw the maiden he instantly fell in love with her. The maiden looked up with her dark eyes and pale face and when she saw the goodness in Miquelet's face she too fell in love with him at once. "She is the most beautiful flower in your garden," he said to the Moorish king. Out of politeness the king could not refuse his visitor the gift of the maiden, much as he wanted to marry her himself; so he let her out of her prison and the happy couple sailed away.

'They were halfway back to Majorca when one night the devil appeared from nowhere and whispered evil words into the ears of Miquelet's sailors, filling their hearts with envy. "Why should Miquelet have all these riches and a beautiful bride-to-be?" said the *dimoni*. "Has he worked as hard as you? No! He hasn't done anything to deserve it, so be rid of him and keep these treasures for yourselves!" So the sailors waited until Miquelet came out of his cabin just before dawn and then *plaf!* threw him overboard into a rough sea. They told the maiden – whose name was Catalineta – that Miquelet had fallen into the water accidentally and, simulating great sadness, they took down the white sails and changed them for black ones. Their wicked plan was to take the ship with Catalineta and all the rich cargo to some faraway land and enjoy an easy life to the end of their days. But things don't always turn out as one would wish, and despite their efforts to turn the ship around, the winds and the rough sea drove the boat straight into Miquelet's harbour as fast as an arrow. When the king and queen saw the black sails from the palace balcony they were filled with grief and rushed down to the dock. They believed the wicked sailors' story and took Catalineta to live with them to ease their sorrow.

'They need not have despaired, however, for Miquelet was not dead. No sooner had he fallen into the dark waves than two shadows had appeared from nowhere and lifted him out of the water. The shadows carried him over the seas and left him on the edge of a cliff near his home town, vanishing as quickly as they had appeared. Miquelet looked down at the dark menacing waters that crashed against the shore a hundred feet below and trembled at the thought of the death he had just escaped. Then he began to walk home through familiar pinewoods and fields until he reached the palace gates. But he did not knock on the door for fear that his parents would think he was only the ghost of Miquelet and not let him in. Instead, he waited outside the palace for days on end, until one night Catalineta looked out of her window and saw him, and the love she felt for him revealed the truth of his presence. And so, after a joyful reunion with his parents, they were married and had a huge banquet with all the dishes, glassware, spoons and tablecloths presented by the Moorish king and lived happily ever after. Miquelet was so good that he forgave the wicked sailors, saying that only the *dimoni* was to blame, but he never returned on board a ship or went near the edge of a cliff just in case he should slip and fall into the water. Perhaps they are all still alive, unless they are dead; in which case we'll meet them in Heaven. Amen.'

During those long summers of my childhood we were sometimes taken to the next beach along the coast, where instead of rocks and pebbles there were long stretches of sand. It is the scene of one of my earliest memories.

I still remember how cool and damp the sand felt under my knees. I was making a sandcastle with my brothers, and when I looked up the sea was sparkling, flat and blue, forming pale streaks in the semicircle of the port. It was a beautiful natural harbour — it still is — with a narrow mouth that sheltered it from the rough seas, and a lighthouse on either side; the docks for the fishing boats were built in the far right-hand corner, with a naval base a little beyond them. On the left of the harbour the land rose gradually until it reached quite imposing heights with jagged cliff-edges of grey rocks and a belt of thick pine trees behind. The half-moon of the harbour was ribbed with sand and, in those days prior to mass tourism, was as clean and deserted as a scene in a Caribbean holiday brochure.

Suddenly there seemed to be a lot of people on the beach, people who were not dressed for the seaside, women in their aprons carrying small children, men in dark clothes. They were gathering round a small fishing boat that had been dragged up on the far left of the bay, near the spot we had chosen for our sandcastle. Trouser legs and skirts covered the field of my vision and the little boat disappeared behind them. But then I saw a shiny coffin being carried from the road behind us towards the place where the crowd was form-ing. People were crying, 'Ai, bon Jesús!' and crossing themselves, and the coffin was laid down on the sand. The crowd moved to one side and there was a hush. Now I could see more clearly. Two men were carrying a large bundle wrapped in sackcloth from the boat to the coffin and when they reached the coffin they lowered the bundle into it. Their necks had bulging veins from the effort. The lid was put in place, but as the coffin was too small, the dead man's feet stuck out in the air, like a chicken's from a shopping basket.

I was told later that the poor man had suffered a terrible accident, which resulted in his falling into the sea, tangled up in the tree that crashed down with him. For three days they had been looking for his body and at last it had appeared, miraculously well preserved, considering the heat and the water. Now he could be buried and rest in peace under the earth. His widow and children would be able to go into mourning – two years of black for the widow, followed by a year or two of half-mourning; a few months or a year for the children, depending on their age – and the whole family would stay at home during local holidays and celebrations until the mourning ended. The widow would now clean her home until it was spotless, scrubbing the floors, dusting the doors and shutters, rubbing the window panes with bits of crumpled-up newspaper, polishing the brass until it shone like the Virgin Mary's halo in the church. Then she would have the open coffin placed in the parlour with the radio set on a corner table and the framed wedding photograph looking down from the wall. Madonna lilies and a few leafy branches would surround the corpse, and neighbours would sit with her and say the rosary, while others would come and go all afternoon, embracing and comforting her with phrases that time had smoothed into pure sound. Then the men would come to carry the coffin away on their shoulders: her cousins, her neighbours, her brother-in-law, all dressed immaculately. Everything would be just as it should. His body had not been saved by two passing shadows as in the old fisherman's *rondalla*, but – who knows? – perhaps his soul had and he was looking down on them from Heaven, for he had been a good father and husband.

I thought of him often as I grew older, and still do every time I drive past the scene of his accident, even though I don't know his name or anything about him except the circumstances of his death. He was felling a tree by the edge of a cliff and had tied himself with a rope to the trunk just in case he should slip on the uneven ground as he sawed. He had taken all the precautions. The tree was supposed to come down backwards, and he had started sawing on the side facing the sea. But he must have been thinking about something else, he cannot have concentrated enough on what he was doing, because he began to saw the trunk under the rope that tied him to it, not above it. The tree began to double over, and somehow it fell the wrong way, dragging him down the cliff with it. His misfortune has all the cruelty of a bad joke, all the power of a myth, all the essence of religious symbolism. He was like Helle or Icarus falling into the sea, and the boat bringing him to the port was Charon's boat crossing the Styx. The rope and tree were a crucifix, the woodcutter's saw was Death's sickle. His end makes me think of this line in one of Rubén Darío's poems:

> *La muerte es de la vida inseparable hermana*
> Death is the inseparable sister of life

That is how I see it now, but at the time I knew only that something terrible had happened and held my mother's hand tight. We quickly left the beach and piled into the old taxi that had brought us down to Sóller Port, and after driving through flat farmland and orange groves, past houses with bright bougainvillaeas and geraniums round their front doors, the car turned right and slowly, noisily, struggled up along the thin grey winding road to the top of the hill. There suddenly the sea came into view again and it was all downhill to our home. Home with the cats and the palm tree, the vegetable garden and flower beds, and everything always the same.

Which meant, of course, Christmas stockings and Easter eggs and the English crockery in the dining-room cupboard, my mother's wonderful reading voice, mealtimes and Sunday strips. 'Sunday strips' was the special breakfast my father would sometimes prepare for us on Sundays, to give my mother a rest. It consisted of long slices of bread –the middle slices of a round, rather flat loaf – with about ten strips of different spreads, jam, honey, peanut butter, cheese, tomato, whatever was available, and the table was set with special care for the occasion. Life was pleasant and full of little bits of fun, the seasons rolled slowly by marked by the changing weather and vegetation, activities and celebrations, and in the secluded world of my home I felt safe.

Only a few childhood fears have survived from those days – though plenty were to come a few years later – which I could add to the sight of the shiny coffin on the beach. One was an edition of *The Pilgrim's Progress* with its grim copper-plates of dark forests and monsters; another was an illustration in a *Children's Encyclopaedia* of a tidal wave about to crash over two minute people standing on the shore (why weren't they at least trying to run away?); and there was also a recurring nightmare of a giant pursuing me through a lemon grove while I ran and remained always in the same place. The first two I could simply avoid. The third could be 'removed' by my father. If I woke up with a nightmare and he came into my bedroom to see what the matter was, he would look for the nightmare on my scalp, his fingers feeling their way through the jungle of my hair, until he would suddenly cry out: 'I've found it,' and walk out of the room with a closed fist telling me he was going to throw it down the lavatory. It always worked.

My bedroom, which in those early days I still shared with my brother Juan, eighteen months my junior, had two windows at right angles to each other: from one I could see the mountains, from the other the sea. Neither view contained any buildings. On one side were terraces of olive and carob trees, dry red earth, myrtle bushes and pale grey rocks above which the sun rose; on the other a green mass of pine trees and the blue water into which the sun dipped, leaving a red or purple afterglow. This was the land of Miquelet and Catalineta, terraced, tended and irrigated over three centuries by the Moors, delivered from its Islamic occupants by the Catalan King James the Conqueror in 1229, stripped of its mosques and synagogues soon after; an island of fishermen

and sailors, farmers and shepherds, mystics and saints, cartographers and explorers, its shores protected against the
Berber pirates by sturdy lookout towers. From my window, I
could easily picture the fisherman's stories, but other characters also had a place in those framed landscapes, characters
who did not belong to that land, like the Pre-Raphaelite
fairies, princesses and heroes from our bedroom bookshelves,
so that even that timeless Mediterranean view was part of my
English world. Part of the world of Beatrix Potter, Airtex
vests, Viyella shirts, dumplings and tea. Items and habits that
had no convincing translation.

I soon understood that languages were closed worlds, that
their translation could never convey the exact emotion of one
word into another language. To say that the man in the port
was dead, was simply not the same as saying he was *mort*,
even if both words have the same meaning. The emotional
connections between sound and meaning cannot be disen-
tangled, for in doing so they are lost. In my experience 'dead'
was like a dull pain, like the quiet end of a smile. 'Dead' was
my half-brother David who had died four months before my
birth, leaving no trace, in Burma. *Mort* was the sudden tolling
of bells, deep mourning, the whole village scuttling up the
hill to the church, a gloom beyond words, and the young
men carrying the coffin on their shoulders, their hair plastered down with *brillantina*, their spotless Sunday clothes the
pride of their mothers or wives.

I spoke Majorcan, which is a variant of Catalan, with
everyone in the village, and Spanish with people who were
either from the mainland, or lived in Palma – where under
the dictates of the Franco regime the Majorcan 'dialect' had
become almost relegated to the kitchen. Majorcan is now
flourishing again, as is its sister language Catalan, but at the
time it was not done to speak Majorcan in certain circles, and

the Majorcans, who had been under Nationalist control throughout the Civil War, did not seem to feel the bitterness of the prohibition as keenly as the Catalans did – or perhaps, being islanders, and peace-loving by nature, they held a more philosophic attitude to invasion and conquest. Besides, as we were foreigners – and looked it – we were addressed automatically in Spanish. Even today people are surprised to hear me and my brothers speaking Majorcan as one of them; perhaps they feel that I have taken something from them that was too intimate to share with strangers.

But, rightly or wrongly, I did take it, and it is now a part of my being that opens up when I speak the language again, or when I hear the Moorish-sounding music of the island where I grew up. Like all bilingual children (trilingual, if I count Spanish) I moved easily between two separate worlds, changing my gestures, my facial expressions and my intonation as required, almost switching identities when I switched languages. At home my mother made hot cross buns on Good Friday, and my father told us that Jesus survived the Cross and was seen in Rome many years afterwards. Was I the same person who had listened in wonder to him, as we ate our buns by the fireplace, when that same evening I piously watched the Good Friday procession with my Majorcan playmates? There went the beautiful Virgin Mary, swaying gently on her platform, covered in a veil of black gauze behind the figure of her dead Son – Death the inseparable sister of Life – while the villagers trooped behind holding long yellow candles and chanting, '¡Perdona a tu pueblo, Señor!' Lord, forgive your people! Would I ever reconcile my two worlds?

The answer came many years later on a starry December night, when the strongest young men in the village arrived at the house looking smart and smelling of eau de Cologne, to help my brothers and my husband carry my father's coffin, first along the winding road to the village and then up the steep hill to the church; when at the door of every house people stood silently and watched the funeral cortège of the old English poet who had chosen to live among them for fifty years; when I stood next to my mother by the altar looking at the coffin from which a sprig of laurel jutted out, trapped between the lid and the box; when I took my place in the row of the deceased's relatives, to be kissed on both cheeks by the whole village as they trooped by in single file, and to be comforted with those age-old phrases that had never before been addressed to me; when the gravediggers who buried the coffin early the following morning, passed a bottle of brandy round and wiped their tears on their sleeves. 'Dead' and '*mort*' became the same that day, and my two worlds joined in one.

III

The Midwife

The coffin on the beach was my first experience of death. At the other end of the scale is my first memory of birth. Both are imbued with a sense of wonder and awe, made all the more poignant because they belong to a time before the net of language and organised behaviour had put a filter between myself and reality; when my visual world consisted mostly of boulders that were warm to touch and trees that were good to climb, and the long lines of ants that crossed the dusty path outside our kitchen. And the intense blue of the sea.

The memory is of Blanca, the village midwife, holding a baby on her aproned lap, in a dark damp room. The baby's face is pink and wrinkled, with a shock of black hair. I touch his tiny foot and cannot believe he is real.

This was at a christening party in the village. I must have been four or five years old and had been taken there by my mother. There was a fountain nearby surrounded by bright green ferns and moss, and the water made a soft splashing sound as it fell into the little canal that took it downhill. The main door of the small stone house was wide open and the entrance hall was full of people. Among them was Blanca, with her round face and her hair combed as usual into thin plaits and wound round her head like a Russian peasant's. The baby's father was handing round cigars and being slapped on the back by his friends as they arrived or left. Everyone was drinking sweet wine, even the children, and the men talked in loud voices, and laughed and shouted. Blanca came up to us and said to my mother, 'Come upstairs to see the baby. Yes, yes, you can bring the little girl too, come.'

We followed her up some bare cement stairs with no rail. The staircase grew darker as we went up and the sound of the voices downstairs seemed to belong to another world. When we got to the top of the stairs Blanca opened a door, which I hadn't even noticed in the dark, and we went into the bedroom. The walls bulged here and there with years of whitewashing, and the floor sagged worryingly. The colours in the room stood out despite the gloom: the olive green of the closed shutters; the wine-colour of the damask curtains and the matching bedspread; the long white christening dress draped over the back of a chair by the window. Then I saw a beautiful woman with wavy black hair lying in bed, her face still pale from childbirth, lips slightly swollen, dark rings under her eyes. Her baby was sucking earnestly from her large white breast, its hand clasped round her index finger. I could not see the baby's face but his hair was black and wavy like his mother's, black and wavy like the sea at night in one of my storybooks. When she saw us she smiled and I remember how she pulled the baby off her breast for us to admire his face, revealing a large shiny nipple. Then she handed him to my mother. He wriggled and made comic grimaces. His face was pink and he was only a bit bigger than my dolls. He had a wide bandage wrapped tightly round his tummy.

The next thing I remember is Blanca sitting on the chair by the window with the baby, making a soothing guttural sound as she patted him on his back. She signalled to me to come closer, so I went up to her, with some hesitation, and she let me touch the baby's foot with my hand, and stroke his cheek. That image of Blanca holding the baby has stayed with me, together with the unfamiliar smell that filled the room – the smell of birth and new life, a mixture of breast milk and baby's pee and eau de Cologne.

In those days, before understanding why, I already knew that Blanca was not like other women in the village – and not just because she spoke Majorcan with a strange accent, and rode a bicycle, and laughed easily. There was something else about her that made her specially attractive and mysterious, something that made babies stop crying the moment she picked them up, and older children stand in awe of her. Was it her gold tooth that sparkled when she smiled? Or her large hands, with their patches of snow-white skin, as white as a newborn baby's? Or was it the small, covered basket she carried with her, out of which sometimes – but not always – came a gift of a sweet or a piece of fruit?

At times Blanca seemed to me like one of the fairy godmothers in my English storybooks, with her round face like a full moon and her kind smile; other times, when her smile abandoned her and she looked pensive, even stern, she made me think of the strange 'Balanguera', the Fate-figure in a popular Majorcan song, who weaves the thread of our lives 'like a spider of subtle art'. We used to sing that song in the school playground, and I knew La Balanguera had magical powers because she could 'see the shadows of the past', and knew 'where seeds lie hidden in the winter' – I loved the song's haunting melody and the repetitive *fila, fila* of the chorus:

> *La Balanguera fila, fila,*
> *La Balanguera filarà*

> La Balanguera spins and spins
> La Balanguera will go on spinning

What I sensed in Blanca, but could not yet fathom, was the power that emanated from her independent spirit, a power so well rooted in her being that it could never be weakened by outside influences. For there was nothing unearthly about her appearance, nothing extraordinary or celestial about her at all. On the contrary, she was earthy and straightforward, with a laugh that would have shocked a fleet of angels.

She lived with her husband, Antonio – a man I vaguely remember as good-humoured and rather elegant – on the other side of the long hill that formed our western horizon. Their house stood all alone on a stretch of rocky coast, like a solitary watchtower, and from her back terrace, looking out to sea, Blanca could watch the sun sink into the Mediterranean in the evenings, leaving a stream of colours behind it, or feel the water's dark presence on moonless nights when smugglers unloaded their goods on the rocks five hundred feet below, and owls hooted from the tree-tops; and when the stars mapped out the future – as above, so below. To the left and right the rugged coast stretched south and north into the distance, gradually turning into a soft grey-blue line that was often covered by a band of sea-mist. In front of the house, on the other side of the main road, a large expanse of pale land, dotted with olive trees and grazing sheep, sloped up towards the dark oak forests, and behind these rose the bare crags of the tall mountain, where the Majorcan black vultures nested and scanned their ample territory.

This was the same corner of the island where, almost seven centuries earlier, Ramon Llull – mystic, poet and philosopher – had contemplated the mountains and the sea and

visualised the world as three interrelated spheres: the divine,
the human and the natural. It was Blanca's landscape he was
describing when he wrote:

> Between the vineyard and the samphire cliff
> love seized me and made me love God;
> and live among sighs and tears.

Blanca enjoyed the solitude that still pervades this Llullian
scenery today, this place of contrasts and harmony where
nature seems transformed into pure feeling. It has always
seemed to me a perfect site for someone who, though in different ways from Llull, was also a free thinker; and for
someone who, like the mediaeval Majorcan mystic, was in
close touch with the mysteries of life, through her experiences of birth and death. For Blanca was not only a bringer
of life, she was also a layer-out of the dead, whenever her
help was required to prepare the corpse of a villager for
burial.

She loved Majorca – she fell in love with it the moment she
set eyes on its sleepy coast from the ferry that first brought
her over from Valencia – and in her house above the sea she
could live at ease, far from the furtive looks of inquisitive villagers. Because she came from the mainland, she was classed
as a *forastera*, an outsider, and her personal history was not at
all clear to them when she first arrived, in the early forties.
While Blanca sat and watched the sunsets in peace, the
women in the village brought their stools out on to the pavement outside their homes and discussed her while they did
their needlework.

'They say – I have heard this from a reliable source, you
know – that they are not married. Why do you think she has
had no children herself ?'

'Oh, yes, they're lovers, they're not married at all. In fact, she's really married to someone else!'

What did Blanca care? She would soon win their hearts and their approval. And she was right. In time, Blanca became a well-respected person, a figure of authority among the women of the village, and any personal grudges about her marital status were set aside. She was, in the words of a mutual friend, *una mujer maravillosa*, a wonderful woman.

In 1953, when I was ten, Blanca delivered my youngest brother to the world. Her husband had recently died and she came to live with us for a while, to be with my mother for the birth and help look after the newborn baby afterwards. I was fascinated by the mixture of expertise and gentleness with which she performed all her tasks. I remember how she gave him his bath, the way she tested the water in the metal tub by dipping her elbow in it, unfolded her oilcloth apron and put it on as carefully as if she was a doctor about to perform an operation; how she placed all the utensils in a neat row, the soap, the sponge, the comb, the towel, the talcum powder. And then how she undressed the baby and immersed his tiny body in the warm water, her strong hand under his neck, and observed the wriggling of arms and legs with interest. There was none of the loud cooing and fussing with which my baby brother was greeted by all the other Spanish women who saw him – Blanca was different.

Over the years she became not only a family friend, but a woman whose life I came to value and admire when I got to know her better, and as I enter the past today, in this Barcelona eye hospital, she stands out brightly among the more nebulous figures of my early years. She belonged to a particular type of Spanish woman whose mind and spirit had fed on the liberal ideas of the Second Republic; women who never forgot the sense of personal emancipation and achievement they enjoyed during those years, and whose strength of character allowed them to remain free thinkers throughout the long oppressive years of the Franco regime.

The last time I saw her was on a hot summer afternoon in the early eighties, when I visited her in a nursing home in Sóller – the town in whose port I had seen the coffin when I was small. I had heard that she might not live long and was anxious to see her, now that I was over on the island for the children's summer holidays. My father's health was also declining, and I knew Blanca would be pleased to have news of her old friend, Don Roberto, and of my mother.

I parked the car in the town square and made my way down Carrer de sa Lluna – Moon Street, a long narrow road lined with shops on either side – in the direction of the nursing home. I knew it was somewhere among those backstreets, so I entered the shady maze, where the worn grey stones of the pavements always shine like polished pewter. Round every bend the same two rows of houses seemed to re-appear, unassuming two-storey buildings whose very lack of outward distinctness was a sign of their unvarying occupation by generations of the same faces, of the same voices, of the same hands repainting the shutters the same colour. The ancient silence of those narrow streets was broken by an occasional reminder of the present: the sound of a TV serial coming from behind closed shutters, the metallic beat of a pop song.

Many houses had their front doors wide open to let in the afternoon breeze, sharing the privacy of their entrance hall with neighbours and passers-by, as if to say, 'We have nothing to hide and are proud of it.' These Majorcan *entrades* always look rather formal and are generally furnished with a couple of upright chairs made of leather or criss-crossed flax, and a dark chest or a table covered with a white embroidered linen cloth, displaying the traditional Majorcan patterns of blue flowers with large petals, wide chalices and gracefully curved stems in daisy-chain stitch. All the pieces of furniture are placed against the whitewashed wall, together with a few large, leafy pot plants. In the back you sometimes see a tiled staircase with an iron railing and shiny metal knobs leading to the upper floors; in one I noticed a statuette of a Madonna wearing a very pale blue mantle, placed in a niche on the wall, a smaller version of the image that stood in one of the side chapels of the village church and had made such an impression on me as a small child.

Despite the heat of the afternoon, two old women were sitting on low chairs outside one of the buildings, busy with crochet-work. I asked them where the convent was, the convent that is also a nursing home, I explained.

'Turn left at the corner,' said one of them, 'then left again when you get to the ironmonger's.'

The other woman went on crocheting without looking up at me, except briefly when I said *gràcies*, thank you.

I knew these women would not end up in a nursing home. Their daughters or granddaughters or nieces or daughters-in-law would take care of them until the end, and think nothing of it, for that was how things were. I can remember a conversation I once heard in a doctor's waiting room in Barcelona, in which one woman was telling another how a male cousin of her father-in-law had moved into her flat, an old man in a wheelchair whose only living female relative she was. She had to nurse him night and day, wash him, feed him, dress him, and she had not even known him when he was fit and well. 'What could I do?' she asked. 'I couldn't very well turn him out after his wife had died and he was left alone. He'd had a stroke, so what was I to do? Send him to a nursing home like a pauper? And just when our youngest daughter had got married and we were going to turn her room into an office for my husband! Just as we had saved up enough money to go with our grandchildren to Disneyland!' Sighs of understanding and resignation filled the waiting room. Of course, there is often a substantial reward in the will – the olive groves up the mountain, or the house by the port, or the flat in town – but then, that's also how things were and always had been.

Not for Blanca. For although she had no children, she did have a niece, and probably other relatives whom I had not met. Yet she prized her independence above all things, and did not want to become a burden to anyone; so she had sold the small house in the mountain village where she had lived since Antonio's death, and invested the money in being looked after professionally during her last years.

I soon found the ironmonger's, a shop where we came to buy tin milk cans and earthenware pots and candles when I was small; it now displayed electric blenders and steam irons in its window. Opposite the shop was the street I was looking for, with the façade of the convent taking up a long stretch of it. Before I reached the entrance, I looked through an open window on the ground floor and saw the dining-room tables with blue and white check tablecloths. I was pleasantly surprised. The front door was wide open and in one corner of the *entrada*, by the staircase, was a statue – was it of St Joseph? – surrounded by plants and vases of flowers. A nun in white overalls led me up to Blanca's room.

She was not expecting me. When I reached the door I saw her lying in a narrow white metal bed looking out of the window at the jungle of potted palm trees and lily plants in the courtyard below. Perhaps the sight reminded her of her family home in Valencia where she grew up, of another cobbled patio, or a back garden with orange and lemon trees and a shallow irrigation canal down its centre. In my mind I pictured her mother sitting upstairs by a balcony window with her embroidery, and her father below – white linen suit and dark moustache – sipping anisette and discussing politics with his friends round a white marble table, some time in the early thirties. They would have been talking about the new Republican legislation and the impact of wage increases on employers, or the recent laws for agrarian reform, or the strikes and uprising of miners in the north. There must have been a great deal to talk about in Valencia at that time, with the country becoming more and more radicalised to the left and to the right as a result of its deep economic troubles and social tensions.

The fact is that I cannot think of Blanca without placing her within the historical framework of the Second Republic, which lasted from the abdication of King Alfonso XIII in 1931 to the end of the Civil War in 1939, because of the way it influenced her life. On the one hand, its new left-wing policies of social change gave her an opportunity to become independent and develop her free-spirited personality. For despite the instability of the first five years of the Republic, the seeds of democratic reform had been sown, and many of its measures had time to improve people's lives and modernise their attitudes. Its constitution, approved in December 1931, separated the Church from the state and accepted regional autonomies – the Catalans were granted their Estatut d'Autonomia in September 1932; the Basques finally approved theirs in 1936. In particular it changed the lives of thousands of women who came out of the kitchen to study, to work in factories, or to have careers.

The Republic and its social changes marked Blanca's life in another way. The separation of the Church from the state had led automatically to the acceptance of civil marriages and, for the first time in seven centuries, a divorce law was passed in Spain in 1932. It was thanks to this law that Blanca was able to divorce her first husband and marry Antonio.

This is her story, as I know it.

Blanca must have met Antonio during the late twenties or early thirties. They fell in love instantly, but their relationship did not last. Antonio came from a wealthy Majorcan family with generals and other respectable figures in his background, and Blanca was his social inferior, a working-class woman from the mainland, with Republican views and a mind of her own. Perhaps, to put in a good word for Antonio, his family had threatened to disinherit him if he married her. Whatever the reason, Blanca must have been deeply hurt when he left her, and very angry. She met another man and married him on the rebound. But Antonio could not bear to see Blanca wed to another and began to pursue her relentlessly. Their love flared up again; Blanca and her first husband divorced, and she married Antonio. Her first marriage was a traditional church marriage; her second, after her divorce, took place in a register office, and probably very quietly. Even during the days of the Republic civil marriages were frowned upon by the conservative circles to which Antonio's family belonged.

When the Civil War ended and Franco came to power, binding Church and state together again, the Republican divorce law was abolished and civil marriages were no longer valid. This meant that thousands of couples who had married in a register office under the Republic had to remarry in the church if they wanted their papers to be in order – technically, if neither spouse was Catholic, their civil wedding could be recognised but such cases must have been extremely rare, and to apostatise formally from one's Catholicism during Franco's dictatorship was a complex procedure and very detrimental to one's social reputation. The annulment of all Republican divorces had serious consequences, and many sad stories resulted from it. Some women, or men, were forced back into a broken marriage. Others, who had remarried after their divorce, like Blanca, found that their second marriage licences meant nothing at all. Of these, some were abandoned by their new spouses – there were cases of women with small children unable to claim pensions or help of any kind – while others continued to live with their partners regardless of the law.

Blanca and Antonio stayed together, but they could do nothing towards legalising their situation, since Blanca's original church marriage was now indissoluble; nor could her first husband remarry while she was still alive. So she spent the rest of her life 'living in sin' with her once lawful husband. They were happy enough. Antonio, a man of some distinction among Palma society, liked spending hours at the easel, painting watercolour landscapes of the fantastic scenery surrounding his house on the coast. Blanca worked as the village midwife and was devoted to him; but in Antonio's family, and among many of their acquaintances, she was considered Antonio's lover, not his wife.

When Antonio died, he left her the small cottage in the mountain village to which they had moved when he became ill, but the main bulk of his estate, including the house on the coast, went by law to his Majorcan family. Even if he had wanted to leave it to her, his family would have been legally entitled to claim it back. Blanca had no right to make any claims; she was not officially his widow.

Those who were closest to Blanca assumed that the fact that she had no children was to avoid the added complication of illegitimacy. But one day, many years later, my mother told me about a conversation that had taken place some time in the early sixties, which she had never repeated to anyone. She was driving down to Palma with Blanca and an American man who was staying with us – we called him the Mushroom Man because he was working with my father on the subject of hallucinogenic mushrooms – when our guest suddenly asked her, 'Do you have any children, Blanca?'

'No,' she answered.

'Have you ever had any?'

'Yes, once, a boy, but he died.'

The Mushroom Man, overwhelmed by her frankness, pursued the matter no further. How typical of Blanca, my mother said, to have kept this sad event to herself, and how typical also to have told the truth when asked.

Her story, of which I know only the bare bones, is one of many sad stories that had to wait over forty years for their conclusion. For most of their protagonists, including Blanca, the recognition in July 1981 of the Republican divorces and civil marriages came much too late.

When I said her name she turned round to face me with a frown; then she recognised me and smiled. I had not seen her for some years, and it took me a few moments to get used to the way she looked now: frail, much thinner, her hair almost white, her cheeks, once so ruddy, sunken. The clinical whiteness all around her and her own silvery-white hair gave her an almost supernatural aura. Now she really looked like La Balanguera, or an all-knowing sibyl. I went over to her bed, sat down and began to say the things one says: how are you, is the food nice, are they looking after you well here? And so we began to talk. Although she had finally grown old, she still had that husky voice, that low drawling laugh that seemed to defy every obstacle in life, every pain and misery, every pettiness; she still wore her hair combed in long plaits which she wound neatly round her head. I had picked some flowers for her in my mother's garden – pink and orange zinnias, crimson dahlias, roses and a few sprigs of jasmine – and I could see how they were bringing back memories of the mountain village, of the days when she lived there and delivered children to the world.

'Your father used to call me La Decana,' she said, all of a sudden. '"*Buenos días, señora Decana*," he would say. "You are the doyenne of this land, and you rule over all the women of the village!" He made me laugh! I couldn't rule over a flock of sheep!'

Yes, you could, I thought. I remembered the story of how one night, when a burglar tried to break into her house on the coast – probably a smuggler who had clambered up the rocks to escape from the Civil Guards – she had frightened him away by wrapping herself up in a sheet and waving her arms about like a ghost. She could be both authoritative and gentle, which is why she made such a good midwife.

I reminded her of the christening party.

'Yes,' she said. 'That must have been Maria's boy – Maria of the Fresh Fountain.' Nobody used surnames in the village; everyone was known by the name of the family house, or a family nickname whose origin was often unknown. 'Your mother and father had been living in the village a couple of years by then, and you used to play with Catalina, the baker's daughter. She was at the christening too, and I remember you both came up to me and said, "Can we have another sugared almond? A pink one?" You were both very small, but I remember you wanted pink ones. "They all taste the same," I said. But no, they had to be pink!'

'I'd forgotten about that,' I said to Blanca. 'But I do remember how good they were. A nun once told me that if I went to Heaven I would be given sugared almonds that would never melt in my mouth. Never!'

'Ah, those nuns,' whispered Blanca, in case there should be one passing by as we spoke. 'They did say some strange things to children. But I suppose they meant well.'

Someone groaned in a nearby room and we both returned to the present. There was a smell of disinfectant in the room, a smell of fragility and approaching death. A dark crucifix hung above Blanca's metal bed. She looked at the flowers again.

'Ah, *¡cuántos años!* How many years have passed!' she sighed. 'You were only a little girl then, and now you have three lovely children of your own.' She was quiet for a moment. Then she added, 'Sometimes, when I read the newspapers, or watch the news on the television, everything seems to have changed so much! It makes me feel tired.'

'But things are better, don't you think? Now that we have a democracy.' I was stupidly trying to make her look forward, make her contemplate a future that was no longer hers. 'We've had to wait a long time for the good things,' I insisted.

'*No hay mal que cien años dure* – no evil can last a hundred years!' she answered, dismissing the subject with a smile. 'Now tell me about your daughters . . . Who do they look like?'

She played with the fringe of her bedcover and I remembered the white bedspread she had crocheted for me when I got married, made of thousands of small squares linked together. I had often seen her at work with her sewing after she retired, sitting alone on the stone seat by the front door of her cottage, under the shade of a leafy vine. She sat with her legs set slightly apart and her feet firmly on the ground; in one hand she held the crochet hook, in the other the thread, and the white ball of cotton jumped about like a kitten in her little basket.

*

I left knowing I would never see her again, and from the way she kissed me goodbye I knew that she felt the same. Not because there was any sorrow in that kiss: it was more like a calm farewell, a blessing for my future. As I walked back through the narrow streets and watched the town resume its activities after the afternoon lull – the women out to buy what was needed for dinner, the children playing hopscotch or marbles on a corner of the pavement – I could see how Blanca had fitted into this closed society, and why she had stayed here to grow old among people who probably still considered her an outsider and still viewed her story with intolerance. There was a certain freedom within the boundaries of this closed land. This was an island, and the mountain village was like an island within the island, where life was ruled by the cycles of its natural habitat, and by rituals so ancient that nobody could remember their origin. With the end of the Republic and the beginning of Franco's long dictatorship, one flag was taken down and another hoisted on to the pole in the town hall, but little else changed. What went on in mainland Spain was remote in every sense of the word. In this primitive place, only the earth and the water and the elements seemed to govern people's lives, whose cycles were marked by christenings, weddings and funerals; and meanwhile, in her narrow metal bed, Blanca remembered the beginnings of many lives as she prepared for her own end.

IV

Water-fairies and Altars

If I close my eyes, I can almost feel the soft warmth of the winter sun on the nape of my neck, and hear the sheep bells and the occasional shouts of the shepherd somewhere up in the olive groves above our house, and the long silences between his shouts – back in the quiet days of my early childhood. I find it easy to enter that uncluttered memory chamber.

As the months and the years went by, and I turned six and seven and eight, I began to appreciate the rhythm and cycles of rural life, the tastes and smells that went with each season, and the way things worked in the village. Outside the confines of my English home, where copies of the airmail *Times* in their light blue wrappers were vague reminders of the comfortable land of my grandparents, there was nothing to distract my thoughts from my natural surroundings and I became immersed in a primitive way of life that flowed predictably from one event to the next, like the water that flowed from the fountains, like the water that ran down the torrent to the sea.

It was a genuinely rural society, almost untouched by twentieth-century modernisation or even the industrial revolution; where carts were much more common than cars, cooking was done on charcoal fires, and women still fetched water from the fountain for their daily needs, unless they had their own well in which to collect the rainwater that fell off the roof. Nor was there any electricity in the village – unless you called electricity a dim orange glow produced by a privately owned generator, with not enough voltage for any domestic appliances; irons were heated over the charcoal fires, and those who had iceboxes cooled them with the large blocks of ice that arrived in the bus at half past three in the afternoon, wrapped in sackcloth. When we had an Aga imported from England and installed in our house in the late fifties, it was considered such a novelty that people would drop by during their Sunday-afternoon stroll just to have a look at it. But by then things were already beginning to change, and soon the tourist boom would take all the young workers away from the olive groves and the fruit orchards to work in the new hotels that lined the sandy shores on the other side of the island. The rugged land, which had for centuries been a source of production, would soon become a landscape to be consumed by tourists – to feed the mind and not the body; and the efforts of men and women, once dedicated to its cultivation, would be channelled into providing new services for the viewers.

In the late forties, when I was growing up in the mountain village, the link between man and nature – man's control over the elements – was far more apparent than it is today. It was a way of life that, with hindsight, risks being classed as picturesque or quaint, but at the time was not like that at all, especially for the village people themselves. The forties were difficult years for them, with few comforts in the home and little to buy in the village shop: a few sausages hanging from the ceiling, a few tins of sardines, a sack of potatoes, another of dried broad beans . . . . The country was still suffering the aftereffects of the Civil War, with rationing and a rampant black market. Women would take the bus down to the capital with bottles of olive oil hidden under their skirts and come back with packets of rice or sugar. The Spartan living conditions matched the toughness of the land, the dark clothes of the women, their seriousness and reserve. They matched the sullen expressions of the men whom I sometimes saw playing cards and dominoes in a cloud of smoke at the café.

At weddings and christenings and village feasts, after a few glasses of sweet wine, men and women abandoned their normally serious expressions to laugh and tell loud jokes. But there was one person who never laughed, a young woman who lived in the farmhouse just above the main road, on the way out of the village towards our home. She must have been mentally handicapped. I used to see her standing outside the front door, or sitting on a chair, with a piece of bread in her hand, watching people go by. She had a protruding purplish lower lip and short straight hair parted at the side and held back with a hairgrip. In any village gathering, or in church, she stood next to her good-looking mother, too shy to speak or even look up.

By this time I had completely forgotten the Devonshire geography that had formed my visual world until the age of three. The pleasing lines of dark hedges on soft green fields, the rambling roses, the fairy-tale banks of the river Dart with its wild flowers and bushes, all those images had been blotted out of my mind by the stark shapes and colours of my new Mediterranean home. Here a wide valley rolled down from the steep mountainside as far as the sea-cliffs, with rows and rows of terraces held up by dry-stone walls – the only way in which the reddish-brown earth could be retained and give nourishment to olive, almond and carob trees. The sun rose from behind the mountains and set in the sea, and the valley changed colour during the day as sun and clouds journeyed across it. Frequent changes of weather meant that nothing ever looked the same for very long: the olive trees turned dark green with black trunks after rainfall, or silvery grey in the wind, and the mountains could disappear altogether in a sudden mist.

In the middle of the valley, which was like a large bowl with one side broken off where it met the sea, a village of pale brown stone houses clustered round a small hill, with the church of St John the Baptist and the graveyard on its summit, and the town hall at its foot. Our house was situated a little beyond the village, facing the southern rim of the bowl, behind which lived Blanca and Antonio in their house on the coast. Here and there, on the sides of the basin that surrounded the village, were large farmhouses called *possessions*, each with at least one very tall palm tree to mark its location and remind one of its prestige – and of the presence of water. Most of the land surrounding the village belonged to these farmhouses, whose owners, the *senyors*, generally lived in Palma, whereas the *amo*, with his wife the *madona*, ran the house and the property.

On the eve of St Anthony, 16 January, bonfires were lit at night in various parts of the village – a Christian adoption of an old pagan ritual to celebrate the New Year. But the most exciting bonfires were on Good Friday, when they were lit in the *possessions*, and from the village all one could see were the bright orange flames licking the dark semicircle of mountains. The farmhouse situated furthest to the right, which had a view of the church door, would wait to catch sight of the silent candlelit procession leaving the church after Mass, and would then light its bonfire; the next farmhouse, on seeing the flames of the first bonfire, would light up too, and so each farmhouse would light its pile of wood and brambles until the full semicircle was completed. I was fascinated that people could communicate through distant signs; that they could make fires speak to one another, sending messages of fraternity from one powerful house to the next and at the same time showing off their wealth through the size and brightness of the flames. But, above all, that they could communicate to the villagers, who were slowly walking down the hill towards the town hall and up again on the other side, that the farmhouses were the ancient guardians of the mountain and were there to protect them. Is this power to communicate another reason why we say 'tongues of fire'?

Fire could also be destructive and frightening. One summer afternoon, when trees and bushes were parched after months of dry weather, I was in the village with my friends when a fire began to spread in some terraces above the village. The smoke was dense, forming clouds that hung over the mountainside, spreading a strange heat and the smell of burnt leaves. People were gathering quickly, running to the scene with empty buckets which they filled with water in the fountain by the road. In minutes, a human chain was formed all the way up a path towards the fire, and I have a clear recollection of the buckets being passed from one person to the next, up the chain. Some men were shouting, giving orders, and we children huddled together, at a safe distance, comforted by the authority they projected.

There were also tame fires in the mountain, useful fires: the fires of the charcoal-burners who spent weeks at a time in the oakwoods high above the village, sleeping alone under the stars, tending their pyres like priests of some mysterious oracle. But no flames came out of those large round piles of wood because they were covered by earth, to give the wood a slow combustion and allow it to turn into firm black charcoal. I once went up the mountain with a young girl from the village to take provisions to her father who was up there burning wood. I remember that as we walked up the winding path the ground was covered with small dry oak leaves and we had to take care not to slip on them. Then we came to a flat clearing and saw the charcoal-burner sitting alone on a rock, looking tired and unshaven. In the middle of the open space was the round pile of wood with a thin streak of blue smoke rising from it, and in a shady corner I saw an old blanket and some tin plates, and an earthenware water-pitcher. The dark man took the pitcher and offered us a drink of the cool water which, he said, came from a nearby spring. I had heard about the *dones d'aigo*, the water-women who lived in the springs, and wondered whether he had seen them, flitting around the wood at night, but was too shy to ask.

At different levels of the mountainside, underground water, channelled through man-made tunnels, flowed out into the basins of stone fountains placed like shrines at the dark mouths, with fern and moss and ivy growing profusely around them. And beneath the smooth dark ripples lived the *dones d'aigo*, the water-women, fairies who came out only at night, like bats, to roam the woods. In ancient times they had lived in broad daylight, filling the woods with mysterious powers, giving speech to birds, trees, water and wind, carpeting their groves with wild flowers. But the arrival of the True Cross had condemned them to darkness: they had vanished, like the thick grey mist that sometimes sweeps through the trees in the early morning. The earth had swallowed the *dones d'aigo*, but it is said that they created marvellous palaces underground, with lakes and waterfalls, with spacious halls where they sat sadly in the shadows and wove watery garments for their flights into the upper world. Each one guarded a mountain spring, each was the living spirit of its water: the Fresh Spring, the Profuse Spring, the Spring of Lies (called this because if you drank from it you might start telling lies); their glassy currents ran down to the public washing places in the town, where women scrubbed their clothes on the grey stone slabs and dipped them into the running waters of the basin; or formed new fountains in the town, or were channelled into large reservoirs belonging to the mountain farmhouses and from there sent downhill to other farmlands and groves.

For although the farms owned olive groves, and flocks of sheep, and olive presses, their most treasured possession was the water from these springs, without which the fruit trees and vegetables could not grow. Some *possessions* had their own springs, others owned rights that gave them perpetual use of the water on certain days of the week, when they would accumulate it in the reservoirs for irrigation. These water rights were often a source of trouble: they could cause rifts between good neighbours, feuds between families who had been close for generations; they led to spiteful remarks in the café made by men wearing berets and brown corduroy trousers, and to silent looks between women at each other across the street. But for us children, water was always a source of joy. On summer evenings it flowed down the narrow cement canal set about four feet from the ground above the main road and it was fun to dip our fingers into it and watch little bits of twigs and leaves pushing their way along, getting stuck, loosening, continuing their journey down to the big farmhouse on the way to the cove, with its rows of orange trees and tomato plants.

When we were thirsty on the way up from the beach, we would sometimes stop there to ask for water. Or if we were playing in the village we would walk into one of the open *entrades* shouting, '*Ave Maria!*' and out would come the lady of

the house, drying her hands on her grey apron, and saying in
a kind voice reserved for children, 'What do you want,
children?'

'*Mos dóna un poc d'aigo, madona*? Can we have some water?'
we answered. The word *aigo* (pronounced eye-go), 'water' in
Majorcan, seemed to me a perfect word, a word that I still
associate with summer thirst and the cool mineral taste of
pure spring water or rainwater, and with the *madona*'s words
as we drank: 'Don't drink so fast, it will do you harm!'

It was my world, and I understood it; I could see how
things worked, how the lives of the village people blended in
with the mountain, the farmland and the sea. It wrapped
itself neatly round the kernel of my home – so different from
the homes of my village friends – where my father worked in
a room filled with books, or was out in the garden picking
tangerines or digging up weeds; where my mother sometimes sat and read by the fireplace with a cat on her lap, or
was busy cooking in the kitchen, or else was out in the garden
watering the lettuces or picking flowers to put in a pretty vase
on the dining-room table; where at night my parents would
listen to the BBC on our large wooden radio, while my brothers and I cut out illustrations from English or American
magazines – coloured pictures of a faraway land of telephones, red sports cars and electric washing machines that
did not seem quite real to us – and then pasted them with
care into our scrap books.

Real life for me was what went on outside the green
wooden gates of our home. Once a week a sheep was slaugh-
tered by the village butcher and once a year – for St Martin's,
in October – most families killed a pig to make sausages for
the months to come. My mother never allowed us to see the
actual slaughtering, but I remember hearing the frantic
squeals of the pigs once or twice, and thinking they were

never going to stop. Later in the day, we sometimes went to the house where the *matança* was taking place. By then the pig's throat had been cut, its blood collected in a pot, its meat cut and classified, its entrails carefully washed and dried. The women of the family sat round a table, outdoors, mixing spices and meats in large yellow bowls, their hands red and shiny from paprika and animal fat, while the men, who had done the slaughtering and the butchering, turned the handle of a large grinding machine, or carried platefuls of finished sausages into the house. There was a smell of meat and blood and spices, and an exhilarating atmosphere of pagan feast.

Many other events made up the village calendar. Almonds were husked and cracked in September for making Christmas *torrons*; olives were picked in November for pickling while they were still green, and pressed for oil in December when black and juicy; spinach and cabbages were grown in backyards, refuse was fed to the chickens or to the mules and their droppings in turn fed to the earth. The fisherman's wife came up to the village in the mornings when there was enough fish to sell. She stood outside the town hall blowing a conch that was heard up and down the streets, because those were days before mechanical noises had invaded their homes, before televisions and telephones closed houses upon themselves, when people's ears were alert to every sound and could tell what was happening around them. The fisherman's wife was thin and wiry and rather bad-tempered and had given up changing her mourning clothes in the months between the death of one distant relative and another; her dark figure, her tanned, sinewy arms, made the red and blue fish all the more colourful as they gaped and stared at death in the old wicker basket.

School started in late September, when those long summers finally came to an end and the dark carob beans had been collected into sacks that were stacked against the pale stone walls of the terraces; when our bathing clothes had been put away in a chest with the beach towels, hardened and faded by sun and salt; when the fisherman came up from his seaside hut to live in his village home.

The school was run by three or four Franciscan nuns. The girls' class was known as *costura*, which literally means 'needlework', and in fact we did little else there, as far as I remember, except pray and learn the catechism. It was halfway up the steep hill that leads to the church, the last building in a row of houses, with three very tall steps of worn grey stone leading up to the entrance, where we pulled a thin dangling chain and heard a faraway tinkle, followed by a shuffle of feet and the sound of the door clicking open. Before letting us in, the nun would look down the hill to see if anyone else was coming up to school and take a quick look at the world outside. My younger brother Juan would be taken off to the boys' room on the right and I went into the room on the left. A tiny patio at the back of the building – no more than three square yards, as I realised when I revisited the school some thirty years later – was our playground, divided in two by a piece of string. On one side, the girls played, on the other the boys. At the end of the patio a few steps led up to the *excusat*, a hole in the ground with sackcloth for a door and bits of cut-up newspaper or brown wrapping paper hanging on a hook on the wall. One for the girls, one for the boys. We girls skipped and played hopscotch. The boys played marbles or leapfrog, or else rushed around kicking each other and shouting.

In one of my mother's photograph albums there is a black and white snapshot of me and Catalina, the baker's daughter, whom Blanca remembered seeing at the christening party.

She is wearing a tight-fitting coat with a neat row of buttons on either side of the front panel, puffed sleeves and a large round collar. Her hair is tied in tight bunches high above her ears, with large white bows (of course, they may have been pink, like the sugared almonds). I have my arm round her shoulder and we are both laughing. Catalina and I sat next to each other in the girls' classroom, learning our times tables and filling our exercise books with rows of *mi mamá me ama* ('my mummy loves me') and *la pipa de papá* ('Daddy's pipe'). The nuns lost their temper very easily, if you got a stitch wrong or a word wrong when reciting the ten command-ments, and especially if you swore by mistake – even saying *'Punyeta!'* which was a very satisfying word to use when you were annoyed, and meant no more than 'Bother!' – so there was always some girl standing or kneeling with her face to the wall, arms stretched out, being punished for something she had done. But nobody seemed to care; there was no real anger in the nuns, and I recall no unhappiness, even when kneeling on the cold floor. Sometimes they took us on excur-sions into the pinewoods by the sea, and as a great treat would tell us stories about the Majorcan St Catalina Thomàs, who was born in the neighbouring village of Valldemossa, and had even spent a few months of her life living with an aunt in our village before she became a nun. St Catalina, known affec-tionately as *Sor* Thomaseta, was given a very hard time by the devil, who played lots of dirty tricks on her to tempt her and lead her astray. She used to take meals to her father, who worked in the olive groves in the hills above her house, and as she walked up the rocky path the devil would suddenly appear and trip her up, spilling all the food on the ground. Once he even pushed her over a high cliff not far from Blanca's house, on the road to Palma, but two angels came flying down with a blanket and saved her from falling.

Catalina and I used to sing a song about her namesake. Translated, it went something like this:

> Sister Thomaseta, where are you?
> You'd better hide somewhere fast
> 'Cause the devil's looking for you
> and will throw you down a shaft!

In the classroom they encouraged us to take example from the Virgin Mary and Baby Jesus. They were so sincere in their belief that I was soon drawn by their enthusiasm and came top of the class in religion. The Virgin Mary became my idol, so beautiful, so pure, so perfect! The statue in the church, with her sky-blue mantle, her long wavy blond hair, her sweet smile, her neat hands and feet, elated me. It was as if I was being lifted up into the starred ceiling of her niche, as if I was one of the cherubs surrounding her. Those lovely soft cheeks, those eyes looking ecstatically up at Heaven as I looked ecstatically at her. She was above languages, you could speak to her in Latin, Majorcan, Spanish, English – she understood them all, because when you prayed your words changed to some other concept of communication, they became pure emotion. Perhaps, I thought, I could become a saint when I died, and sit close to her in Heaven. Catalina had given me a small metal image of the Virgin Mary, and I made little altars for her on the olive terraces above our house, or in some quiet corner of our garden, in secret crevices that I would tend with care; I gathered tiny blue flowers that grew like weeds by the roadside, petals of geraniums and roses and daisies, and formed a patterned tapestry all around her. One day I went down the garden to the place where I kept the little figure and found it had gone. To this day I wonder what happened to it, for I did not dare tell my parents or my brothers about my loss. I knew I could not bring my Catholic devotion into my English world. The nearest we ever got to religious practice at home was singing 'O Come All Ye Faithful' round the Christmas tree, first in Latin, then in English; and I remember how my father, when it came to 'born the King of Angels', always raised his voice and sang 'born the King of Israel!'

At that time, however, there was little difference in my mind between the Virgin Mary and the *dones d'aigo*, between the angels who rescued St Catalina or the fairies from my storybooks; they were all part of the world of fantasy that children create for themselves at an early age, while the line between reality and fiction is still nebulous. Sometimes these fantasy figures could cross the line into the real world of the mountain village and hide among the olive trees or in caves by the sea. But the countryside, however beautiful, was not an enchanted countryside for me: it was real, and often harsh, even if it was full of things to fire a child's imagination, like the golden oil that came out of the bitter black olives, or the smell of the orange blossom when the trees had been irrigated, or the crystal-clear water flowing down the open canals.

Today, those canals have been replaced by plastic under-ground pipes, and consumption of water has increased so disproportionately as a result of the tourist industry – because of the demands for swimming pools, showers, washing machines, luscious gardens and golf courses – that every summer there is a shortage. Water is still the subject of many heated discussions, but the feuds have moved from the café table to the lawyer's desk, while water lorries race around the island trying to meet the demands of holiday-makers from the north of Europe who have never needed to be careful with the precious liquid. So much else has changed: many of the old village houses have been sold to foreigners to be used as holiday homes, and many new houses have been built; the new generations of rural Majorcans no longer work the land, but instead have become hotel managers, waiters or builders who speak to one another on mobile phones; the Franciscan nuns have left the village, and our *costura* is now a private residence; there are no more charcoal-burners; the fisherman's wife is long dead. Yet every time I go back to the mountain village to visit my mother and my brothers, who still live there, there is at least one moment, either in the early morning, when all is quiet except for the sound of birds pecking at the fruit trees, or at night, when the moon lights up the olive trees across the valley, when suddenly the memory of what it felt like to be a child here flashes through me. Like an old song returning.

V

The Prima Ballerina

I am standing on the corner of a street in Palma, the island's capital, in my sailor-suit uniform, waiting for the school bus. This image of my childhood belongs to another episode and another place.

Every morning, the bus picked me up at seven thirty, and as I waited, with my heavy satchel resting on the pavement, I watched the men go off to work, clearing their throats and spitting as they came out of their front doors, turning their jacket collars up against the damp morning air. Some of them carried long sandwiches wrapped in newspaper and tied with rubber bands, and they set off on foot to catch the tram farther down the road, or climbed on to a bicycle or a dusty moped. The street was slowly waking up, the bakery and the milk shop had their lights on but their iron grilles only half open. To pass the time I would search the pavement for cigarette stubs, which my neighbour María Jesús and I collected to give to a tramp. María Jesús had red curly hair and her father played the trumpet in a military band. She lived across the street from us, but did not come to my school; in the evenings, when the school bus brought me back home, and all the children who lived in flats came out to the street to play and eat their piece of bread and black chocolate, María Jesús and I would sometimes go to see whether the tramp was sitting in his usual place – a deep grassy ditch on the edge of a disused plot of land. I liked him. He always thanked us politely for the tobacco and asked us how we were getting on at school.

I was ten. My parents had moved to Palma so that we children could go to better schools, and during that time the house in the mountain village became our second home, where we went for weekends and school holidays in my mother's black 1930s Renault. People would stop and stare at her as she drove, not believing their eyes. 'Look, look,' they would shout, 'a woman driving a car!'

We rented two flats, one above the other, in a new quarter on the outskirts of town. The lower flat was where we lived, and in the top flat my father had his workroom, and our maid, who had come down from the mountain village to live with us, had her bedroom. It was in the guestroom of this upstairs flat that my brother Tomás was born, one January night in 1953. When we woke up the following morning, my brothers and I found a note from my father pinned on the inside of our front door. It was written in Spanish for the benefit of the maid, who must have spent the night downstairs with us, and it said: '*¡Ha nacido un niño muy robusto!* It's a very robust little boy!' The word 'boy' came as a shock – I had been so sure it would be a girl, a baby sister who would side with me against our two dreadful brothers – and why 'robust'? Was he huge and muscular? I wondered. Would my mother be all right after having given birth to such a child? But when I walked into the upstairs bedroom, led by Blanca and my father, my mother smiled and said, 'Hello, darling,' and suddenly I knew that everything was all right. She pointed to a wicker basket at the foot of the bed. Blanca lifted the white blanket that almost covered the baby's head and said, 'Look, look at your *hermanito!*' And, as if by magic, there was another one of us, with that familiar look about him in his tiny features – and not robust at all, I thought.

The flats were part of a grey-blue apartment block, built in the spirit of the Reconstrucción Nacional that characterised the fifties in Spain: dull cement-finished buildings, with no balconies overlooking the street, shoddy finishings, and floors covered with mock-marble tiles that looked like raw meat. But the area also had its charm. Parts of our street and of the wider street that cut across it still contained a few pre-war houses – modest single-storey buildings with flat roofs, and names like Villa Paquita written over the front door, that had probably been holiday homes when they were first built – sandwiched between the apartment blocks, and from the back terrace of our flat we had the view of a derelict farmhouse with a curious pink chapel attached to it, and a field in which turkeys and chickens wandered about pecking the ground and a goat nibbled at grass and weeds. In those days the town of Palma ended only a few streets further north from ours, with large areas of uncultivated land where a few abandoned almond trees blossomed in January and a dense carpet of poppies and yellow daisies covered the ground in spring.

When the men had left, the women came out in their long dressing gowns and bedroom slippers to sweep the bit of pavement outside their front door; their tinted and permed hair always showed an inch or two of dark roots. Often two or three of these women would be sweeping at the same time, but they never said anything to one another, as if they were fierce rivals in a competition for the cleanest bit of pavement, or perhaps because the dressing gown imposed a law of silence on them, building a wall of privacy around their territory. When the weather was warm, they would also bring down a bucket of water to sprinkle over their clean patch and keep the dust from rising.

An atmosphere of privations and scarcity pervaded the city; much more palpable here than in the mountain village, where the regenerating forces of nature made up for the material and intellectual limitations imposed on all Spaniards. Over a decade had passed since the end of the Civil War and people were tired of getting nowhere, of having to work extra hours and during their holiday time to make ends meet, and of seeing no prospects of a better future. And yet on a large scale things were beginning to change. Rationing was being lifted, industry was beginning to turn its wheels again, and Spain was slowly emerging from its isolation. The Cold War had made the West reconsider its hostile opinion of the Spanish dictatorship in the light of its deep anti-Communism and its strategic situation in the Mediterranean. Ambassadors were returning to Madrid. And in 1953 Spain signed a treaty of mutual co-operation with the United States, by which the Americans were allowed to build air and naval bases in the country in exchange for financial and military help.

But in the meantime, the women went on sweeping their pavements in silence, dreaming of the day when they could buy a refrigerator like the ones they saw in American films – after mutilation by the censorship authorities, who sometimes removed whole scenes that did not conform to their high moral standards – and go to the hairdresser's once a week to style their hair like Rita Hayworth in *Gilda*. In the meantime, too, Franco was making sure that this timid opening up of the markets in no way endangered the ideological commitment of the new generation of Spaniards to his one-party state. The school-books in my satchel held the key to all

that: it was through his educational system that Franco
ensured a tame acceptance of his policies.

Our school was run by a French order, and was supposedly a little more open-minded than the other schools in
town – it was the only school in Palma that had agreed to
admit me without a baptismal certificate. Academically it
was quite acceptable, especially for Latin, maths, and French
and Spanish grammar, but no school escaped the rigours of
the National-Catholic educational system. The union of
Church and state was at the very root of Franco's Fascist
ideology, the Church having been traditionally associated
with authoritarian, right-wing ideas, and having, moreover,
been the target of appalling left-wing attacks during the
recent Civil War. Every one of the yellowed pages of our
religion, history or reading textbooks reflected some aspect
of the ideology of the Movimiento, and exalted the civic,
moral and political values on which the new generation of
Spaniards, unscathed by Republicanism and Masonic influence, was to feed and grow. History books selected events
and characters through which they could stress the sense of
patriotism that was at the core of Fascist nationalism, skim-
ming quickly over any great military defeat, like the Spanish
Armada, or the ephemeral periods of enlightenment and
liberalism, which were always due, we were informed, to
scheming foreign heretics who crept like snakes through the
green grass of Spain. Ferdinand and Isabella were used as
the role models of Spanish political and religious unity, their
emblem, a yoke and arrows, being adopted by the Falange,
the Spanish Fascist party created in 1933 by José Antonio
Primo de Rivera, and the only legal political party in Spain.
We wrote endless dictations about the glory of the Spanish
flag and the greatness of the Empire, and were told that
democracy was the ruin of a nation: 'If every citizen were

allowed to hold his political opinion and act accordingly,'
said our Spanish history book, 'instead of an organised country we would have social chaos.' We were also taught that the
Spanish language was superior by far to English and French,
'which are such worn and eroded languages, that they are
heading for a complete dissolution'. And that the Jews, who
hated the Spaniards and were political spies and conspirators,
had secret dealings with the Moors and murdered Christian
children: for those and for many other reasons the Catholic
Kings had thrown them out of Spain for ever.

It was Señorita Mercedes, the history teacher, who was in
charge of our political education, of making sure we understood the ideology and structure of Franco's glorious regime.
She was one of the few lay teachers in the school and an active
member of the Sección Femenina, the women's branch of
the Falange. She was tall and pretty, in her mid-thirties, with
an oval face and short black hair. She wore a dark brown tai-
lored suit buttoned up to the neck, thick stockings and
lace-up shoes, and she was a spinster. Señorita Mercedes had
a habit of suddenly putting down the history book from which
she was reading to us, or turning away from the blackboard
where she had written down the names of all the Gothic and
Visigothic kings of Spain, to tell us her own stories of the
Civil War, of how she had seen the Reds burn down churches,
how she had heard accounts of the slaughter of nuns and
priests by the Enemy. I never quite understood who the
Enemy was, who were these Reds she told us about in a trembling voice. They sounded like invaders from another
country. It never occurred to me that they were actually
Spanish, ordinary men and women of different political
beliefs who had come to the defence of the Republican government in power and had fought for freedom and
democracy. It was impossible for me to conceive that these

people – indiscriminately described by the victors as barbaric Reds – were still living in Spain and went to work like everyone else on their bicycles, with a sandwich wrapped up in newspaper.

These wartime accounts were the best part of the lesson, because Señorita Mercedes was a wonderful raconteuse. My favourite was the story about the eggs, which began with the sirens announcing an air raid, and our teacher, then a young girl, running down to the shelter with her family. The building had been hit, and when they returned their kitchen was in ruins, everything had been destroyed. But – lo and behold! – an egg basket with half a dozen eggs in it was still miraculously hanging from a beam among the smouldering ruins. 'It was a miracle! A miracle!' she would cry. Of course, the air raids over Madrid were carried out by Franco's forces in an attempt to break the siege of the city, which had remained Republican throughout the war. But we just assumed that anything bad, like throwing bombs on homes, was always the work of the Enemy, the *rojos*. Señorita Mercedes and her family must have had a traumatic three years trapped in a 'Red' Madrid.

Our history book, *The Holy Land of Spain* (subtitled *An Exaltation of our National History*), also included moving stories of modern martyrs during Franco's National Crusade. The first martyr, of course, was José Antonio Primo de Rivera, founder of the Falange, who had been executed by the atheist Reds and whose face was as familiar to us as the face of Franco, but there were other lesser-known victims whose stories made us all shudder with emotion. There was the story of poor little Martín and his brother Agustín who lived in Teruel. When the Republican army conquered this city, Martín and his little brother refused to be evacuated with their family to Castellón. They were desperate to rejoin

Franco's forces. So they fled. Snow was falling heavily as the two little boys started to make their way across enemy territory, Martín carrying his younger brother in his arms, because he had 'fallen asleep' – the quotes were there to make us feel uneasy. By the time they reached the Nationalists' lines, little Agustín had died of cold.

> Martín refuses to believe that his brother is dead. He shakes him, kisses him with all his might, holds him tightly against his chest: nothing; he raises his arms: nothing, they fall to his side, lifeless. But Franco will regain Teruel, and forever after Agustinillo's martyrdom will add a sheen of glory to the streets of this heroic town.

And when the final victory came:

> Halleluiah! Our land opened up to receive the seeds of Peace in its womb! Marxism, like the ivy that chokes its prey, had tried to spread all over Europe, beginning with our beloved Spain, but like Islam, like Protestantism, it found its grave in our country! All the people came out of the churches rejoicing, raising their voices in gratitude to Heaven and chanting Halleluiah!

Señorita Mercedes was also our gym teacher, and that year the Sección Femenina organised a Provincial Gymnastics Competition for Girls in Palma. She wanted to put our school down for it and managed to convince a rather reluctant Mother Superior that there was nothing wrong with baring our legs in public. After all, we wore long navy blue bloomers under our skirts, and besides, it was important to show that the school was a firm adherent to the spirit of the Falange, and its principles of caring for the body as well as the soul.

The Mother Superior clearly did not believe in this principle, and had lectured us more than once on the dangers of 'certain immoral dance movements'.

Señorita Mercedes prepared us ferociously for two months. Twice a week we put on our dark blue bloomers, white blouses and white plimsolls, and went into the gymnastics room to train like soldiers. In her long pleated skirt and white blouse she looked younger than she did in the classroom, and she instructed us with almost fanatical fervour. The movements had to convey a military precision: arms up and open, legs apart, one two, open, close, open, close! But we also had to smile, to project the inner joy of living in Franco's Peace.

The great day arrived and we were driven down to Palma to take part in the competition. I remember the thrill of standing in that huge room, an indoor *pelota* court, singing '*Cara al sol*', the Falange hymn, with hundreds of other girls, our hands firmly outstretched in the Fascist salute. I could see my mother and father looking rather serious in the audience – whenever I see documentaries on public gymnastics during the Third Reich, I can understand why. And we won, our school won the first prize for the Balearics. I remember Señorita Mercedes on the way back to school in the bus, sitting arm in arm with one of the older girls, her eyes brimming with tears of joy.

The only reason we had won the competition was that five or six of us went to Olga's ballet school, and had learned how to hold ourselves straight, point our toes and move our arms gracefully. Three evenings a week, after school, I would walk into the centre of Palma, to Olga's Academia de Ballet Clásico, a large room fully equipped with mirrors and bars and a wooden floor, and a black upright piano in a corner played by a lady called Pepita, who kept her coat on all winter. Olga was Latvian, from Riga, and had come to Majorca in the late forties. I did not know much about her then, except what she used to tell us sometimes after our class, when we sat in a circle on the floor and watched her doing her own exercises. She would raise her leg incredibly high in a slow *adagio* and say, 'Look at you sitting there! When I was a star in the Riga National Opera, I had to work eight hours a day, e-ve-ry day! But then the Russians invaded our country and I was forced to leave . . . The only good thing about the Russians is their ballet, the only good thing!' Other times she would describe her country to us – with its lakes and forests and its long sandy beaches – and tell us how the river in Riga froze in the winter.

Once a year Olga put on a show at the main theatre in Palma and we danced round her to a full orchestra, dressed in tutus and gauzy dresses made specially for the occasion. The theatre would fill with parents and friends of parents and at the end of the show my father would run on stage with bouquets of flowers for everyone.

I idolised Olga, and made up my mind to be a ballet dancer like her. She was slim and pale, with very long, cinnamon-coloured hair which she wound round her head in plaits, one of them flat against her skull, the other propped up by hair-grips, like a diadem. Sometimes she would come and spend the weekend with our family in the mountain village and there, when the weather was good, she would wash her hair on the terrace, using rainwater from the well, which we heated up for her on the charcoal fire. My mother and I would stand by and throw warm water over her head with a saucepan, but the part I loved best was the drying operation, with both of us wringing her hair as if it were a sheet or a towel. Then it had to be combed and untangled, and finally

Olga would sit on a garden chair, her face in the sun, a cigarette in her mouth and her eyes closed. Those were the only times I saw her look happy and relaxed.

Normally, Olga was excitable and passionate, as if her spirit were rebelling against the fierce discipline that dancing imposed on her body, and she would shout or burst into tears at the slightest provocation. She was so unlike anyone I had ever met – her supple body, her temperament, the faraway look in her eyes. After a few years in Palma, she married a tall, gentle, American musician called Glen and went to live in Ohio. I remember her wedding, the beautiful white gown and her cinnamon-coloured hair gleaming in the dark Palma church. They looked so happy. But Glen, with his sweet smile, was taking my idol away from me, and I was not sure whether to laugh or cry.

It was only a few years ago that Olga told me the story of how she had come to Majorca. She had stopped over in London on her way to Spain and we had dinner together in a hotel off Piccadilly. In her early seventies, with a long history of hip operations and other health problems, she still looked spectacular. A peacock-blue dress and cape, fine eyebrows pencilled over her made-up face; her hair, only slightly greyed, still combed in the same way; and her ballet-dancer feet turned gracefully outwards in a pair of dangerously high heels.

'I was born in Riga in 1921,' she began, in her slow, rather slurred voice, the Latvian accent still strong after forty years in the USA. 'You know, Latvia was the richest of the three Baltic states because of the port of Riga, and all the industry around it. People would come over in the summer from Poland and Lithuania to work in the fields. It was a good place to live, and I had a happy life there. My father was Latvian and my mother was Estonian, but at home we spoke

Russian, which was their common language — my father had been educated in Moscow. In 1939, when I was nineteen, I finished my *gymnasium* and my ballet training, and joined the National Opera of Riga. I became a prima ballerina, you know, and all the best roles were for me — I was Odette and Giselle and Helena . . . I was a good dancer, and I always wanted to be better. Ballet was all I ever dreamed of, it was something that was always deep in my heart, here, in my heart . . .' and she put her hand on her heart and closed her eyes.

'Then came the war and everything started to change,' she went on, her eyes fixed on the pale white wine in her glass. 'The war in Europe took away all our prospects and hopes, as well as human lives. In 1940 the Soviet forces occupied Latvia and made it part of the USSR. It was a terrifying year, the Russians were so brutal, so many people were deported to prison camps, or executed, or tortured. They took away our silver currency, our flag, our identity . . . But a year later the Germans arrived and pushed the Russians out; they gave us back our flag, our currency changed to German marks, and things were much better than they had been with the Russians. I still remember the day the Germans marched in — Latvian flags were flying from all the windows and balconies, and people were singing the Latvian national anthem at the top of their voices. Look,' Olga rubbed her hand over her arm, 'I still get goose pimples when I remember! We saw the Germans as our liberators, our saviours. Of course, they rounded up all the Jews and Poles. But they did nothing bad to us; to them we were Aryans, and they treated us well.

'It was during those years of the German occupation that I met Dr Oliver, a Majorcan who had come to Riga with the Blue Division — you know, the army of volunteers sent by Franco to help Hitler defeat the Russians. They ran a hospital in Riga where they treated the casualties from the Russian front, from Novgorod and the siege of Leningrad. Dr Oliver was a very cultured man. He loved going to the ballet and the opera, and was a great admirer of mine. Sometimes he invited me round to his hospital for tea with other members of the ballet, and we became good friends. We spoke in German, and he told me about Majorca – it sounded like Paradise. He was a truly good person, with a very big heart, and he helped a lot of wounded soldiers – I don't care what people say about the Fascists and the *falangistas*, the "blue-shirts". Dr Oliver was one of them, and I never knew anyone as kind as him. The poor soldiers came back with dreadful wounds and even more dreadful frostbite, and it was heart-breaking to see so many young men with amputated limbs. And during the retreat Spanish soldiers helped quite a few Russian girls escape by giving them Blue Division uniforms with which to dodge the authorities. The Russians, they were the evil ones!

'On the fifteenth of April 1944, the Blue Division left. The day before, Dr Oliver had given me a piece of paper with his address in Majorca. He said, "Where I live, there is no war and life is peaceful. If you ever need help, come to us, my family will help you." I was sad to see him go, but thought no more of him for a long time, because the war didn't let you think. How could I ever get to Majorca anyhow? My friend Anna, who had a job in the offices of the Spanish hospital, had persuaded one of the Spanish soldiers to marry her so that she could get a passport. She had her wits about her and was well organised; she stayed on in Riga for a few weeks after the departure of the Blue Division and then travelled to Germany and from there to Spain, before the Russians had even arrived in Latvia. But I waited too long, always hoping that things would work out, dancing at the Opera, unaware of how dangerous things really were. I've never been a realist, you know that! My parents also stayed on.

'Meanwhile, the Russians were pushing their way back, and the Germans moved out of Latvia. On the last possible day, my father managed to get some papers together and we left Riga on a train bound for a German refugee camp. But there was so much confusion at the station that I ended up travelling alone, in a crowded train, not knowing where I was going or what would become of me. I didn't know where my parents and brother were. I was sent from camp to camp, and in some of the camps I had the opportunity of dancing for the German officers, who in exchange would give me champagne and caviar and treat me like a princess. Those were the only good times I remember. I was in Austria for a while, and after 1945 was sent to a displaced persons camp in the British sector of Germany. There too I was able to dance sometimes, in theatres or cafés, in special shows organised by the cultural departments of the Allied forces. I was always looking for my family. I had photographs of them and showed them to officers, to people who had come from other camps. Finally, after many months, when I had already given up hope, my mother found me. She had already managed to find my brother and father, and we were all reunited. It was a wonderful moment . . . But I was restless, desperate to continue with my professional career.

'In the early days of my refugee life, in Pomerania, I had coincided with a Latvian choreographer, a friend of mine from the National Opera in Riga. In 1947, when he joined the Sadler's Wells Ballet he sought me out and asked me to come over to England. The invitation was enough for the British officials to organise my travel papers, but when I got to London, my friend told me he was not permitted to employ me because I was a DP. It didn't matter that I was a good

dancer. He tried very hard to help me, but I ended up scrubbing floors in Archway Hospital. I was so unhappy! If I had
joined the ballet I could have got myself a house and asked my
family to join me – they were still in the DP camp,
waiting . . .

'I began to think that in many ways the Nazis had been so
much more helpful to me than the Allies; they had at least
appreciated my ballet, my art. One day I suddenly remembered the Spanish doctor from the Blue Division. I wrote to
him and told him all my problems. He wrote back and said,
"Come!" So I went! He helped me start up my *academia*. I will
always be grateful to that family. They did all they could to
help me . . . All right, they were Fascists, ultra-right types,
but that did not make them bad people, on the contrary!
They were generous and good to me, especially Dr Oliver.

'Shortly after I came to Palma, in 1949, my father died in
the German camp. He died of malnutrition and a broken
heart. My poor father, he could take no more . . . My brother
ended up in England with my mother . . . And Glen and I
moved to the States. By then, of course, I had given up my
dream of becoming a prima ballerina again – time was against
me. Glen has been very good to me, you know how difficult
I can be . . . but I always went around with a broken heart,
like my father . . . I tried hard, but I was never able to get my
life together again. And I could not get Latvia out of my
mind – its colours, its sounds, the happiness I had known
there . . . The same thing happened to so many people.'

What Olga did not tell me that night – but which I had
found out when I grew older – was that when she first came
to Palma she fell in love with Dr Oliver's son. They had a
short and stormy relationship, complicated by the fact that the
doctor's wife did not want a foreigner for a daughter-in-law.
Poor Olga – one more rejection to add to the list! But Glen

adored her, and took her as she came to him, with a heart that had been broken again and again.

In our school-books nothing specific was ever said about the Nazis and the Second World War. The Blue Division, named after the blue shirts worn by the *falangistas*, was mentioned briefly as having taken part in a battle between the forces of light and darkness, the forces of darkness being the same Reds who had caused such miseries to Spain. But Germany, and Spain's ideological connections with the Third Reich were conveniently glossed over in the educational programme of the fifties, leaving us with a lot of questions unanswered – except, of course, that questions were never asked. We had to memorise everything and there was no opening whatsoever for debate, particularly when it came to what our history teacher liked to call our 'political education'.

I could hear the school bus hooting before it turned into the street where I waited – an ugly brown vehicle with a square nose. Francisca kept a place for me by her side, and though we were not allowed to talk, we would communicate in sign language when we thought the nun wasn't looking. 'Have you learned your history?' 'No! Was it for today?' Francisca would tilt her head and smile kindly. She would take the history book out of her satchel and give it to me to read, showing me the underlined phrases I had to memorise for the lesson. 'The National Crusade saved our Homeland from the wicked Enemy' and 'Generalissimo Franco is Head of the Spanish State and Head of the Falange. He achieved the sacred unification of our Catholic Fatherland.' Francisca had the smoothest skin I have ever seen, a very pale olive colour that contrasted with her dark eyes and black wavy hair, which she tied up in bunches with navy blue ribbons. Of all the girls in the school she looked the loveliest in her dark blue sailor dress, the pleats of her skirt always perfectly ironed, her handkerchiefs immaculate, pressed and bleached by the maid and with a few drops of eau de Cologne to add freshness to them. Her books had no smudges, she was top of the class in every subject, and her laughter sounded like the tinkling of bells. Like many of my friends she wore a gold ring with one of her milk teeth as a gem. She also wore a gold chain with a crucifix, a gold bracelet and pearl earrings, all of which had been given to her for her First Communion. Francisca was my best friend and I was trapped in a fascination for what seemed to me moral and physical perfection. Even if, like the Holy Mother Catholic Church, she could be possessive and demanding, my love and admiration for her were unconditional. I never told her about my neighbour María Jesús and the tramp – she would not have approved, even though our textbooks were full of stories about charitable rich girls who sold their dolls to give money to the poor, or took food and medicines to the sick. She would have argued that, if anything, we should give him bits of bread and that we should learn to distinguish the deserving poor from the undeserving.

Francisca was the epitome of the middle-class Spanish girl of the fifties, the product clearly aimed at by our textbooks and the Spanish educational system of the time: she was tidy, obedient, helpful, deeply religious and in due course would no doubt be willing to fit into the domestic role for which all Spanish girls were destined, that of marrying, slavishly looking after their husbands, having as many children as God would send them, and bringing them up to be patriotic (right-wing) and religious (Catholic). As José Antonio put it: 'Man is overpoweringly selfish; whereas women almost always accept a life of submission, of service, of self-sacrificing contribution to a task.' Her mother and father were always warm and friendly to me whenever I went round to her flat,

but Francisca never came to ours, nor was she allowed to
take ballet lessons. Her mother, a tall, good-looking woman,
argued that Francisca's health was too delicate, and it is true
that she was always being taken to the doctor, who diagnosed
her as being *floja*, weak, a fashionable diagnosis at the time,
which meant boxes and boxes of vitamin-complex injections.
I suspect the real reason was that, like the Mother Superior,
she did not like the thought of her daughter baring her legs in
public.

The school bus made its way down Calle Blanquerna, past
the printer's workshop, past the dry-cleaner's, the stationer's
and the butcher's, all of which still had their iron grilles rolled
down. The nun sat at the front, on a seat that was turned
towards us, and every now and then she would stand up and
say, '*¡A ver!* Let's see!' It was such a long drive that we used to
count how often she said, '*¡A ver!*' just to pass the time. When
the bus reached the avenue we usually had to stop at the crossroads where a policeman stood in his parapet directing the
traffic, always giving way to the crowded orange trams and
blowing his whistle fiercely to accompany his arm movements. We all looked sleepily out of the window as the bus
proceeded down the avenue, with its wide central pavement
bordered by plane trees, past the melon market, where gyp-
sies were taking the fruit out of carts and piling them up into
huge mounds, and past the barracks by the seafront where
young soldiers guarded the entrance under the sign TODO
POR LA PATRIA – Everything for the Fatherland. By now all
the students had been collected, so the bus turned up the
avenue again and then took a long straight road out of Palma
towards the school. There were no more flats here, only
small, run-down houses with geraniums growing in old tins
by the front door, and toothless old men sitting on their
doorsteps smoking – probably immigrants from the poorer

regions of Spain – and little brown dogs running about without collars, and thin cats sitting on walls. On some buildings the mournful head of José Antonio Primo de Rivera had been stencilled on the façade, with the yoke and arrows, and ¡ARRIBA ESPAÑA! written underneath. The bus groaned along the pale grey pot-holed road, and in the distance I could see the purple mountain range behind which was the sea and our mountain village home. We passed carts coming in from the country with vegetables for the market, and lorries piled high with scrap metal, and mopeds and bicycles, and a few cars – mostly 1940s or 1930s models, like my mother's Renault. Through the bus window I watched that silent film every morning and evening, and a grey cloud of sadness always hung over it.

Looking back, I try to imagine what Olga must have felt when she arrived in Majorca, after her grim experiences during the European war. Was she affected by the atmosphere of sadness and depression that prevailed? Or was her own sadness far too great for her to notice it? Even when I saw her at the end of her life, she still carried a deep grudge around with her, as if she had only just lost her position as prima ballerina in the National Opera of Riga – she was still a displaced person.

In the bus, Francisca held my hand and smiled at me as the nun said, '¡A ver!' for the eighty-seventh time.

VI

J i m e n a

It was through Olga that we first met Jimena. She lived near the ballet school and did the cleaning there once or twice a week. At that time our maid had returned to the mountain village and my mother needed someone to help with the housework. Olga referred her to us. 'You will like her,' she told my mother in her Latvian accent. 'She is so *simpática*, so honest, so hard-working! And she is always saying to me, "If you hear of someone who needs a cleaner, let me know." ' Jimena became much more than a cleaner to us – a friend, almost one of the family. She is now in her eighties, and since she is not sure what day she was born – all the records of births, marriages and deaths in her home town were destroyed in a fire at the end of the Civil War – she decided some years ago to share her birthday with my mother, on 22 February. 'Your mother and I are twins!' she says.

Whenever I see Jimena we end up talking about the old days, when I was at school in Palma and she used to come to our flat to wash those ugly floors that looked like raw meat and fry up the fish she had bought for us on the way, at the market. We remember how sometimes she brought one of her two boys with her, and he would sit quietly in the kitchen while she worked; and how, after cleaning our flat, she would go round to Olga's. 'Poor Olga,' says Jimena, every time I mention her. 'She never had any food in her flat because she spent all her money on cigarettes and taxis . . . I did not say anything, but I could see how difficult things were for her. Sometimes I would pinch a little bit of your mother's tea and take it to her, to cheer her up. I wouldn't have dared take it for me, but it was for Olga, may God forgive me! Olga had a head full of dreams, nothing but dreams!'

When I was a schoolgirl Jimena never had time to talk much. I would watch her work, her black jersey sleeves rolled up above her elbows, her large hips swaying from side to side as she came and went with a pail of water. She would speak to my mother at the end of her work, while she folded her apron and rolled down her sleeves; then she would give me a kiss and say, '¡Adiós, mocetona!' on her way to the door. I loved that word, mocetona, the diminutive of moza, which means 'young girl' or 'lass'. It comes straight from the heart of mainland Spain, from the rural areas of olive groves, vineyards and little white houses to which Jimena belonged. And the way she said it, with such open sensuality, struck a chord somewhere deep inside me in those pre-adolescent years. If anyone had told me then that Jimena was one of the Enemy described by Señorita Mercedes, I would have found such a suggestion preposterous. How could that warm, kind woman, who worked so hard, be one of those evil people who had wanted to poison Spain?

Over the years I learned that Jimena and her family had been Republican sympathisers during the war; and on one occasion Jimena had insinuated to my mother that things had been hard for them at the end, in 1939. Neither of us ever questioned her, however, and she never offered to talk about the past. Until just the other day.

I was in Majorca and Jimena had come up to stay with my mother for the weekend. Jimena and I were in the kitchen, preparing a meal for the evening. I wanted to know how she made her roast chickens taste so good.

'It's very easy,' she said. 'You take the chicken and rub it with a little piece of chicken cube, to give it a bit more taste. Now we need to slice the onions. Are those all the onions you have? Help, we're up against the Church! You'll have to send one of the children to the village to buy some more because we'll need all these and we can't leave your mother's kitchen without a single onion. Now, we put the sliced onions under the chicken with some rashers of bacon. Oh dear! I nearly forgot the lemon, my head's going, that's for sure. I used to be a very good cook, but now . . .'

'You're still a good cook, Jimena – what about the white wine?'

'Don't rush or you'll be late! The wine, *hermana*, you add at the end, when the other things have done their work, see? But I tell you, my head's not what it was, I keep forgetting things. Of course, after all the difficult times we lived through that's not surprising . . . Those years when I used to come to your flat. Oh what times they were, *muchacha*!' Jimena laughed – she always laughs nervously when she remembers those days. 'We were always so hungry! Nobody could fool me with all that talk of National Reconstruction. The reconstruction was for the others, not for us. My hair is white and I know what I'm saying. Now, then, let's take the red peppers out of the oven, they will be soft enough by now. Just leave them on a plate for later. Don't let me forget them, you know what I'm like . . .'

There was a long pause. Then Jimena said, 'Having to keep silent was the worst part of it. If you came from a socialist family you had to keep quiet, and keep all those things inside you, rotting. For forty years, after they had taken everything away from us, we were not allowed to speak. Now things are different, people can say what they feel, but then, well, you were too young to understand, of course, and besides, at school they must have filled your head with all that Movimiento and Falange stuff. But, you see, only those who had been Nationalists during the war were able to prosper when it ended – people like Dr Oliver, just to take an example, because he had been in the Blue Division, and all those religious types who were openly on Franco's side, well connected with the Jesuits, and whose wives did charity work for the Sección Femenina . . . people who were well plugged in.'

Jimena put the chicken in the oven. The sun poured in through the yellow curtains and we heard a flock of hungry seagulls screaming up the mountain towards the olive groves. She sat down again at the kitchen table and put her hand, now deformed by arthritis, on her cheek. Her eyes were watery, but not with tears, just old age.

'We mustn't forget to add the wine,' she said. 'I forget everything these days.' Jimena smiled, bit her lower lip and shook her head. Soon the chicken began to sizzle in the oven,   · the smell of herbs and onion and all her special ingredients filled the room. Suddenly she said, 'Of course, there are a lot of things I will never forget, so long as God grants me life. My children won't listen to me, they tell me I'm mad,' and she twisted her index finger on her temple. '*Loca.*'

Slowly, in the sunlit kitchen, Jimena told me the story of her life, which had begun in a village south of Madrid, near the wine-producing town of Valdepeñas. She told me about her

father, Joaquín, the village carpenter. How one cold
December morning with the sky a dazzling blue, he stepped
out of his house near the village square holding his newborn
baby in his arms and followed by his nine other children.
How her mother watched them leave from her rocking chair
by the fireplace, shaking her head and smiling, for she had
finally persuaded her husband to take the baby to be baptised. She did not mind his left-wing ideas, but she put her
foot down at the thought of leaving her babies unchristened.
Every time one was born it became more of a struggle to convince him. Perhaps this would be the last.

Jimena watched the little white bundle in her father's large
hands as they crossed the village square, past the fountain,
past the trees and benches, and walked into the church. He
removed his beret and the girls unfolded their black veils and
put them on their heads. The boys put their hands in their
pockets or rubbed their chins awkwardly. The church smelled
of incense and damp, and the gold leaf decorating the niches
shone dully in the candlelight that illuminated the figures of St
Sebastian enduring his torment, of the Virgin Mary carrying
her Child, of St Teresa in her black nun's habit holding a quill
in one hand and a book in the other. The priest was waiting
for them by the font. Jimena's father handed the baby to
Jimena, who was to be the godmother, then thrust his hand
inside his coat, pulled out a Republican flag – red, yellow and
purple – and wrapped the baby tightly in it. 'Here's my
Republican son,' he said to the priest. 'Now christen him if
you must.' ('The funny thing is,' Jimena added, 'that this
brother turned out to be a real right-wing type when he was
older!')

The village where Jimena grew up was in the province of
Ciudad Real – part of Don Quixote's La Mancha, where
windmills turned into giants – which remained under

Republican control throughout the war. It was also one of the few Spanish provinces where the Agrarian Law of 1932 had been fully and successfully implemented; it meant that all unworked estates measuring over fifty-six acres had been taken over by the Republican government and redistributed to peasant co-operatives or individual peasants, after compensating the original owners. So the atmosphere in the village was one of social reform and belief in the Republic, after centuries of suffocating feudal laws.

Joaquín's workshop was in the back of the house, next to the *corral* where the family kept the hens, the goats and the donkeys. His eldest son worked with him, making threshers, as well as pieces of furniture and coffins. Jimena loved the workshop, the smell of sawdust and the sounds made by the saw and the hammers, and she would often help the men by holding the planks steady when they were sawing or stacking pieces of wood. But when they were making a coffin and she saw the black lining waiting to be nailed into it, she would stay well away until it left the house.

They were reasonably well off, what Jimena called 'the second level of society – not the rich, nor the very poor'. They employed a boy to look after the donkeys, her father had land and her mother owned two houses.

'My mother was very well educated, she had been to school in Barcelona, you know,' said Jimena. 'She could read and had beautiful handwriting, so everyone in the village would come to her when they needed a letter written or read to them. There was also a man in the village who read very well and whenever he got hold of a newspaper he would sit in the square and we would all gather round him to listen – especially during the war. Of course, we had a school in the village, and the *maestra* did what she could, poor thing, with all of us in one room. But she only came twice a week, because she also taught in another village, and we didn't have any books or anything like the sort of thing my grandchildren have nowadays. So we didn't learn much. It's your mother who has taught me to read and write, now that we are both widows and can spend more time together. Did you know I can read magazines and newspapers now, and I can sign my name and string a few words together? Your mother is a good teacher.'

When she was not in school Jimena played in *corrales* with her friends, or in the square, or went into the fields outside the village. Sometimes, on Sundays, or when it was someone's name day or a religious feast, there were meals in the open, with friends and neighbours. She remembered the smell of the *chorizos* grilling on the hot coals, and the taste of the dark green olive oil on wide slices of bread, which was baked at home once a week. 'There was plenty of food where we lived, before the war,' she said. 'Simple food, but plenty of it. I suppose we were lucky.'

The girls also stayed at home much of the time and learned to embroider and to sew. In the summer they would take little stools out on the pavement to sit and gossip while they did their needlework. In the winter they sat round the wood fire, or kept warm with heated terracotta tiles which sometimes cracked open with a loud bang. Jimena was good at sewing, and when she grew older she would tack up clothes for her neighbours and hand them back ready for the sewing machine; they would pay her with a ham or a *chorizo*, or a tin of home-made biscuits.

The boys enjoyed a much greater freedom. There was a river near the village and sometimes, in the summer, if there was enough water running down it, they would go swimming there. But the girls were not allowed to swim. 'Women weren't allowed to do anything,' said Jimena. 'We were like slaves, always doing all the work; the men did nothing, *hermana*. The Republic didn't change that – men are always men. And you know, people were also very religious, even in my family, even during the years of the Republic. One of my cousins became a nun – lots of girls did in those days, either because they couldn't get a *novio* or because their *novio* had left them, or because their families forced them into a nunnery – one mouth less to feed. A lot of boys studied to become priests too, but many did it just for the education and left the seminary before being ordained. But us girls, we were always being watched by our parents, especially when the boys started looking at us . . .'

Jimena had had plenty of admirers: not only was she very pretty, she was open and talkative, and she danced the *jota* better than anyone. Her first love was a tall young man with dark hair, who had recently moved to her village to live with his aunt and uncle. She first noticed him on St John's night, when he was throwing sticks into the bonfire that raged in the middle of the square. He stood there alone looking at the flames and she immediately felt the glow of his gentleness touch her heart. 'It was a *flechazo*, like an arrow piercing us both. But he came from a much poorer family than ours and my parents would never have allowed me to marry him. Once, during the village *fiesta*, my brother dragged me away because he saw us dancing together. It wasn't anything like these modern dances – when you dance a *jota*, well, you know, it's just a lot of jumping about and moving your arms right and left. We didn't even touch one another, but I suppose my brother could see we made a good couple – and there was nothing I could do or say, it was useless to protest. Another time I bumped into him in the village square when he was coming out of the barber's shop. There was nobody else around. "I've fallen in love with you", he said, "and no other woman will do for me. Say you'll marry me, Jimena.

I'll go and sort the papers out right away if you say yes." And do you know what I answered, *muchacha*? I said, "You'd be wasting your time," and turned round and walked straight home. I felt very sad, there was a knot in my throat . . . but you couldn't go against your parents' wishes in those days.'

Then the war came and the young man left the village in uniform never to return.

'When the war broke out in 1936 the village was at first divided into Reds and Fascists – or into Republicans and Nationalists, if you prefer – depending on what doctor you went to in the village. Yes, it was as simple as that. One doctor was a socialist and the other was a Fascist. The socialist doctor was a cousin of mine called Hilario who had worked in Madrid. But Ciudad Real was not taken by the Nationalists and remained within the Republican zone throughout the war, so those who had at first sympathised with Franco had to keep a low profile.

'Instead of saying '*¡Adiós!*' everyone now said '*¡Salud!*', because *Adiós* sounded too religious, but otherwise life in the village was not so different. Of course, we used to hear terrible stories, especially at the beginning, of what was going on in the larger towns – killings of nuns and priests, burning down of convents, dreadful things! But later the Fascists got their own back – I tell you, a hundred times over!'

By the time the war had begun, Jimena's parents had arranged for her to marry a cousin, whom she had always liked very much, though not in the same way as she had liked the tall dark man. Her cousin was now officially Jimena's *novio* and would come courting most evenings; but there was little conversation between them. Most of his talk was with Jimena's father, Joaquín. 'And my father would make sure I was in my room before my cousin left the house to go home,' Jimena said, laughing. 'There was no sex or anything like that in those days, only an occasional kiss and holding hands. I had not even reached that stage with my cousin! Parents had to supervise the courtship very carefully, because if a *novio* left a girl she would never find another one. Evil tongues would spread the word that she had given in to his desires and that he had punished her weakness by abandoning her. And if a girl got pregnant before the wedding and the wedding went ahead, it had to take place at night and the girl had to dress in black. That's the way things were, *hermana!*'

Jimena's wedding was planned for June 1939 but by then the war had ended and the whole family had left the village. The night before they left, the cousin came round to the house and tried to persuade Joaquín to leave Jimena behind. But Joaquín would not hear of it: he was too afraid of what might happen to her if she stayed in the village. The revenge of the victors knew no limits.

Jimena turned her attention to the plate of baked peppers and started peeling them. She held each one by the stem and pulled off the browned skin, revealing the juicy red flesh underneath. Then she placed them side by side on a clean plate and stared at them. Her eyebrows rose and she shook her head.

After the fall of Madrid, in March 1939, which marked the end of the war, the Nationalists quickly occupied all the remaining Republican zone, from Ciudad Real to the eastern coast, where thousands of Republicans were trying to leave the country by sea. All the men returned home from the front line, on foot, in lorries, in carts, and now the Nationalists in the village began to speak up and strut about the place making the Fascist salute. 'I'll never forget the day a boy – he can't have been more than fourteen – wearing the

Fascist blue shirt and black tie, came in to fetch my father,'
Jimena said. 'It was late one afternoon at the beginning of
April 1939, a cold, windy day. He took him away and there
was nothing we could do to stop him, though he was only a
child. All night long we waited for news, fearing the worst.
The next morning they brought my father back, half dead.
They had hung him with a rope by the feet and given him a
terrible beating. An aunt of mine was asked to go and clean up
the blood. After that my father was never the same. He was a
broken man, very shaken and he couldn't hear very well. He
must have been about fifty-five at the time this happened.
My cousin Hilario, the doctor, was not allowed to keep his
practice after the war or even work as a doctor – he was
lucky not to get shot. So was my father. Things were very
bad, a lot of people were arrested . . . You could see women
walking to Infantes to visit their husbands in the prison there.
Some were pregnant but had to walk all that way to try to
keep their men alive with whatever food they could lay their
hands on or buy after selling all they had: embroidered sheets,
anything . . .

'Soon after my father's detention we left the village. A
Civil Guard who happened to be a friend of his came to the
house and warned him that we must leave; what they had
done to him was only the beginning – if he stayed he would be
executed. We left immediately for Majorca, where an older
brother had already managed to settle. Money was useless
after the war, it was worthless from one day to the next, and
people had to mortgage property and things to get some cash.
But the Fascists took everything from us: our home with
everything in it, even an olive grove we owned outside the village – one of the best olive groves in the area. We had to leave
the village quickly, all of us. We left with nothing. With one
hand in front and the other behind, as they say. I never saw my

cousin again, except once, just a few years ago, when I was already a widow and he was a widower. It happened quite by chance, when he was on a visit to Palma, but I was too shy to say anything and I don't think he recognised me. I would have liked to speak to him, to ask him how things went for him after the war, to catch up with things. I will always be left with that question inside me, I will never know how he got on after I left. So many people were dispersed. It's very sad.'

Jimena's family managed to reach Valencia – some two hundred miles away – partly on trucks and partly on foot, and then took the ferry to Palma. Not all on the same boat: Joaquín travelled separately in case he got into trouble with the Majorcan officials. Jimena's mother travelled with her eldest son, and Jimena went with two other sisters and three small brothers. All the boats were packed with immigrants from Murcia and the south of Spain in search of work, carrying mattresses and bundles of clothes. When Jimena saw the island from afar it did not impress her the way it had impressed Blanca some ten years earlier. To Jimena it was just a large rock to which she was being exiled, and she wished she was back in her village preparing for her wedding, sitting outside her front door gossiping with her friends as she made her bridal gown.

'Once we had docked in Palma port,' said Jimena, 'my sisters and I walked down the gangway. I could see my mother and father standing in the crowd with my eldest brother, and it was good to know they had reached the island safely. My three younger brothers made a dash for it, dodging the police and disappearing into the crowd. My sisters also somehow managed to get through without a problem, but the *guardias* stopped me. They asked for my papers and when they saw them they said there were some missing. Then they grabbed me, one holding one arm and another the other. Before I could even speak to my family the guards marched me down the main street in Palma to the prison, where I was held overnight with a whole lot of other people. They were deporting us all to Barcelona. There was some paper missing, I'm not sure what it was, I can't remember, I just know that without that piece of paper you couldn't enter Majorca. They just wanted to be difficult, to frighten me. Luckily my older brother, the one who had settled on the island before us, was allowed to visit me and give me an address of some friends in Barcelona. I spent about a month there, with people I didn't even know, but there was no way of sorting any papers out. So I decided to try again. I took the ferry, and this time I managed to hide behind two priests as I walked down the gangway. Nobody stopped me.

'When we first settled in Palma we had a terrible time. We were *forasters*, people from the mainland, and the Majorcans looked down on us. I earned 10 *céntimos* an hour – one *peseta* a day. There was a lot of poverty everywhere. I'll never forget that on one of the first days my father and I went to the flea-market to buy two low chairs. When we got them home we found they were full of bugs. There were always bugs everywhere in those days. We were hungry and humiliated and the worst thing was that we had to be quiet, we could never speak out and say what we wanted to say. If they had known I was a socialist, they would have shaved my head and given me a dose of castor oil. It was like the Inquisition. Did you know that they sent priests round to the houses of the *forasters* regularly to check on us, and if there had been a crime or a robbery they searched our houses to see whether they could accuse us of it? But, as I said before, the worst thing was not being able to speak for so many years. It's bad to bottle things up.'

Soon after their arrival on the island, Jimena married a Majorcan, a hard-working man by whom she had two sons. He was a socialist, and when he came to court her he would talk to her father about what had happened to the socialists in Majorca during the war.

The story was almost over. She looked at me with her lips tightly closed. Then she said, 'He was a very quiet person, a very good man, but he wasn't a fighter, you know that. Joan was always too timid, too resigned, too . . . It's been hard, we've had some very bad times.' Then she began to smile and the smile turned into a laugh. 'I told you before: we were always hungry!'

'Shall we pour the wine over the chicken now?' I asked.

'Oh, the wine! said Jimena. 'You should never let me talk so much, *hermana*!'

Jimena is able to laugh at the absurdity of life because she is open and talkative and could still dance the *jota* if she heard one. She lives in a council flat and has a decent enough pension, thanks to the socialists, she tells me. Her favourite occupation is listening to the news on television and finding out exactly what is going on in Spain – she would have made a good politician, given the chance. Now I wonder how many of the women I saw as I journeyed to school on the brown bus had also been left on the losing side at the end of the war. It is always the women who first come to my mind when I think of Spain in the fifties. Women sweeping their bit of pavement, or buying two eggs and a tin of sardines in the corner shop.

VII

Sister Valentina

The school of the Dominican sisters was an impressive building made of pale grey stone, with blue-grey shutters, railings
and doors. Inside, the walls were white, the floor tiles a light
creamy colour, the ceilings high with dark beams. On the
way to the classroom with our satchels, our navy blue coats
still buttoned up after the bus ride, we walked through long
corridors and large halls that smelt of disinfectant, with chairs
lined up stiffly against the walls, always silent and dark and
empty of life. They made me think of the chambers of the
soul in St Teresa's *Interior Castle*, or of the empty caverns of
the soul described by St John of the Cross: a void waiting to
be filled with the light of God. Religion had acquired a
sombre lustre since my serious education had begun, and the
uncomplicated joy of my geranium-petal altars seemed like a
thing of the distant past.

At that time of the morning we sometimes met Father
Moll coming out of the chapel where he had been hearing
confession from the nuns or from some of the girls who
boarded at the school. I hated him. He held out a limp hand
to be kissed and we had no alternative but to take it to our

lips, though it was damp and hairy and had an unpleasant smell. Once I tried to slip away but he put his left hand on my shoulder while the others were kissing his right hand, forcing me to stay. When my classmates had gone, he asked me, 'Did you say your morning prayers to little Jesus when you woke up?' I nodded vigorously, not sure where to look. 'You know little Jesus expects more of you than of anyone else because you have not yet been christened and your soul is in danger, don't you?' I nodded again, and kissed his hand quickly before running off. How many times did they all have to remind me of what was gnawing at me day and night?

I was in a state of perpetual anxiety about my salvation, unable to reconcile what I was being assured was the only truth in the world with my parents' agnosticism. In the mountain village there had been an equilibrium between my two different environments, each with its own myths, stories, traditions and languages. Neither one had ever claimed total supremacy over the other, and in my mind both coexisted in a peaceful way within the elemental setting of the terraced valley. In my new urban life the balance had been upset. Not only was I being indoctrinated politically by the educational system of the time, and made to believe that Franco was some sort of saint who had delivered Spain from the brutal Enemy, but I was being indoctrinated religiously and made to believe that if I did not embrace the Roman Catholic Church I was damned for eternity. This brainwashing was so powerful that I was overcome by a deep sense of unworthiness at not being a Catholic, and by a real fear of dying before being baptised and ending up in Hell. Sister Valentina's diatribes, aimed at making us better Christians, left me trembling.

'Can you imagine what it would be like to be burning for ever?' she would cry. 'For ever, without a single moment's respite, without the pain ever abating? Have you ever tried

putting a match to your finger, just for a split second?
Remember how it felt, then imagine what that pain would be
like all over your body, never ending, for ever and ever and
ever. Let the eyes of your imagination open the gates of Hell
and watch the fierce flames raging. Imagine yourselves there,
among those fires and devils and fearful shadows, imagine
your souls entering that place, which you will, if you happen
to die in mortal sin!' The nun's clear, melodious voice carried
with it a hint of her own delirium, of nights spent awake with
such thoughts, of terrible mortifications, of hair shirts worn
tight under her night clothes – and her questions were left
suspended in the air of the classroom, followed by a long,
heavy silence. She walked up and down the aisle in her
immaculate, cream-coloured habit with a black overall hiding
her natural shape, and her face framed by the stiff white
toque. The large rosary that dangled from her waist made a
soft tinkling sound in the thick silence. Christ's head on the
little crucifix was bent with despair for humanity, and
I wished with all my heart I could be worthy of His
redemption.

Language also became an issue. In school we were only
allowed to speak Castilian, in other words, standard Spanish;
Majorcan, like its sister language Catalan, was officially
banned by Franco and considered with disdain as a dialect of
uneducated peasants. Until then, it had never occurred to
me that one language could be superior to another, but now,
if we ever spoke Majorcan, the nuns would cry, '¡Habla en
cristiano! Speak in Christian!' In the mountain village the
Virgin Mary had seemed to me an approachable divinity with
whom I could communicate freely in any of my three languages, or even without words. Now I prayed to her
in Christian Spanish: I could see her only as an icon of
Franco's Spain.

Only one member of the Church hierarchy managed to make me feel slightly more comfortable with my situation. His name was Father Velasco and he was the complete opposite of Father Moll. He was tall, energetic, he had penetrating blue eyes, and he even drove a car. We sometimes caught a glimpse of his trouser legs – a venial sin, no doubt – as he got in or out of his little grey car. His hands were dry and strong and he ruffled our hair and laughed when we clustered round him. I liked him because he seemed so much more open-minded than the other priests I knew. He once told us that there were historical doubts regarding the date of the Three Kings' adoration of Christ; the event may even have taken place when Jesus was three or four years old, he said. That was the sort of thing I was used to hearing my father say at home, and it made me feel for a brief moment that perhaps the two worlds were not so impossibly apart, after all. Father Velasco never picked on me the way Father Moll did, nor did he give me the looks of pity I was used to receiving from the nuns. He turned out to be the worst of them all.

Every classroom had a large crucifix on the wall behind the teacher's desk and a framed photograph of Franco next to it. On another wall there were two large maps of Spain: a political map with its fifteen regions (sixteen, if you counted the provinces in North Africa) in different colours and a geographical map showing the main mountain ranges and rivers, which we all knew by heart. The desks were double, with a flat ledge for the inkwells and slanted tops on which to write; but we sat in alphabetical order, which meant my neighbour was always Elvira Gamundí, not Francisca Perelló, my possessive bosom friend. Francisca sat two rows behind me, watching everything I did and making sure I did not get too friendly with Elvira. When Sister Valentina gave us religion, I was even more aware that her eyes were fixed on the back of my head.

'Sacrifices!' cried the nun. 'We must always offer sacrifices to our Lord, to make up for all the suffering we cause Him with our sins!' And with her long bony hands she would write these words of St John of the Cross on the blackboard for us to copy into our religion exercise books.

Niega tus deseos y hallarás lo que desea tu corazón.
Deny yourself your desires, and you will find what your heart desires.

'Jesus suffered in silence just for you, and you must do the same,' she said. 'Even if you are young, there are plenty of ways, approved by the Church, in which you can mortify yourselves for your sins and faults. Now then, which are they? Francisca?'

Francisca was quite openly Sister Valentina's favourite pupil. We all turned our heads to watch her as she recited, 'Going without something you like, doing a favour to another little girl who is never friendly to you, eating what you don't like to eat, and doing the jobs your mother asks you to do without complaining.'

But I knew there were other things that Francisca did, like putting tiny pebbles in her shoes, and that she had told Sister Valentina about it. And that Sister Valentina had scolded her, but only gently, with a smile of complicity. Francisca had told me all this one day in the bus, going home. She and Sister Valentina were inseparable, Francisca with her smooth olive complexion and shiny curls, and Sister Valentina as pale as white candle-wax.

I had tried penitence myself, in an attempt to emulate my friend, but never got further than pinching my arm rather half-heartedly or kneeling on the cold floor of my bedroom for a while, when I thought nobody was watching. Common sense prevailed over my religious zeal, although at the time I thought it was weakness.

Most of the nuns in the school came from the mainland, and Sister Valentina was from a village near Ávila, in the heart of the old kingdom of Castile. Her voice was clear and musical, without the heavy nasal accent with which Majorcans spoke Castilian, or the singsong of Galicians or Catalans, or the exaggerated expressiveness of the Andalusians. The way she spoke transported me to what I imagined her native land was like, full of sturdy castles, monasteries and town walls with battlements cutting into the clear sky, and storks nesting in the towers of the village churches. Our history books told us that the Spaniards had built many fortresses in Castile from which they rode off to reconquer the lands stolen from them by the Arabs — with the help of St James, whose body had been discovered miraculously off the shores of Galicia. The Reconquest lasted for centuries but was blessed with the certainty of the true Faith, just like Franco's great crusade against the Reds.

Sister Valentina was young and pretty, with delicate features and pale pink nails, always well trimmed and tidy. She did not always talk about Hell and sacrifices. Sometimes she told us beautiful tales from the New Testament or about the lives of saints. But even then I noticed a trace of dissatisfaction in her voice and in her pale eyes. I assumed that we were the cause of that annoyance, but now I wonder what sufferings lay behind those eyes. Perhaps the memory of a father anguished by poverty, a coarse man with a beret, smelling of sweat, cheap tobacco and wine, who pulled out his belt and beat his children when he was drunk and spent his evenings and Sundays playing dominoes in the village tavern; four or five children to a bed, a thin mother dressed in black, and bread and garlic soup for dinner. Or had a tall, good-looking man,

as attractive as Jimena's first 'courtier', taken her innocence
and then abandoned her?

Perhaps Sister Valentina had regarded the nunnery as her
only means of escape, the only way she could break free from
the shackles of her wretched home or the threat of an equally
unappealing married life. In the restrictive society of postwar
Spain, joining a religious order was probably the only free
decision a woman could take, a decision nobody could contest. When the girl in the dairy shop opposite our flat in
Palma decided to become a nun, she stopped pouring milk
into the tin cans at the counter and retired to the back of the
shop for a while, to avoid contact with the outside world,
until her novitiate began. Sometimes, when her older sister
drew back the dark blue curtain that separated the shop from
the living quarters, to fetch a crate of yoghurts or a barrel of
milk, I would catch a glimpse of her sitting quietly with her
mother, smiling absently: she had become an almost supernatural creature, an untouchable person whom one could not
criticise for giving up her duty to the Spanish nation (which
was to become a submissive wife and a devoted mother of as
many children as God would send her) because she had
retired from this world to marry God and wear His wedding
ring. Of course, Sister Valentina may have had a true vocation,
she may have experienced that mysterious light, that voice
from Heaven, that sublime moment of understanding we read
about in the books of saints.

Whatever her reasons for taking the veil, Sister Valentina
channelled all her energies into forming the souls of the new
generation of postwar Spaniards under her care, just as
Señorita Mercedes worked on forming our political ideas.
Although she was probably too young to have been a nun
during the war, she was not too young to have heard first-
hand accounts of the actions carried out against religious

orders by anarchists and other extreme-left groups during the Civil War, and would have embraced the anti-Red feelings that prevailed in the early fifties in Spain.

The collective memory of the trauma suffered by all devout Catholics in Spain during the thirties operated in favour of Franco's postwar alliance of Church and state, which made it easy for him to establish and perpetuate an attitude of revenge and smug superiority among the victors. When Sister Valentina was a young girl, the hatred between the classes had become a hatred between 'believers' and 'unbelievers', with all the contradictory issues that such an oversimplification implied. The Church had become the people's enemy, a symbol of the old oppression of the rich over the poor. But the war had changed all that: there was no room for unbelievers in the new, ultra-Catholic Spain.

In such an atmosphere, the presence of a northern European girl from a Protestant family among their all-Catholic herd was too much for the Dominican sisters and their missionary zeal. I have recently discovered that on the last day of the summer term before I joined the school, the Mother Superior had called a special assembly to announce my arrival the following autumn. 'It is your duty as Catholics, as members of this school and as Spaniards,' she said, 'to try to guide a poor lost sheep into the shelter of the Roman Catholic Church. We must all do our utmost to save the soul of this young English girl, who knows no better, from the flames of Hell. Every effort must be made. Try to persuade her gently, almost without her noticing, through the sheer force of your friendship. God and the Virgin Mary will rejoice at her conversion and reward the whole school with Their blessings both in this life and in the life hereafter.'

In the three years I was there not even Francisca gave away the Mother Superior.

From our classroom window we could see the tall dark pine trees that surrounded the school grounds and the little grotto with the statue of the Madonna set among sea shells where we went to recite the Hail Mary every day at noon.

Closer to the school building, just outside our window, was the open space where we skipped and sang during break, with two girls turning the long thick rope that whipped the dust off the ground, and the rest queuing up to enter the moving arch. One of the most popular songs was '*El cocherito leré*'. Every time the girls turning the rope said '*leré*', a cheerful but meaningless two-syllable sound, the one who was skipping had to stand still while the rope was turned twice in the air above her head. Thirty years later, my own children sang the same song:

> Last night the coachman *leré*
> the nice young coachman *leré*
> said he would take me *leré*
> out for a ride, oh, *leré*!

> But then I answered *leré*
> I do not wish to *leré*
> 'cause riding coaches *leré*
> makes my head spin, oh, *leré*!

There was another skipping song that went:

> Rice pudding!
> I want to get married
> To a *señorita*

> From this town.
> She must know how to sew
> And embroider too,
> She must know her times tables
> Better than you!

We also sang a few religious songs. I remember one about St Catherine, with a beautiful, haunting melody, in which one girl (St Catherine) had to kneel down while another (an angel) held her arms forming a circle above her head, like a halo, and chanted '*Sube, sube, Catalina*, Rise, rise, Catherine'. The thought of an angel asking me to rise up to Heaven made my skin crawl with excitement. Heaven after death was what I longed for more than anything, even though I knew it was unattainable for me. I had no hope of ever going to Heaven unless I became a Catholic.

Among the dark prints of monsters and devils in the edition of *The Pilgrim's Progress* that had frightened me so much as a small child, there was a beautiful coloured plate in a Pre-Raphaelite style called 'Christian and Hopeful arrive in Heaven', in which the two men are being covered in white gauzy robes by two angels, while two other angels hovering above them are placing crowns over their heads. More angels gather around the men, playing trumpets and harps, or throwing rose petals at them from a little basket. The whole picture was like a sudden burst of celestial light, but this, I now realised, was a Protestant Heaven and therefore a sham. How could people be so blind? I felt sorry for Bunyan, he really seemed to believed that his Heaven existed when he wrote:

Now just as the gates were opened to let in the men, I looked in after them, and behold, the city shone like the sun; the streets also were paved with gold; and in them walked many men with crowns on their heads, palms in their hands, and golden harps, to sing praises withal. There were also of them that had wings, and they answered one another without intermission, saying, 'Holy, holy, holy is the Lord!' And after that they shut up the gates, which, when I had seen, I wished myself among them.

I wished myself among them too, but unlike Bunyan, unlike the whole of my family, I knew the sad truth: Heaven was open only to Catholics. And there could be no two heavens. Sister Valentina was always pitying the Chinese and the Africans because they would never go to Heaven – that was why the missions were so important, she said. I knew those words were also directed to me.

In our book *Meditations for Girls* there was a chapter on the joys of Heaven, headed 'What is Heaven?' which Sister Valentina made us learn by heart. I was given a little white rosary as a prize for reciting it without any mistakes and I still remember some of it today:

What is Heaven? Dear girl, have you ever sat down to think about the joys of Heaven? Remember what the Catechism tells you: 'Heaven is the sum of all good things, without any trace of evil.' In other words, not one good thing, or two, but all good things at the same time, without ever ending, without ever tiring of them, without ever getting bored . . . Does this give you some idea of the happiness of Heaven? Close your eyes and imagine you are in there, in the most pleasant and beautiful place you could ever dream of, with music composed of the sweetest harmonies imaginable, with indescribable beauties for your eyes to enjoy; your body will shine more brilliantly than the sun itself with the gift of clarity; you will never feel tired, thanks to the gift of agility; nor will you feel pain, or grief or sadness, thanks to the gift of impassibility; and you will be able to pass through other bodies thanks to the gift of subtlety. Think of anything and everything you would wish to have: in Heaven you will enjoy it. You will see and embrace all the beings you loved in this world who have gone to Heaven: parents, brothers, sisters, friends. You will enjoy the company of angels, of the saints, of your Immaculate Mother, the Holy Virgin Mary. Would you not consider yourself the happiest girl in the world if you were able to see Her now just for a moment? . . . Well, child, can you imagine what it will be like to live in her company throughout eternity?

I could just about imagine it by looking at the ecstatic faces of saints who were already safely there. Francisca and I both collected *estampas*, coloured prints of martyrs which we kept in empty cigar boxes. The saints had pale faces, with tired eyes looking upwards and a soft smile on their lips. You could tell that martyrdom was nothing compared to the joy of Heaven.

My favourite saint was, of course, my namesake, St Lucia, one of the many early Christian martyrs, who is represented holding a salver with two eyes placed on it, and a palm in the other hand. I wore a medal of St Lucia round my neck – I had somehow plucked up the courage to ask my parents for it. She is the patron saint of good eyesight, and consequently of seamstresses, because she is said to have had her eyes pulled out in her martyrdom, though I have since discovered that there is no historical truth in that gruesome story. Her day is celebrated on 13 December, just a few days before the winter solstice, and her name comes from the Latin *lux*, so her feast day probably replaced some ancient European ritual to the dying sun. In Sweden St Lucia's Day is an important feast and one December, at about this time, I was taken by my father to a party at the Swedish consulate in Palma, where I was dressed up in a long white robe and asked to wander around a crowded room balancing a crown of lighted candles on my head. And in Italy, where we went on a few summer holidays to visit my half-sister Jenny in Portofino, I collected *occhi di Santa Lucia* – St Lucy's eyes – from the nearby beach of Rapallo, flat shell-like stones, no bigger than a fingernail, with blue or brown circles on them, which I treasured as much as my *estampas*.

But would I ever get to Heaven and escape the eternal flames? Would I ever be able to persuade my parents that I must be baptised? And even if I did, how could I be truly happy there if none of my family were with me? I would be separated from them, worrying for all eternity about their destiny. It was all such a muddle.

When we skipped and sang and formed large rings that turned right and then left, and chased one another in the playground, I could put those anxious thoughts aside. But in the classroom there were too many reminders of my short-comings. Neither of the two Saviours on the wall could have approved of me. For a start I was English, and the English were mostly evil Protestants who, moreover, had taken Gibraltar unlawfully from Spain. And although I myself had not been baptised into any religion, my parents were theo-retically Church of England, and anything Christian that was not Roman Catholic was classified as Protestant. 'Protestants are heretics who deny the authority of the Church and inter-pret the Bible as they see fit,' said our catechism. A man who lived two floors above us was a Spanish Protestant and he always had very badly paid jobs because of his religion, even though he was a qualified lawyer or something equally important. He was tall and thin and rather pale and the neighbours never greeted him or his wife except with a nod. We felt very sorry for him and sometimes he would drop in for a drink with my father. We also had an English friend who ended up in the Palma prison because he was caught distributing Jehovah's Witness leaflets. What would happen to my father if they discovered his theories on the Crucifixion? Would the Civil Guards come to our flat one day and take him away in handcuffs? Franco looked down at me from his photograph, and I tried to see mercy in his eyes.

The crucifix next to Franco was an even less encouraging sight. I knew Jesus was feeling sad for me, the *inglesita* who had to go up to the choir and stand by the organ when the whole school took Holy Communion in the chapel, the little English girl whose Protestant parents would not allow her to join the Catholic Church. Of course He knew, because He knew everything, that I had not actually asked my parents for permission to become a Catholic. 'My parents won't let me,' was what I told everyone, but I was not being entirely truthful. Every day, when I listened to Sister Valentina's lectures, I made up my mind that I would ask my parents that very evening, but when evening came, I always put it off for the following evening. Partly because I did not think my parents would understand my deep concern, but also because I felt I would be betraying them by going over to the other side, so to speak. This was my English world, and when I stepped into the flat after school, smelt my mother's cooking, saw the jar of Marmite, or the tin of Tate & Lyle's golden syrup on the kitchen table – treasures someone had brought over from England for us – and moved about all the familiar pieces of furniture, with books like my *Girl Annual* and my brother's *Swift* comics lying about the place, those problems seemed to melt away. It was only when I turned off the light at night that

Sister Valentina's threats made me get out of bed, kneel down and pray — and try to get my brother Juan to pray too. Our religion books depicted God as a luminous triangle with an eye in its centre, and I could almost see the triangle hovering over my bed.

In one of her less aggressive moments Sister Valentina told me that if I died before being baptised I might be admitted to Limbo, the place where infants went if they died before having been received into the Catholic Church. Even though I was not a newly born infant, she said, I might be able to go there, so long as I died without being in mortal sin. So every night I examined my conscience and begged forgiveness for my many sins, just in case I died in my sleep — quite a common thing, the nuns told us, and one should always be prepared. I pictured Limbo as an enormous white room with a door that opened every now and again to let someone new in. It was a quiet, still, neutral place where at least I would not burn, and where I could flit about aimlessly in a white robe with lots of little unbaptised, nameless infants — for ever. Of course, Limbo had previously been the abode of all those who had died in God's grace before the arrival of Christ. People like Abel, Noah, Abraham, Moses, and thousands of others had been waiting there until Jesus died and the gates of Heaven were opened again after their closure as a result of the original sin. It did not seem such a terrible fate to end up in Limbo. Besides, since I was barred from Heaven I was also automatically barred from Purgatory, where many of my friends were bound to go for a few hundred years at least, if they happened to die in their sleep without having confessed their abundant venial faults.

One day I saw Sister Valentina in the school grounds talking to Father Velasco. He was stooping to listen to her, nodding his head repeatedly as she spoke, earnestly, excitedly.

Every now and then a gust of wind would press her skirts against her thighs. I was looking out of the window during a history lesson, while Señorita Mercedes was ranting on about the Reds, and instinctively, without knowing why, I sensed that she was talking about me.

A few days later I was summoned into an office in the middle of the day. A nun came up to me in the garden during playtime and said, smiling, 'Father Velasco wants to see you.'

I took off my overall and followed the nun down the silent corridors; her skirt was so long she seemed to skid along the shiny floors. We came at last to the spacious entrance hall. On one wall was a large reproduction of Murillo's *Virgin Mary*. On the other side was the door to an office, where parents met the nuns to discuss their daughters' reports. I had never been in that room. I wondered why he had called me.

'Go on, knock,' said the nun.

I knocked.

Father Velasco greeted me with a warm smile. He was sitting at the desk, and his legs protruded from under the table. I could see the hem of his trousers.

'Sit down, dear,' said Father Velasco. The chair had stiff springs from lack of use. 'Now let me see, how old are you?'

'Twelve. I'll be thirteen in July.'

'Thirteen . . . yes, you'll soon be a *señorita!*'

I began to shake. I turned to look at the door but the nun had gone. I realised he was going to try to convert me.

'You're getting older now, and your soul is in grave danger. We are all human, and our sins unfortunately grow in size as we ourselves grow. But you do not have the advantage of confession to guide you through your puberty and absolve you when you stray from the path of righteousness . . .'

The door seemed further away every time I looked.

'Wouldn't you like to feel the embrace of the Holy Catholic Church? Just think how happy little Jesus would be, and the Virgin Mary, and your own patron saint, who guides the blind through darkness!'

'Oh, yes, yes, Father, I would like to, but my parents won't let me. You know that.' It was the old formula.

'I do,' he answered. 'And I've been thinking about this problem, mulling it over, you know, and God, our Lord, has given me the answer. I'll tell you what you must do. You must stop worrying about it and come to see me twice a week, here, in this office, where I will prepare you for the ceremony of baptism. On the same day you can take your First Communion. Think of that. It's what you want, isn't it? I know it's what you want.'

'Yes, but, it's just that . . . my parents won't allow me to,' I insisted.

'That's just it. You must do this without asking them. You are old enough, you have use of reason now. Nobody can take your free will away from you.'

He stood up and ruffled my hair, as if to say, 'You can go now.'

'I'll speak to my parents,' I said, stubbornly.

'Free will' was a phrase with a double edge. The more I thought about it on my way back to the classroom, the more I understood that he was doing exactly the opposite of letting me use it. If I was going to join the Catholic Church it was not going to be because he had suggested it. I would only do it if I wanted to. But did I?

When I walked down the aisle to my seat, Francisca looked at me searchingly, but I gave away nothing, and during the bus journey home I told her Father Velasco had asked me to translate an English leaflet on Catholic missions in India. I did not want to talk about it.

That evening, before dinner, I knocked on my father's study door. He raised his eyebrows to look at me over his spectacles. 'Supper?' he asked me. I told him all about Father Velasco and how he had suggested that I become a Catholic without telling my family.

He had been listening with his head down, as if to hear me better and concentrate on what I was saying. Now he looked up.

'What do *you* want?' he asked.

'I want to be christened,' I found myself answering. 'Would you or Mother mind very much?'

He took his glasses off and rubbed his forehead. Then he said, 'I would like you to wait until you are fourteen. Then, if you still want to become a Catholic, you have my permission.'

Suddenly I felt as if a huge weight had been lifted from me. I had been given a time limit, an amulet that would protect me against the panic of eternity. A year and a half until my fourteenth birthday was something specific on which to concentrate, a manageable time of waiting. Suddenly Hell was no longer a such a real threat; Heaven was attainable, and Limbo was an unlikely outcome. I felt in control of my destiny. What really happened to me that evening in my father's workroom, without my realising it, was that I lost my faith. I think it remained stuck for ever on the door of Father Velasco's office – for ever and ever, amen.

At the end of that school year I was removed from the convent, spent a year being tutored at home to brush up my English, and was then dispatched with my younger brother to Geneva, the home of Calvin.

VIII

Raining in my Heart

It was not Calvin, of course, but Elvis Presley who filled the spiritual void left by my defection from the Catholic faith. Geneva itself, with its elegant buildings, its dull and prosper-ous-looking citizens, its watches, its lake and its neat, urban flower arrangements, had little influence of any sort either on my soul or on my mind during the years I was at school there, except as a model of efficiency and order. My real world was set within the boundaries of the multinational school where my brother and I first unpacked our suitcases in September 1957, an institution that was culturally dominated by a large group of American teenagers whose dogma was rock and roll and whose trappings were white bobby socks, loafers and upturned collars; where we British formed a small ethnic minority together with Turks, Iranians, Indonesians, Egyptians, Italians, Peruvians, Brazilians, Lebanese and other exotic nationalities.

The school had a park with a playing field in the middle, surrounded by an avenue of plane trees. I liked to walk around it alone, especially in the autumn when there was always a thick red carpet of leaves to walk through, to push gratifyingly with my feet. Even in its scenery, so different from the wild Mediterranean land I came from, this central European country projected the poise and calm of neutrality and order. The proximity of the United Nations, to which Spain had been admitted in 1955, and of other international institutions, gave us a sense of being at the heart of things, and awoke our awareness of poverty and injustice in the Third World from the comfortable viewpoint of the developed West. Once a year we held our own 'Student United Nations' in the UN building itself, where we put forth motions and debated the issues that were in the air at the time: the independence of African nations, the reunification of Germany, the unrest in Southeast Asia, world refugees, the industrial use of nuclear power. We wanted to be citizens of the world. The future that rolled out before us was decorated with streamers of multicoloured flags.

One of the first things I felt when I became a member of that community was that one's nationality was one's presentation card, and the fact that there were so few Britons in the school made me all the more patriotic about my lion-and-unicorn passport and my queen. I had little experience of life in contemporary Britain, having been there recently only on short visits, but I was beginning to understand the importance of British democracy and its total contrast with Franco's dictatorship. Indeed, my whole attitude to Spain had changed completely once I left the convent school, and any belief I may have had in the Generalissimo's good intentions throughout and after the Civil War had melted away at the same time as my belief in Heaven and Hell, leaving me with a long-lasting bitter taste for anything related to organised religion or right-wing ideas. During the year I spent being tutored at home, I began to listen with interest to conversations between my parents about the dictatorship and Fascism. Now that I no longer had to listen to Señorita Mercedes, I took up a clear anti-Franco position, classing him as a 'baddy' who had, moreover, sided with Hitler. And Hitler was ultimately responsible for the death of my half-brother David, who had been killed in Burma during the war.

In my new Alpine surroundings, however, Spain suddenly became the target of an overwhelming nostalgia, what in Spanish is known as *añoranza*. From my adolescent standpoint the wrench was as painful as if I was never to return, and three months until the Christmas holidays seemed a lifetime. I felt homesick not only for my family but also for the smell of the fisherman's nets in the cove, for the stark colours and the rough textures of the mountain village landscape, for my Spanish friends and for the Spanish way of life, its food, its warmth, its immediacy. Being devoid of familiar references made me think about them all the more. And I learned to separate what was timeless and inherent to the Spanish nature from what was the result of the present political situation. It was as if – to echo Claude Lévi-Strauss – this move away from my roots, rather than opening a new universe for me was inducing me to redefine my old world, to consider it from a different mental perspective and invest it with new values and meanings that could only be seen from afar: the more you travel around the world, the more you learn about your starting point, the place you left behind. I decorated my room so that it looked like a Spanish Tourist Board office, with bullfight posters and *banderillas*, counted the days left for my return to the island, and wrote copious letters home. Home was once more the house in the mountain village, to which my parents had returned with my little brother Tomás, now that the rest of us were away at boarding school – William had been sent to school in England three years earlier – and the flat in town was no longer needed.

Many afternoons, after lessons, I would sit with my friends in a small dairy shop opposite the main entrance of the school. On the whole, I chose the company of non-Americans. Among my friends were Elizabetta, an Italian girl from Trieste with a German surname, who was voted 'best-dressed girl' in the school yearbook; my Armenian roommate Aïda, who had huge green eyes and long eyelashes, and whose family lived in Teheran; and a Turkish boy who spoke fluent Spanish because he was a Sephardic Jew – although at the time, being sixteen and far more interested in gossiping about teachers and friends than in finding out about family backgrounds, I never thought of asking him where he had learned the language or why he had a rather odd accent. A few years would pass before I even understood what was meant by a Sephardic Jew.

We always sat at the same table by the window, eating large lemon yoghurts or drinking Coke, and watching the number 12 trams gliding by on their way down to the centre of town, to the smart shops, to the lake with its *jet d'eau*, and to the clock made of real flowers on the lakeside promenade. The Swiss trams were clean and sturdy, so different from the Spanish orange and brown ones that rattled down the Palma streets. There, tram-drivers shouted at pedestrians and car drivers who crossed over the tramlines; women breast-fed their babies on the wooden seats, or stood, holding on to the metal poles with their bushy armpits showing; men, with nicotine-stained nails and their powerful and persistent smell of eau de Cologne and sweat, held their cardboard briefcases and spat. People jumped on and off chaotically. Cyclists held on to the back of the tram for a free ride. I missed the chaos of Spain.

I also missed the spirit of Spain, its essence, all the timeless characteristics of my homeland. The Moorish-sounding folk music of my island, of my Ithaca, the heartfelt laments of fla-menco singers, the power behind the graceful movements of the bullfighters – I began to feel passionate about those things. For the first time I was creating an image of what I had left behind. I was trying to define it.

Of course, the years in Geneva coincided with my time of change into adulthood and my first search for a self-defini- tion. Being on unfamiliar ground, and in need of presenting myself to my peers as clearly as possible, the picture I rather hastily came up with was necessarily influenced more by con- trasts and comparisons than by a sense of growth from continuity. I knew who I was only in terms of who I was not. I knew that I was British although I had never lived in Britain. I knew that my home was Spain even if I had distanced myself from its doctrines.

The question of language was fundamental to my self-por- trait. In Spain I had become used to the permanent duality of my cultural surroundings, and I slipped in and out of my three languages as one enters and exits different-coloured rooms in a house. I thought and dreamed in whatever language hap- pened to rise at that moment from my subconscious, or else in a wordless language of images. But now the emphasis had suddenly shifted entirely on to my Englishness – the daughter of an English poet, at that – and the Spanish element was considered merely incidental.

This new single-nationality identity made me feel unsure of myself. Never having lived in England, except from birth to the age of three, I had large cultural lacunae and, what was far worse, the year spent studying at home proved to have been insufficient to supply me with a proper understanding of how the English language worked and behaved. I loved the Latin neatness and coherence that governs Spanish, which works by means of fixed grammatical rules, and their exceptions are easily memorised. Also, its spelling is phon- etic, so that one can work out how to write an unfamiliar word just from its sound, unless it happens to have a mute *h* somewhere, which can also be deduced if one happens to know its Latin origin. But English was like a wild animal I was unable to tame; I mistakenly tried to find some logic in its spelling, and wanted to rationalise it – how could I tell whether to write 'leaves' or 'leeves'? – but my English teacher in Geneva had little patience. I failed my English language O level twice. In one of my letters home I wrote:

> Mme B. got very cross with me because she says I don't work hard enough at English language, and I get disgraceful marks and my spelling is atrocious. It's not true that I don't work hard, believe me, it's just that I've never been able to write English. Then she said, 'What did your father say about your results?' as if I had to write as well as you do just because I'm your daughter – it made me so angry . . .

For the first time I was experiencing the reality of my father's fame. As far as I was concerned, his greatest achievement had always been that he had fought in the First World War. I was fascinated by the photograph of him in uniform that appeared in his autobiography, in which he had black hair and looked a bit like my brother William, and whenever he received letters addressed to Captain Robert Graves, I was filled with pride. He was my hero, and his miraculous survival in a battle that had happened so many years before my birth, even years before my mother's birth, seemed far more important to me than any of his books. Besides, in Spain, apart from the friends who came to stay with us from England or the States, and the occasional foreign visitor who happened to recognise him in the village café, the general public was unfamiliar with his work. Even those Spaniards who knew him by sight on the island, though impressed by his striking appearance and warm personality, and amused by his old rope-soled shoes and straw hat, had no idea what thoughts were contained in the basketful of papers he carried over his shoulder, or in the books that lined his shelves. He was just *el señor* Graves, almost part of the local scenery. 'Your papá must be a very important man,' they would sometimes say, and leave it at that. But here, in Geneva, I was often approached by people who knew his work and wanted to know more about him through me – teachers, parents of my schoolfriends who were visiting the school. What was he like? What were his working habits? What was he writing at the moment? I began to read his books, because it annoyed me to think that complete strangers seemed to know more about him than I did. Yet all the time I felt his work belonged to a realm of language and thought that was unattainable for me – too dense, too full of incomprehensible words and expressions. My *Pocket Oxford Dictionary* became worn round the edges, its gilt faded, its spine loose.

I began to see that being trilingual meant I had never been able to focus fully on any one of my languages, that each one covered only particular areas of experience, and as a result I could not express myself fully in any of them. I was always groping for words, knowing what I wanted to say but often finding the exact word or expression in a different language from the one in which I happened to be speaking. Moreover, having only spoken English with my parents, my colloquialisms had always been limited to their language experience, to their expressions and references, and the occasional trips to London or visits from English friends had been too short to supply me with the necessary linguistic contrasts. This was my first real immersion in an Anglo-Saxon community, even though the school was international – but there was an added complication where language was concerned, in that most of my English-speaking peers were American. I knew that my own expressions were dated, but I was working so hard on building up my British identity that I instinctively rejected theirs. Everything was 'neat' and 'cute' and girls 'went steady' with boys and you 'flunked' your exams. But I had little to offer in exchange. I had to wait for the holidays when my older brother came home from his English school to catch up on current British teenage jargon.

It was a slow process. The English language was like a dense jungle, alive with rare species and forever growing – it was far from 'heading for a complete dissolution' as my Spanish text-book had declared. It was going to take me many years to feel comfortable writing English, even speaking it, and yet I felt instinctively that English was my mother tongue, the language of my most intimate emotions, the language in which I spoke to animals or to infants. Over the next few years Spanish became associated in my mind with the returns to my home; it became the language of a lively life under the sun, of happy childhood memories and of holiday time – it held in its sounds and images a whole series of feelings for which I found no parallel in English. Later it would become the language of my love life, of my marriage. Was that, I wonder now, the simple explanation for my marital unhappiness? Was I projecting only one part of myself in that relationship? The continual bridging of the gap between Spanish and English was at the same time a continual process of self-examination – often inconclusive – since every act of translation involves weighing out what are the most important aspects of the thoughts or feelings one wants to convey from one world picture to another. All this led me eventually to become a translator, a profession that put a dignified label on the ongoing duality of my existence, and on my lifelong habit of reinterpreting my thoughts for the benefit of my interlocutors.

Nor did I have the excuse enjoyed by those of my peers at the Geneva school who were not English-speakers, although English was, academically speaking, my second language, just as it was for them. For them, doing badly in English was frustrating but not a dishonour. English was simply an obstacle they had to overcome if they were going to be educated under the British or American systems. Some were offered supplementary tuition. Others tried more practical and less strenuous ways of succeeding. Like Abdullah, the son of a Saudi Arabian sheikh, who once brought a beautiful silver sabre back from his holidays as a present for his English master. He could not understand why, instead of accepting it, the teacher had confiscated such a beautiful object. And after he failed his English O level his father flew to Geneva, drove up to the school in a black Mercedes, stepped out wearily and went to speak to the headmaster: 'How much cost English O level?' he asked, drawing a soft leather wallet from his breast pocket.

In that community we were all displaced persons – like my Latvian ballet teacher – and at night, when the lights went out in the bedrooms, and the photographs on the walls darkened into squares of absence, we each revisited our private Ithaca. We would return to our homes in our country of origin, perhaps remembering the way a garden gate squeaked in the wind, or the details of an old landscape print that had always hung in the corridor. I always thought of the cove in the summer, with the sea sparkling in the sun, and the taste of the fish soup served by the fishermen every day in their small café. Or of the tall palm trees by the farmhouses, so majestic, so African.

But during the day everything was different. The Americans, who formed the largest single-nationality group, came from a variety of backgrounds, some with parents working in the oil fields of Saudi Arabia, and many connected with Hollywood, including sons or daughters of famous screen names, others from diplomatic or military families. But they all shared the same self-confident vision of how to proceed into adulthood. They knew exactly how to be fifteen and a half. It was they, the Americans, who set the trends we all followed and who pulled us out of our homesickness and into the fever of the American teenage world. Having grown up with the idea that theirs was the mightiest country in the world, the most advanced and comfortable, their missionary zeal in establishing their Truth above all others was no less sincere than Sister Valentina's: they had brought with them a culture so powerful that we all fell under its spell.

It was a look, a style: blue jeans and college cardigans for the boys, wide skirts and twinsets or blouses for the girls, with the collars always turned up at the nape. Thick cotton socks of brilliant white for everyone. During break-time, we all milled around the front courtyard, the boys carrying their folders carelessly under their arms, always ready to put them down if a basketball appeared on the scene, the girls hugging a neat pile of books as if they were cuddly toys. We were on show, girls and boys alike, openly and innocently trying to attract one another, learning about ourselves through our impact on others, immersed in a sea of sentimentality and romance.

But what really glued us together was the music the Americans brought with them. Rock and roll, which in itself was the product of the encounter of two cultures, became our common language, the language that overruled all others. Its lyrics influenced the way we felt and thought. Its rhythm superimposed itself over the different rhythms of our home countries.

It was like a fever, and even today, when I hear 'Blue Suede Shoes', 'Only the Lonely', 'Dream, Dream, Dream', or any of the Buddy Holly songs, I am back there, I can see it all again: the Saturday-night dances in the hall, the dining-room chairs and tables stacked up in a corner, the girls waiting for the boys to come over and ask them to dance, the excitement of being asked by one of the good dancers – Mike or Álvaro or Tom. During the afternoon we had spent hours going through the latest dance steps up on the girls' floor. We had wandered around in curlers, plucking our eyebrows or painting our nails, wondering what to wear. My wardrobe was not as well stocked as those of the American girls – most of my skirts and dresses had been made by the dressmaker in Palma and were not wide enough to twirl gracefully back and forth when I jived. But, then, I was British, I reminded myself, I did not want to look American. I clung to any strand of certitude I found within my emerging individuality.

I remember the day we heard that Buddy Holly had died in a plane crash. Someone had picked up the news on the radio. Girls were running up and down the corridor, knocking on doors, crying, 'Have you heard? Oh, my God, oh, my God!' We could not believe it, we were devastated, he was such an idol. His records were played over and over again that day, and we cried as much for ourselves, for the pain of growing up, as for him. Somehow his songs had the power to reflect what we all felt, far from our homes, and after his death his 'Raining in my Heart' became the song we all associated with the boarding school; it became our anthem.

As the months and the years went by my picture of Spain gradually became distorted. I had lost touch with its reality, and the gap between my two cultures was now growing increasingly wider. When I invited my boarding-school friends over for summer holidays all they saw of my Spanish world was the picture-postcard beauty of the Mediterranean landscape from the terrace of my British home – for them it was just an appropriate backdrop to Louis Prima's 'Buona Sera', or a would-be film set for a Hollywood romance. How could I share the other Spain, the real one, with them? Sister Valentina, Father Velasco, the Protestant family in the top flat, the novice in the dairy shop, the men with the sandwiches wrapped up in newspaper, the women sweeping the pavements in their dressing gowns – what would all that have meant to my American friends? They would have regarded it only in terms of backwardness, backwardness measured against their well-developed capitalist system. What did it mean to me, now that I saw it from the outside? I no longer felt that I had anything in common with Francisca or the other girls from the convent, and had few Spanish friends from my generation. And yet there was a warmth, a private warmth that was kept alive by my occasional encounters with Blanca, with Jimena, and with the older people of the mountain village who had known me all my life; a warmth unshared, a dormant love that could be stirred by a single strum from a guitar.

In the summer term we went swimming in the lake, showing off our new Jantzen or Lacoste bathing suits, and we lay on the grass with our shiny shaved legs, our dark glasses and our copies of *Bonjour Tristesse*. Sometimes I would think of what I had left behind, and what I would be doing with my life had I not left the island, had I stayed on at the convent, and had my friendship with Francisca continued. It was easy enough to picture: Francisca and I would be walking down the main Palma avenue on Sundays, arm in arm, eyeing the boys as we passed them, pulling down our skirts and pretending to look uninterested. Or we would be sitting in her bedroom reading romantic stories in comic strips. These came in a collection called *Azucena* (Lily) and another called *Romántica*, and ranged from stories of princesses in mediaeval attire to modern stories about wealthy girls who befriended and helped the gardener's daughter, or accounts of the apparitions of the Virgin Mary in Fátima or Lourdes. Occasionally there were stories set in a mythical country where girls called Myrna or Dalia worked as secretaries and ended up marrying their boss; but any description of Anglo-Saxon communities was plastered with typically *falangista* moral values. Translations of foreign literature, especially children's literature, were heavily censored and edited to fit in with the indoctrination scheme for the postwar generation.

Going to the cinema would have been another thing to do – usually on Sunday afternoons – and during the long two-film sessions we would have eaten sunflower seeds, raw sugar cane and liquorice sticks. But films were also censored: all 'sensual' scenes and kisses in Hollywood productions were either cut out or shortened, and their scripts changed and adapted during the process of dubbing. The most famous of these tamperings was the change in *Mogambo* where Grace Kelly and her fiancé, who slept in the same tent, were turned into brother and sister, which made the plot totally incomprehensible. Most American films were *para mayores*, for adults, so one normally ended up seeing some Spanish film about a beautiful flamenco singer who is suddenly discovered by a talent scout and is soon able to feed her numerous brothers and sisters, and live happily ever after.

If Francisca and I had gone swimming together, it would have been on the beach outside their summer villa, on the outskirts of Palma. Francisca was never allowed to come to stay with me in the mountain village. The steep walk down to the rocky cove was far too dangerous, said her parents;

they probably also worried that my family might not observe Spanish bathing rules. On the sandy side of the island, we would bathe under the supervision of her mother and aunts, having to wait three hours after lunch, or two hours after breakfast, to make sure we had digested our food before we put our feet in the water. If we wanted to wander up and down the beach, we would first have to put some clothes over our bathing suits, keeping to the strict regulations that were enforced by patrolling Civil Guards. Notices on the beach huts reminded us of this: 'It is forbidden to remain on beaches, in bars, dances and, generally speaking, out of the water, wearing a bathing suit: this garment is to be used solely for bathing and cannot be allowed beyond its natural destiny.'

How far all that seemed to me from the grassy solarium on the bank of Lake Geneva! Another life, *otra vida*. What I did not realise was how much and how deeply things were changing in Spain at that very moment – particularly on the mainland. The first students of the postwar generation were now filling the universities and beginning to express themselves against state repression: reading forbidden Argentine translations of Sartre and Camus and passing them round from hand to hand; joining the first clandestine opposition parties, printing subversive leaflets, and getting themselves thrown into prison. New Spanish writers were expressing a general feeling of dissatisfaction with the reality of Franco's Spain. People were getting used to reading between the lines. And not far from that lakeside solarium, probably in one of Geneva's dull apartment blocks, Mercè Rodoreda, a well-known Catalan author who had fled from Spain in 1939, was writing some of her best work, re-creating her faraway home, mythologising it, extracting its essence in a way that, perhaps, can only be done from exile.

At the age of sixteen I could understand the nostalgia of the exiled; of those who pined for a country they had been forced to leave. I myself had strong longings for Spain, a country I could not call my own but which was my home, the source of my deepest emotions and my real point of departure; and vaguer longings for the country of my parents, which I did not yet know, but to which I felt passionately loyal. In years to come these teenage experiences would become fixed patterns in my life, so that I always felt like an exile, whether I was in England or in Spain; and when I eventually returned to Spain to marry a Spaniard and live there in a permanent way, the feelings of not belonging and of otherness grew steadily, until I found myself creating an imaginary land where I spent much of my time, separated from reality.

IX

The Translation Class

My years in Geneva were followed by two further years in London where I had a room with a family in Bayswater, studied for my A levels at the French Lycée in Kensington, and ate my lunch-time sandwiches under the dinosaurs in the Natural History Museum. William, my eldest brother, was at Imperial College at the same time, and my parents came over occasionally, so my time there was dotted with family reunions as well as visits to other relatives in England, such as my grandfather and aunt – on my mother's side – who lived in Hampstead, in the old Pritchard family home.

I enjoyed visiting my grandfather. My grandmother had died some five years earlier, and my grandfather Harry lived with his daughter, my aunt Enid, who worked as a solicitor in the family firm, next to the Houses of Parliament, from which he had now retired. He was like a grandfather in a storybook, always dressed immaculately in a suit and waistcoat, with a gold watch chain dangling from the side-pocket, his white hair neatly combed back, his white moustache well trimmed. He sat in his green leather armchair smoking a pipe, or cleaning it with brightly coloured pipe cleaners, and at some point of my visit, after my aunt had served tea – in the same delicate china set that I remembered from my childhood – he would take me into his study at the bottom of the carpeted staircase and show me the family photographs. 'This man here with the big whiskers is your great-great uncle, and this lovely lady here is your grandmother when she was a young girl. No wonder I fell for her, don't you think?' My favourite photograph was one of my mother and her twin brother, aged about five, holding black umbrellas and standing with their backs to the camera. Every time I went into that house, with its stained-glass windows on the landing, and heard the church-bell chimes of its grandfather clock, I was assailed by memories of my childhood visits to England, when this place had seemed to me like something produced by Aladdin's magic lantern, the place where I had seen my first television set and thought it was full of tiny people, where my grandfather would amuse us by producing a rabbit made out of his white handkerchief, and where my dainty grandmother would wander around the house whistling happily to herself – in a way my own mother still does sometimes.

And yet, when I look back on those two years in London, what I remember most about them is the time I spent alone in my basement room in Bayswater, a time of waiting and expectations, like sitting at a crossroads from which I did not know what path I would take, which of my two identities I would pursue. Towards the end of those two years I met someone who would determine the route for me to follow. His name was Ramon and he was a Catalan.

We met in Majorca, at the end of December 1960, when I was seventeen and he was twenty-one. One evening I went along with my brother and our group of friends to a nightclub called Las Cuevas del Molino – the Windmill's Caves – where

Ramon was the drummer in a jazz and Latin music combo. Somebody had said: 'We must all go and hear my friend Ramon playing – he's fantastic!' and there was great excitement. He was sitting on a low stool playing bongos when I first saw him, his hands moving at incredible speed as they formed patterns of rhythms on the drum-heads, spelling out words in a language that was new and wonderful to my ears. The first thing he thought when he set eyes on me was: This woman is going to be my wife. He was right.

After my A levels I returned, as I did every summer, to the mountain village. It was not as quiet as it had been in my childhood. There was now a substantial colony of foreign artists and writers living there all year round, and in the summer the population doubled with British, French and Spanish families, many of them with teenage children, who rented houses for July and August. Visitors were always dropping by, friends came to stay, and in the evenings we teenagers would play guitars and sing under the stars, or walk over to a hotel on the other side of the valley where there was a round dance floor in the garden and a record player. The days were spent on the beach, and we sometimes went out on short boat trips with the fishermen, or explored caves with candles floating on bits of cork. Ramon, now my boyfriend, would drive up on his Vespa to see me whenever he could. It was Paradise.

In September I went to Madrid for what turned out to be a 'gap year' between school and university, a strange time of indecision and change, one part of me wanting desperately to get married as soon as possible to Ramon, the other part feeling tempted to pursue a university course that excited me intellectually but would mean a temporary separation from him. In the end, my *muy inglés* common sense and my mother's powers of persuasion (for which I can never thank her enough) triumphed over my more emotional needs — reason over desire, as Sister Valentina would have said — and after an entrance exam at the British Council in Madrid, I was offered a place to study modern languages at St Anne's College for the following autumn.

Everything about Oxford seduced me — from the wood-panelled rooms of the old colleges to the smell of its libraries, from the French films we saw at the Scala cinema to the lectures and tutorials where my mind was stimulated and challenged as never before. For the first time since my British education had begun I was accepted by my peers as one of them, and felt comfortably poised between my two worlds.

As I studied the complexities and peculiarities of the Spanish language and turned the pages of its literature, I was able to understand intellectually what made up the very essence of Spain, its language and its people. From Oxford I now looked at Spain from what I knew was a privileged position of freedom. Unlike my contemporaries at Spanish universities, where undergraduates were denied access to all literature that was considered subversive, and where it was impossible to take an open view on the country's recent history, I was allowed to read and discuss what I wanted. I was even able to study Catalan literature and language, when in Spain no university offered such a course, and the libraries held vast collections of Spanish literature, from microfilms of mediaeval manuscripts to Communist-Cuban poetry. Even so, this bookish vision of Spain was no real preparation for the ordinary living of life; and when ordinary life proved difficult in later years, the world of texts and books became my escape to a safer place.

One of my favourite moments of the week was our prose class, which took place in a room in New College, round a

large, rectangular table made of very dark wood. The surface
of the table was smooth and shiny, and it always felt cold, even
in warm weather. I also remember the pretty stained-glass
window looking out on to the quad, and the cupboard standing in one corner, and the centuries gently weighing down on
us. We sat with our notebooks and pens, listening to our
tutor as he introduced us to the world of translation, making
us savour each word, take note of its history, capture its various layers of meaning, understand its function in the
sentence and allow language to breathe out its content.
Opposite me – so strange to think of it now – sat the man
who, some thirty years later, would become my second
husband.

In one of those classes, we were working on an 'unseen'
passage from *Fortunata y Jacinta*, a novel by Benito Pérez
Galdós, set in Madrid in the second half of the nineteenth
century. That afternoon, as we discussed the text, the words
we studied filled the austere room with the sounds and colours
of an actual city where I had lived for almost a year before
coming to Oxford. They brought to my mind the streets of
old Madrid, the red tiles on the rooftops, the balconies with
orange butane gas tanks tucked away in a corner and laundry
billowing in the wind; and I could see the faces of the men and
women passing by, and hear the sound of their voices. The passage for translation began with this long sentence:

> *Jacinta veía las piezas de tela desenvueltas en ondas a lo largo de*
> *todas las paredes, percales azules, rojos y verdes, tendidos de puerta*
> *en puerta, y su mareada vista le exageraba las curvas de aquellas*
> *rúbricas de trapo.*

"'Jacinta saw the pieces of material unrolled in waves along
all the walls,'" someone suggested.

'*Piezas* is not really "pieces" in this context,' said our tutor. 'Rolls.'

'Yes, but then what will you do about "unrolled"?'

'Unfurled?'

'*Desenvueltas* has another meaning . . .'

'Self-confident, free and easy,' I said.

'Right. And when applied to women, it can be used in a more pejorative sense, meaning "loose". Do you think Galdós was thinking of that when he chose the word?' asked our tutor.

We came to the conclusion that he probably was, since these images are a reflection of Jacinta's state of mind. Jacinta is a devout, pretty, timid middle-class girl, who is married but is unable to have children. Here she has left the shelter of her bourgeois neighbourhood and is walking through the streets of one of the poorer quarters of old Madrid, on her way to adopt a little boy whom she believes is her husband's love-child by Fortunata. She feels out of place, anxious, both jealous and afraid of Fortunata's sexuality, and distressed at the thought of her own infertility. It therefore seemed obvious that the author had intended to make that meaning come through. But was there any way of making it come through in the English? Could we justify the use of an additional adverb or adjective — 'loose' or 'loosely'? Was not the image of the waves enough to impress on the reader that this is a metaphor with a double meaning of freedom and moral laxity? Would we be justified in saying 'unfurled in loose waves . . .'?

'Aren't all waves loose by definition?' somebody asked.

'Yes, but not all women are.' Chuckles and smiles spread around the table.

'Are we not straying from the point?' asked our tutor.

'"Jacinta saw the rolls of material unfurled in waves along all the walls, blue, red and green percales, stretching from door to door, and her dizzy eyes exaggerated the curves of those rag flourishes,"' said Julia summing up — Julia had black curls, and a beautiful smile parted her full lips. She made me think of Fortunata.

'That's good, Julia,' said our tutor. 'Of course we could also keep the word "rubric"; but although this is originally the same word as *rúbrica*, the Spanish term is used much more commonly to mean the flourish that identifies a signature, whereas in English . . .'

Every group of words was a challenge to transport as much as possible of its original sense into the target language. The frustration was often unbearable. For all its precision 'rag flourishes' just did not bring across what '*rúbricas de trapo*' did. The Spanish phrase was much more expressive, vibrant and musical, with the accent on the first syllable and its rolling *r*, and the rest of the syllables cascading down like a waterfall. Besides, in Spanish the word *rúbrica* is associated immediately with a signature, so that the image becomes clear at once: one large collective signature of the illiterate proletariat of Madrid. In English it all sounded rather lame. But perhaps we were reading too much into the Spanish text?

And so the class continued, with our minds racing, our thoughts unstoppable. This excitement of moving between languages was the mainspring of my life. Years later it became my way of escaping from daily existence — translation was always a journey to another place.

Sitting in that ancient room with my peers, the polished table like a deep pool guarding our private thoughts, I saw myself walking apprehensively like Jacinta down those same streets of old Madrid — behind Puerta del Sol — on my way to my first guitar lesson with Señor Áureo Herrero, in the autumn of 1961. The lesson was at nine o'clock at night, and

I carried my guitar through an anarchy of dirty, noisy streets, with washing hanging darkly out of tiny balconies; I remembered the smell of urine and barrel wine, and the occasional whiff of sardines being fried for supper; and I remembered noticing young couples courting in the doorways, kissing and touching each other sensually and furtively before the girl had to run upstairs for dinner. I had never been so close to the real people of Madrid, the authentic unmixed *pueblo*. At that time, a vast population of immigrants from Andalusia and Galicia filled the suburbs and the shanty towns of Madrid; but here Madrid families had lived for generations. These *madrileños* spoke in that slow, proud *castizo* way that makes every conversation a display of wit and imagination; they were like actors, waiting for their cue and then holding the listener's attention, aware of the importance of timing and rhythm for the effect of their words. They spoke as Galdós' characters might have spoken; but unlike the people in his novel, these lived in the real world, and the families who were still residing here in the winter of 1961–2 did so because they could not afford to leave. Everybody's dream was to buy a flat in one of the newly built private housing estates of the outskirts. It is only quite recently, through imitation of other European countries, that Spaniards have started redecorating and refurbishing old flats that they once considered an outward sign of poverty. Today, an attic apartment with wooden beams at the top of an old building in Lavapiés, with its view of sagging red-tiled roofs and geranium-packed balconies, is priceless. In those days, no buyer would have looked twice at it.

The streets went up and down, with steps and archways and dark corners, until at last I reached number fifteen Calle Ministriles. Through the glass door of the porter's lodge I saw three or four men in overalls and a large woman, who was eating a piece of bread and *chorizo*. She came out and studied me with curiosity. I suppose I could not help looking foreign.

'*¿El señor Áureo Herrero?*' I asked.

'Áureo, ah, yes. Well, you see, you go up to the second floor, and it's there, at the end of the landing, door number ten. You will see the number on a plaque by the door. *Puerta diez*,' she repeated.

The stairs were wooden and irregular, the walls were damp, with plaster flaking off, covered in graffiti: names, hearts, drawings, some done in pencil, others scratched into the soft plaster with a knife. As I expected, the second floor turned out to be the fourth floor, because it was preceded by an *entresuelo* and a *principal*. I stood outside number ten for a minute or two, recovering my breath. I could hear a lot of noise inside, people laughing and talking in loud voices. When I rang the bell a little old man with wiry grey hair opened the door and the noise grew louder. He wore a thin velvet bow tie and a dark red dressing gown; his eyes were small and sparkling, and he had deep furrows on his cheeks.

'Come in, come in,' he said.

He led me into a room that had been divided in two by a flowery curtain – presumably to create an extra bedroom or some storage space. It was full of people of all ages, including a very small baby and an old woman in a black coat, with her yellowed grey hair drawn back into a bun, who sat quietly in a corner. On a tall Formica table stood a very large, very shiny television. I saw the usual black and white images of Franco looking at plans for a new factory, and through the din of the family reunion heard the familiar voice of the evening newsreader, with its rather pompous, rhetorical tone: '*Su Excelencia el Generalísimo Franco . . .*' On top of the television set there was a framed photograph of a girl in her long First

Communion dress, holding a rosary and a mother-of-pearl prayer book in her clasped hands.

'You must excuse me, but my family from France has arrived unexpectedly,' said Señor Herrero.

'Oh, then I'll come back another day,' I said.

'No, no, no. *Faltaría más*, I would not hear of it. You have come all the way here. We'll go into the music room. My wife will look after them.'

As I followed him out I had another look at the family gathering. I saw Señor Herrero's wife, a large woman with red hands, thick short hair and wearing a sleeveless house-coat, the classic Spanish *bata*, over her skirt and jumper. She was sitting on the edge of a chair, as if ready to jump up at any moment to do something in the kitchen, and was talking affectionately to a pretty teenage girl, touching and admiring her fashionable ready-made clothes. 'So, Cristinita, have you got a *novio* yet? Just make sure a Frenchman doesn't take you from us, eh? There are plenty of nice men in Madrid, do you hear me?'

Cristinita gave her a blank look and shrugged her shoulders.

The rest of the party, except for the old grandmother in the corner, stood about or sat around the dining-room table, the women holding brand-new handbags, the men looking rather uncomfortable in their smart clothes, loosening their ties, smoking American cigarettes and sipping brandy.

Emigration had recently become common. As a result of the economic boom of Western Europe, thousands of Spaniards were emigrating to France, Germany, Belgium or the UK, happy to take over the jobs rejected by the native workforces, often earning in one hour what in Spain they earned in a ten-hour day. The Spanish government set up special overseas radio programmes for them and sent out 'cultural embassies' (groups of folk dancers and flamenco singers) to entertain them and revive their *añoranza* – and to make sure they sent their savings back home. I wondered whether the television set had been paid for in French francs or from my guitar teacher's small income. I also wondered whether Cristinita would enjoy a more permissive life in France than she would if she lived in Spain.

Being nineteen at the time, and in love, and coming from a family where no restrictions had been imposed on me – ever, as far as I can recall – it saddened me to see how Spanish girls of my age and even much older were trapped in unhappy relationships even before marriage. I am not referring to the old-fashioned rigidity of family life, the constant reminders of the importance of a girl's virginity by mothers and aunts, the control of one generation of women over the younger. Those were things common to all European countries until the sexual revolution of the sixties, and in Spain were so much a part of Catholic family life that nobody thought anything of them; it was even considered normal for one's boyfriend to pay the occasional visit to a brothel – after all, men had far greater sexual needs than women, or so the girls were told by their father-confessors. What shocked me was what I saw going on between couples once the relationship became formal: the dullness, the lack of excitement – so well por-trayed in *El Jarama*, the novel written by Sánchez Ferlosio in 1955 – that clouded those long courtships. Women were influenced to such an extent by the moral precepts on which they had been raised during the forties and fifties, and the men were so conditioned to expect total submission from their partners, that if they ever tried to break these strictures and express their individual needs, they would feel evil and impure, and their boyfriends would probably leave them for someone more passive and unselfish. Besides, just as women were raised to be submissive and not complain, men were allowed to have their moods, to be fussy with their food, to be authoritative – the worst examples of mother's darlings. Courtships were too formal and too long, and most couples walked up to the altar without really having got to know each other at all. The situation was particularly hard on women.

Women like Conchita.

She had a dressmaking school a few blocks down Calle Ferraz, where my English friend Stella and I shared a flat. Every afternoon at about six I walked out of my front door saying '*buenas tardes*' to Ambrosio, the porter, or to his wife Macarena, who were always there watching who came in and out. Ferraz is a wide street, on the western edge of the city, leading from Plaza España to the north of town, and it was alive with shops of all sorts: a dairy, a stationer's, a little supermarket and two *droguerías* – shops that sold cleaning materials. I remember that one of the *droguerías* was very small and dark, and was run by an old woman who was always in fits of laughter at the smallest thing. Her wares extended beyond the classic bleach and soaps to earthenware pots, plastic flowers, and a variety of oddments hanging on strings from the ceiling. It also had a stocking-mending service, advertised in a small printed notice on the door: *Se cogen puntos de medias*. For ten or fifteen pesetas, ladders were invisibly mended.

The dressmaking school was in one of the many solid, rather sombre blocks of flats, dating from the turn of the century, that made up Calle Ferraz. It had a tall glass and wood doorway into which a smaller door had been fitted to allow for easier pushing and pulling. A naked bulb hanging from the hall ceiling destroyed any hopes of grandeur one might have conceived before entering the building. To the right was a wide staircase with cracked grey tiles and a wooden banister, and to the left, next to a sign saying *Portería*, was another: Academia de Corte y Confección, *bajos*. You went down a dimly lit staircase to get to the *bajos*, the basement, and then walked along a corridor until you reached the door of the 'academy'. It consisted of a long thin room, with four or five sewing machines, and a large table for cutting, on which there were scissors, bits of blue marking chalk and stacks of brown tissue paper for making patterns. In one corner there was a birdcage containing two canaries, and in another a large radio, which was always on. There was only one window, high up at street level, with iron bars, and all one could see out of it were the legs of passers-by.

Conchita always sat by the radio listening to the *radionovelas*, the serials, and every now and then would glance up at the passing legs. She was plump and pretty and wore plain straight dresses that always looked rather tight, or skirts with frilly blouses, and high heels. She must have been in her late twenties. Her long dark hair was loosely tied back at the nape of her neck and when you spoke to her she had a habit of repeating the last sentence you said, in a mumbling voice, as if she was praying.

There were breaks in the *radionovelas*, with publicity for aspirins and for furniture shops offering wonderful bargains at cost price, and at that point Conchita would stand up and wander round the room checking our work. She lived with her aunt, the *portera*. She once explained to us that her mother had died when she was very little, and her father had taken her to Madrid to be raised by his sister, a spinster. It was obvious that she despised her aunt. If one of us dropped a piece of cloth or thread, and bent down to pick it up, she would always say, 'Leave it, my aunt will sweep it up.' I imagine she had to vent her frustration on someone. After all, she

was financially emancipated, and ran her own dressmaking
school, but she herself was a prisoner, like the canaries in the
cage. She was not allowed out alone with her fiancé, Carlos,
to whom she had been engaged for nine years, except to the
cinema on Sunday afternoons, or for an occasional stroll
before Sunday lunch, and she had no way of changing her situation; she did not even want to do so.

One day, one of the girls, who was making her own bridal
gown with Conchita's help, asked her, 'What about you,
Conchita, when are you getting married?'

'When Carlos gets a pay rise. There's an old man in the
firm who might be retiring in a year or so.'

'But you have your academy. Surely, if you put your two
wages together . . .'

'Ah, but Carlos won't let me work after we get married.
There'll be the children, if God wishes.'

'Of course, I understand.'

'And, besides, there's my aunt to consider. Even if we got
married now, with his low pay, how would my aunt survive
without me? She has the *portería*, but you can't live off that.'

'You'll have to take her with you, of course.'

'Of course. We can't very well leave her, can we? She has
no children herself. But then, we might not find a flat, we
might have to live with his parents.' She paused, looked at the
hand-stitched ruffle she had been evening out and said, 'Do
you know what I say? *Más vale no calentarse la cabeza con
problemas.* It's best not to heat one's head up with problems!'
And she laughed.

As the minutes went by in that basement room, listening to
the sentimental stories on the radio, I felt the oppression of
her situation as strongly as if I was the prisoner. I knew how
those relationships were, how the man always had the last
word, how women had to be patient and never argue with

them, and I grew angry with Carlos, with the aunt, with the whole system. Yet once she was married the little independence she now had would be gone. The government's insistence on the traditional role of women as housewives and mothers was reinforced by the Marriage Prize, a sum paid to all women who gave up their job when they married, and the Birth Prizes, which were given to couples with large numbers of children. For all the Conchitas of Spain it was practically impossible to oppose the force of *franquista* ideology. Even sexual education was manipulated by the regime. Books by accredited doctors and learned priests, written as guides for women on the threshold of marriage, claimed that most women were naturally frigid, and that sexual intercourse had to be viewed as a necessary sacrifice for the great reward of procreation.

We saw Carlos only once. He came into the academy one evening, and Conchita looked up from her work without the least trace of excitement. Then she got up from her chair, put down her sewing on the table and slowly walked over to him. He stood at the door, looking like so many other men in Madrid, with a thin moustache and a trench coat tied tightly round the waist, like Humphrey Bogart. His thinning hair was severely plastered down with Brylcreem, and he had an arrogant look in his eyes. He looked uncomfortably round the room, overwhelmed, like one of Penelope's suitors, by the female power of the sewing room. The two went out to the corridor and talked for a few minutes. When she returned it was still impossible to see any hint of emotion in her face.

Every afternoon, after one of the radio serials, came a roll of drums and a deep male voice announced, '*El consultorio de Elena Francis.*' This was an agony-aunt programme, which had a devoted female audience all over Spain and discussed the problems of love and courtship from every possible aspect.

The old *falangista* message of submission was always there, even if it came disguised in lighter language: 'The mission of Spanish women is to bring our men their slippers with a smile, and turn their mischievous little children into patriotic Spaniards!'

We never heard the letters received by the agony aunt, only her answers. Her voice was wise and soft. This was the sort of thing:

> My advice may seem a little harsh, but it comes from the bottom of my heart: break up with your *novio*; he does not love you. When a man seeks certain concessions in a woman, the sort of concessions he is asking of you, this is a sign of how little he values her. Believe me, dear friend, he is only interested in your external appearance, otherwise he wouldn't even dream of making such a preposterous suggestion to you. As for you, don't you feel your feminine modesty rebelling instinctively against what he considers so natural?'

Conchita looked up at the window. I wondered whether she had written the letter that had provoked that answer. Just to break the tedium. Fortunata trying to impose herself on Jacinta.

Remembering this episode, I looked up from the table in the classroom. Could all this world of Madrid be encompassed in an Oxford translation class?

Certainly, my linguistic explorations enabled me to describe the tedium of Spanish life, to express my views on a repressed society which I had observed as a spy – for I was really an outsider there, but one with the necessary inside information to form a creditable opinion. Oxford was giving me an education and shaping my instruments of expression, but would such an education help me to feel at ease within that society when I returned to live there? Did I really know the Spain I was about to enter as an adult? The essays I wrote and the texts I translated were only a partial preparation. I wrote about the passions portrayed by Lorca, the contained but powerful expressions of sensuality in nineteenth-century novels, the photographic realism of Galdós, the importance of personal honour in Golden Age drama, the deep Catholic piety of some authors and the anticlericalism of others, the colours, the tragedy, the closeness to death everywhere. From Manrique's mournful Coplas to the sharp humour of Cervantes, from the beauty of Garcilaso's poetry to the metaphysical words of the saints and mystics, I learned to see Spain as a country of brilliant minds, of originality that fed on the warmth of a tightknit society. And yet, although these sentiments could be analysed and discussed, they were not truly lived and experienced. They were only words on paper.

One sentiment I shared with Spaniards of the 1960s was an ingrained fear of the authorities, and perhaps, being a foreigner, I felt this even more keenly than they did. For they had never known anything else, and were used to the fact that there were certain things one just did not say over the phone, whoever you were speaking to, because tapping was a normal procedure; that there were certain comments one simply never made to strangers; that one did not discuss one's political opinions in a public place. The only way they could voice their protest was through the jokes that went from mouth to mouth like wildfire as reactions to the latest political event or scandal. During the year I spent in Madrid I first became aware of this fear. Being a foreigner did not mean I could make fun of the regime or criticise it openly. Spain was my home. And when, in May 1962, the English girl with whom

I shared the flat in Calle Ferraz offered it as a hiding place to some university students who were in deep trouble with the police, I packed my bags and went back to Majorca. I admired her act of solidarity, but she had nothing to lose – at most, she would be asked to leave the country – whereas I could not afford to have my name on a blacklist. None of this was taught at Oxford.

In the dark college room, we were reaching the last paragraph.

Las bocas de las tiendas, abiertas entre tanto colgajo, dejaban ver el interior de ellas tan abigarrado como la parte externa, los horteras de bruces sobre el mostrador, o vareando telas, o charlando. Algunos braceaban, como si nadasen en un mar de pañuelos.

'"Through the doors of the shops, like open mouths among all those rags, she could see that the interiors were as motley as the exteriors, with clerks leaning on the counter," or – what is *varear* exactly?' asked David.

We looked it up in the dictionary:

'*Varear* comes from *vara*, a rod, and can mean various things. It can mean to beat with a rod, as when one beats a carpet or a blanket to remove its dust. It can also mean to measure with a rod.'

I remembered the times I had gone with my mother to choose materials for our summer dresses, and the swift, precise movements of the clerk's arm as he pulled at the roll of material with one hand and moved the rod up and down with the other, counting the metres under his breath.

' "Measuring materials with a rod, or chatting. Some of them moved their arms about as if they were swimming in a sea of scarves," ' I said.

The hour had passed. Books were closed and we wandered out into the quad and through the entrance to the bicycles by the gate. I breathed in the English air. I would go back to my room in college and write to my boyfriend – whom I never called my *novio* if I could help it. The word had too many snares, implied too many impositions, meant too many things I did not believe in. I was with him and, yes, we were getting married. But I still felt that *novio* did not describe what he was to me. Fiancé sounded even worse. Both words made me feel trapped, a prisoner of the web of language. Perhaps life's situations were more complicated than a translation class: they defied the use of dictionaries.

X

Persephone in the Underworld

When I was twelve and we lived in the flat in Palma, my brothers and I all went down with the measles. We had to stay in bed for days on end, and our rooms were kept dark to soothe our watery eyes. The only light in my bedroom was a red electric light bulb, which made the dolls on the shelf look like devils.

Since we were not allowed to tire our eyes with books, my father and mother would take turns to read to us by the light of a torch, or to tell us stories. One day, or night – there was no difference between the two in that dark room – my father came in and sat on the chair next to my bed. 'In this red light you look like Persephone in the Underworld,' he said.

'Like who?'

'Like Persephone, spring goddess of the Greeks,' he explained, putting his hands on his knees with his elbows sticking out to the sides, which meant he was going to stay for a while. 'And the Underworld, also called Tartarus, was where Greeks went when they died, and where Hades, the god of the Underworld, had his Palace.'

'Is it a story?'

'Yes, a very good story. Let me see. The palace was very dark, because there was no sun in the Underworld; only a dim red glow, as dim and as red as the light in your bedroom, that came from the depths of the earth, and lit up the halls and colonnades. Now, Persephone was not dead, but her uncle Hades had fallen so madly in love with her that he had abducted her one day while she was happily picking poppies with her friends in a sunny meadow. Persephone had kicked and screamed, wept and protested, but Hades had paid no attention and dragged her straight down a chasm.

'Meanwhile her mother Demeter, goddess of the cornfields, was frantic with worry, and looked for her all over the world.'

'I expect she was as frantic as Mother was when we lost Juan last year and then found him eating bread and olive oil in that house – you know, the house where he was being looked after by the people who found him.'

'Oh, just as frantic. Or perhaps more so. Anyway, when Demeter discovered who had taken her daughter, and where she was, she went into a terrible rage. So great was her anger that she forbade all trees to yield fruit and all corn to grow until she had recovered her daughter. All the gods, including almighty Zeus, pleaded with Hades to give her up, because the Upper World would come to an end if there was no fruit or corn with which to feed the human race. Hades saw the logic of the argument, and gave in. "On one condition," he said, "that Persephone vows that she has not eaten anything since she came into my dark kingdom. For anyone who has tasted the food of the dead cannot return to the world of the living." Persephone swore she had not eaten anything, not even a crust of bread, in all the time she had been there. So Hades let her go, knowing she would not have lied to him.

'So, in the dark lands of the Tartarus, Persephone was smiling for the first time since her uncle Hades had dragged her away. She was pleased to be leaving the land of eerie spirits and groaning voices where the light was dark red. She said goodbye to Hades, and Hermes, the messenger of the gods, who had been sent by Zeus to collect her, helped her into his chariot. But when everything was ready for her departure and Hermes was about to crack his whip, a ghostly gardener appeared from behind a tree and said in a ghostly voice, "Persephone has tasted the food of the dead! I saw her eat seven pips from a pomegranate while she was wandering through the palace gardens!"

'Persephone gasped as she remembered the occasion; how she had been so intrigued by the firm golden fruit, which she had never seen before, that she had opened it, and on opening it had discovered all the shiny little red seeds separated into different compartments by a fine yellow skin. She had tasted a few out of curiosity . . .

'In the end, after a lot of arguing, a compromise was reached between all concerned. Persephone would spend three months of the year with Hades as queen of Tartarus and the remaining nine with her mother in the Upper World. Though some say she spent six months above and six months below.'

'Was she very sad?'

'She was at first, because she loved the Upper World so much, but once she became used to the changes, she enjoyed both lives. Even the most pleasant of places can become tiresome if you know you can never leave them. When she was in the Upper World, she would sometimes stop her singing or her dancing, or the games she played with her friends, and think for a moment about the silence and the peace of the Underworld. Sometimes she even looked forward to the dim red light of her uncle's palace!'

During the years when I was at university, I became
Persephone. I spent half my time in the dark underworld of
silent wood-panelled libraries and mediaeval stone, and the
other half above ground in the sunny Mediterranean with my
boyfriend, listening to jazz, talking to friends, swimming in
the blue sea. After my initial reluctance to be parted from him
and return to England, I had grown to love each of my worlds
separately, like the Persephone in my father's story. My pomegranate may have been Pablo Neruda's *Twenty Love Poems*, with
seeds as shiny and beautiful as these: '*Puedo escribir los versos
más tristes esta noche*, I can write the saddest lines tonight'.
After tasting them, I had become a willing prisoner of the
world of Spanish literature.

The fact that my father was professor of poetry during the
years when I was an undergraduate did not make me feel
uncomfortable. By then I had largely overcome the feelings of
inadequacy instilled in me by my English teacher in Geneva,
although my *Pocket Oxford Dictionary* was still my constant
companion. I had also read a few more of my father's books
and his *Collected Poems* was at my bedside. Besides, a new bond
had been established between us during our trip to Athens in
the summer of 1961, a bond that added a thick layer of
friendship to that of filial and parental love. He had been
invited to attend the première of the opera *Nausicaa* by the
Australian composer Peggy Glanville-Hicks, which was based
on his book *Homer's Daughter*, and I was to be his travelling
companion. 'See that he doesn't lose his passport or his
money,' said my mother, as we parted at Palma airport.

It was probably the first time we had ever been alone
together for a whole week and I enjoyed every moment of it.
From the start he was in a playful, almost euphoric frame of

mind. When we arrived at our hotel – the old Grand
Bretagne, in the centre of Athens – we checked in and took
the lift to our rooms. Halfway up, there was a power cut and
the lift came to a halt. It was hot and dark, and although we
could hear men shouting downstairs in the hall, nobody
seemed to be doing anything about it. A few endless minutes
went by, and the other people in the lift began to sigh and
mumble and grow restless. My father whispered in my ear,
'Let's *will* the light to come back, shall we? – This is awfully
tedious.'

I did as he suggested, and immediately the lift started rum-
bling up again.

'Well done!' he said.

He was in that sort of mood most of the time: amusing,
mischievous, happy, and I went along with it, weaving a new
relationship between us in which I was no longer just one of
a brood, and where I did not have to compete for his attention. Even though there were a lot of people around him all
the time – fussing over him, wanting to speak to him – I was
always by his side, in restaurants, walking up and down the
steps of the theatre at Delphi, lying on a sandy beach. On the
night of the opera we sat in the packed open-air theatre of
Herod Atticus, at the foot of the Acropolis, and the floodlit
Parthenon behind us looked as if it was suspended in the
night sky. My memories are also of delicious meals with
retsina wine at sunset, of boat trips to small islands, of postcards and souvenir shops, of good-night-darlings said in a
new way.

In Oxford, another situation emerged. For the first time
we were meeting as adults, each in our distinct roles, as
separate people. To see him on trial, as it were, in a crowded
lecture hall, addressing my contemporaries and telling them
the same things I had heard him talk about so often at home

round the dinner table, gave me an opportunity to consider
his ideas more objectively. His lectures on poetry covered
wide areas, but they always revolved round the central pre-
occupation of his life – the origin and meaning of poetic
inspiration. For twenty years now he had maintained the
unwavering belief that in preclassical times in Europe there
existed a matriarchy presided over by an omnipotent goddess – the White Goddess – and he saw in the ecstatic
worship of her followers the birth of poetic inspiration.
Research led him to conclude that this matriarchal order had
been supplanted by the Greek patriarchal system, which still
persists to this day. The patriarchal social system was behind
all our problems, my father would say, as he chopped vegetables or shelled peas in the kitchen. Male thinking – logical
and scientific – took over from female thinking – instinc-
tive – changing the way the world was meant to be. I vaguely
understood, but did not think of these things beyond the context of family life.

Now, as he spoke from the stand in his long black gown,
his face framed by an aura of white hair, he looked more like
a seer or an ancient prophet; his words sounded different. I
listened more attentively and began to see how this could
apply to my own experiences of the world, to the Spanish
political situation for a start, with its all-male powers of
Church and state, and the widespread *machismo* that angered
me so much. Besides, at that time, the appearance of the
contraceptive pill was beginning to change women's lives in
the Western world, feminist ideas were the food of our generation, and we were all wearing long Indian-cotton skirts
and rallying against the Bomb. My father's ideas seemed in
tune with all that. Looking back, I can see myself in my college room, sitting on the bed with its green and blue Indian
cover, listening to Miles Davis or Mozart, and thinking about

these things. As I searched for ways of defining my attitudes to life, I was building my own inner convictions, and saw in these a strong belief in the ancient feminine powers described by my father, powers that needed to emerge and be expressed. In a sense, this was a deeply personal religion that replaced the Catholicism I had so ardently followed as a child. It did not, however, help me come to terms with the sudden death of my half-sister Jenny in February 1964 – no religion could have done that.

In the Upper World, far from the realm of translation and theories about feminine supremacy in preclassical Europe, I helped my boyfriend run the jazz club we had opened in Palma. In the evenings I stood behind the bar mixing cocktails and listening to his eloquent drum solos, the swinging bluesy music of Pepe, the piano player – a lawyer in the daytime – and the moody plucking of Paul, the Danish bass player, who had a drug problem and a missing front tooth. In the summer the trio would expand to a quartet, and sometimes we had guest stars like Ronnie Scott and Tubby Hayes, who could fill the little club till it was bursting at its seams. There were good nights and bad nights – the best evenings came from US Marines whose aircraft carriers sometimes anchored in Palma bay – and the sight I most longed for now was a stack of empty beer crates and thick wads of peseta notes with which to pay our never-ending bills. During the day we spent as much time as we could in the mountain village, swimming off the rocky coast, far from the gaudy crowds of tourists that now swarmed round Palma and its neighbouring beaches at the height of the season.

Mass tourism had appeared suddenly. Almost overnight, it seemed, the one-time solitary sandy beaches on either side of Palma and along the entire eastern coast of the island became an ugly expanse of high-rise hotels and cheap apartment blocks. Tourism was fast becoming Spain's main industry, and what was happening in the Balearic Islands in the early sixties was being repeated on every available stretch of coast of Mediterranean Spain. Everyone was talking about this unprecedented phenomenon, and finding ways of getting as much out of it as possible – even we were, with our jazz club; and although the visitors resembled an army of Vikings, they were welcomed with open arms. Good agricultural land in the centre of the island was suddenly worthless compared to a plot of land by the sea, and it became a joke among Majorcans that the men making big money out of tourism were those who had been left the useless bit of land by the coast in the family will as a punishment for their laziness or bad behaviour.

At first, the older generations of Spaniards were shocked at the sight of foreigners wandering around their coastal towns in bikinis or shorts, and entering their churches wearing little else; old priests in fraying cassocks mopped their foreheads in the pulpit as they preached words of wrath against the Lutheran menace, and the nuns walked with their eyes firmly fixed on the ground. Pious middle-class families who owned holiday houses in coastal villages outside Barcelona, Málaga or Palma now preferred to spend the summer in their town flats, or find a new second home somewhere quieter, rather than have to put up with the scandalous nightlife made up of shoddy flamenco shows and loud orchestras that kept them awake until dawn. But, as they say in Spain, '*los números cantan*, numbers sing,' and the economic repercussion of the tourist industry could not be ignored. It was not long before the dress-code notices on the beaches were pulled down, and even the more intransigent traditionalists learned to turn a blind eye and shrug their shoulders.

But among the younger generation, who had been brought up within such restricted parameters, and so isolated from the rest of Europe, tourism was welcomed from the start. For them it provided an opportunity to compare their way of life with that of the young foreign people they met, to observe the latest European fashions in clothes and music, and to begin to question the rigidity of their own moral codes. Everyone, all over the country, could see that it also meant better jobs for young people, as they left the rural areas in droves for the coast, glad to change a life of hard labour and poor pay in the fields for work in hotels and the construction business. Nor did they worry – why should they? – that many ancient crafts and ways of life would come to an end with their departure, and that ecological disasters would eventually result from their abandonment of the fields. These are not second-hand journalistic comments on social and economic issues: I actually saw these changes occurring over a period of two or three years.

I saw the beaches fill with pale human flesh during the day, until there was not a square inch on which to sit. I saw restaurants open all along the coast, selling *paella* and cheap *sangría* to those who wanted a taste of Spain, while the less adventurous consumed endless Cokes and hamburgers. I saw how, at night, the main square of every village and town near where I lived was taken over by the tourists. In the bars, the old men with berets playing dominoes with nicotine-stained fingers were no longer a familiar sight, the bar-football tables were stored away until the quieter winter months, and the large Spanish family groups, with babies and small children whom I had so often seen late at night in the cafés, now preferred to spend the evenings sitting with neighbours outside their front doors.

The square became the pivot of the tourists' universe, the

meeting-point where nightlife began and ended; for the Spaniards it became a battlefield where a thousand skirmishes took place between the nationalities and sexes, as new conflicts and unfamiliar tensions originated – between men and women and between generations. In Palma, the most popular square was Plaza Gomila (in the sixties, of course, the names of streets and squares were all written in Spanish), situated behind a row of hotels on the western front of the bay. From here people poured out into the neighbouring streets, into little bars with flashing pink and blue neon signs, or made their way to the more elegant *dancings* with a porter in uniform standing under a tasselled canopy; or to the latest *discoteca* where the voices of the Beatles, the Animals and the new Spanish pop heroes blared through loudspeakers and the strobe lights flickered like blue flames; a few ended up in our little jazz club a mile or so further up the seafront. Young foreigners – Scandinavian, British or German – the girls in knotted blouses and miniskirts, the boys in tight white trousers and Fred Perry T-shirts, wandered about hand in hand, wondering where to spend the next couple of hours, not quite sure of anything except the name of their hotel – often not even quite sure what country they were in. Above, shooting stars flashed across the August night sky like rockets. The temperature was perfect. This was the place to be, after a day on the beach, sitting on an aluminium chair at one of the café tables that filled the square, drinking a *cubalibre*.

Foreigners easily outnumbered the Spaniards in the square, and the Spanish men easily outnumbered their women. As a rule, Spanish girls were not allowed out late, particularly working-class girls, unless they were out with some older member of the family, perhaps a married sister and her husband. They would sit with a soft drink or an ice cream, and watch the foreign girls with a mixture of curiosity, disdain and envy; and when they stood up to leave, carefully smoothing down their skirts as they looked discreetly around the square, their tables would immediately be grabbed by a new group of tourists for whom the night was just beginning. When the Spanish girls were safely deposited in their homes, they would find their mothers waiting up for them, sitting in a rocking chair on the balcony if it was a hot summer night, their fathers, who had to get up early the following day, having gone to bed as soon as the national anthem marked the end of the television programme. A daughter's reputation had to be protected at all costs – a sly remark from neighbours the following morning could do immeasurable harm.

Sitting in the square, in that continual *fiesta* atmosphere of flamenco and after-sun lotion, tourists could not imagine that this was an oppressed country, where freedom of expression and other basic human rights were denied to its citizens. Nor could they have any idea how people thought or lived under a dictatorship. They never knew what was happening behind the cardboard set; all they could see was the Technicolor film of their holiday, with images of watermelons, bullfight posters and sandy beaches flashing by to the background music of guitars.

The skirmishes in the *plaza* became part of the colourful party, its rules of engagement being as formal as those of an eighteenth-century battle – and as old. On our way to the jazz club, my boyfriend and I would sometimes stop for a drink with friends, and witness the familiar tactics. Invariably, at one of the tables, a group of Spanish boys would be having a conversation with a group of Scandinavian girls, which always went something like this.

'You like Majorca?'

'Oh, yes, I like Majorca!' This was followed by uncontrollable giggles.

'You come dancing to Cala Mayor?'

'No, no, no dancing.' More laughter.

'I have Vespa. Brr-brr. Vespa. Yes? You come?'

The exchange would go on for a good half-hour, with mumbled asides from the boys like: '*La Tetas para mí, ¿eh?* Big-tits for me, eh?' while Toni, the waiter, wove his way through the tables with fresh supplies of *cubalibre* and *gintonic*.

Toni often had his own '*plan*' for the night too. The object of his plan would be sitting on a stool at the bar with her long legs crossed, smiling at him every time he ran in with an empty tray. From the colour of her skin I could tell how long she had been on the island; if she was very tanned her holiday was soon coming to an end, and she would soon be replaced.

But Toni also had a pretty Spanish *novia*, with black hair combed back into a ponytail, whom I had noticed one morning when we had come to the square to distribute leaflets for the jazz club. She was walking by with a woman who must have been her mother – they had the same shaped mouth and eyes – and both carried heavy baskets with peaches, tomatoes and grapes carefully placed over the top of the market shopping. They both eyed the *plaza* like women scanning the battlefield after the fight, as if they were coming to see what damage had been done to their men, and collect the dead for burial. The café where Toni worked had not yet opened to the public, and from the street, the room looked cool and dark and empty. One could just about make out his shape behind the bar, drying glasses that were neatly lined up upside-down on a white tea towel. A younger waiter, almost a child, was bringing out the chairs and tables that were stacked inside, in a corner of the café, dusting the tops of the tables and placing ashtrays on each one. The two women stopped in front of the café, and the girl went into the dark bar, gave Toni a peck on the cheek, which he accepted without stopping what he was doing, and talked to him in a quiet voice for a few minutes. Her mother stood by the door, guarding the shopping bags and mopping her forehead with a handkerchief. When the girl came out she was smiling, her gaze fixed in front of her, her thoughts flitting about in her mind like butterflies. Toni went on drying glasses, raising his head to say goodbye and acknowledge the presence of his future mother-in-law.

She had been reassured. She knew, of course, or at least she suspected, about Toni's *suecas* (female foreign tourists were collectively known in Spain as *suecas* — Swedes — whatever their nationality), but she also knew there was nothing she could do about it. Nothing, that is, except remind him every now and then that she was his and he was hers. This unannounced visit to the café at a time when there was no danger of meeting any foreign girls — they were all asleep in their hotels or sunbathing on the beaches at that time of day — had been a means of testing his reaction to her unexpected presence, and she had been pleased with the result of the encounter.

She was now crossing the main road with her mother, carrying the heavy baskets made of plaited reeds, leaving the battlefield and returning to her position behind the front line. That night, and every night while the tourist season lasted, she would lie awake in bed, listening to the noise of battle, motorbikes and cars on their way to Plaza Gomila, feeling the pain of jealousy like little bits of glass in her chest, yet unable to blame Toni for his behaviour because she could not offer him her body until they were married.

Like Conchita, the sewing teacher in Madrid, the vast majority of Spanish girls had been brought up to guard themselves against any sexual advances of their *novios* before marriage. They had been taught that *la decencia* was the most important asset in a woman, the one condition men covet above all other female virtues and attributes. It had to be projected in their physical appearance, their social behaviour, their gestures, their language, and a tight control over their sexuality.

How could they not see the patriarchal plot behind these rules? Even as I asked myself that question, I knew that it was unfair to ask it. They could not see it, because the power behind it was too great, because it was reason-proof and left no chink of light for discussion. Not only was it a mortal sin to have intercourse before marriage but girls firmly believed that their boyfriends would leave them once they had got 'what they wanted' from them. Above all, they had a very real fear of getting pregnant. The stigma attached to single mothers was enough to ruin a woman's life, and even her family's. Things were not so different from what they had been thirty years earlier, in Jimena's youth, when pregnant brides had to get married in black and at night, and girls whose *novios* left them had no chance of ever finding another one. Abortions were still banned, contraception was still illegal, and girls took it for granted that their fiancés visited prostitutes as often as they considered it necessary. It was the way things were. Men were free to do as they chose; women were not – yet.

In postwar Spain, when prostitution had become a 'national plague', the government had decided to legalise brothels to ensure some sort of health control. A large percentage of prostitutes were war widows who could find no other way of making ends meet, or young girls from Republican families who could not get back into the work market. It was not until 1956 that brothels were declared illegal, partly because of pressures from the Church to dignify women's status, partly because Unesco, which Spain had recently joined, demanded this ban from all its member states. But the general attitude that prostitution was necessary for the sexual education of men was still widespread at the start of the sixties. As was the attitude – extolled on the radio every afternoon by the agony aunts – that for a woman, sex had to wait until the wedding night, and that women's sexual needs were not the same as those of men.

So when liberated tourist girls arrived in Spain in search of a Latin Lover, young Spanish males saw this as a much more attractive and more fulfilling way out of their sexual misery. They developed their hunting instincts. In the mornings, on the beach, they would scour the forest for available beauties and make eye contact with their chosen specimen. At night, under the stars, they would demonstrate the fiery qualities for which they were becoming internationally famous. Later, they would brag about their conquests among male friends, and talk about them with a mixture of pride at having obtained their favours and simulated disgust at the tourist girl's loose behaviour. I heard a lot of that sort of talk from behind the bar in the jazz club.

And yet, for the Spanish girl who lay awake in bed, a *sueca* was not the same as a prostitute. *Suecas* had names and did not get paid; one of them might even fall in love with her boyfriend and expect an open relationship. Some Spanish boys even married the foreign girls they went out with – she would have heard of more than one. While Toni was making love to the Swedish girl in her hotel room, his *novia* would be remembering how he had looked at her that morning while he was drying the glasses in the bar, saying so much without speaking, without even touching her, and she, too, would feel desire for him. Would she then, all of a sudden, think that there was something unfair in all this? Would she, perhaps, jump out of bed, take a good look at her body in the mirror and say, 'I too want to be free to love'?

That would be the turning point, and soon she would join the war Spanish women were about to wage on their men, on their Anglo-Saxon and Viking rivals and on their elders. The Spanish women of that generation, educated on the doctrines of a crowd of moustached male chauvinists, began slowly to rebel, to change, to want what they had been told not to want. Those who had the means would go abroad for a few months as au pairs. The number of female students in the universities increased. A deep ancestral awareness of their womanhood began to push its way through their collective subconscious, as Persephone pushes flowers through the earth every spring. And although it took at least two decades for Spanish women to achieve a certain degree of emancipation, the change had begun and was now unstoppable.

As the sixties advanced, the lofty ideas on which my generation had been brought up, all the lessons that had been drummed into them at school and out of school – that Spain was a moral bastion of the West, that it was immune to the dissolute customs of the rest of Europe, that young Spaniards had perpetuated Franco's crusade against freemasons and Jews – were eventually swept away by the salutary forces of that revolutionary decade. Men and women became increasingly influenced by all the foreign elements they noticed around them, and those older people with aggressively Catholic moral views had to come to terms with a new concept of personal freedom. Constant friction was created between the generations, and the battles that had started playfully in the *plaza* gave rise to less pleasant ones between children and parents; in time, parents had to give in.

On a higher level, the Church and state had also to accept the changes and try to show some degree of adaptation to the new reality of the younger generation. The Church in Spain had become stale and was losing its grip on its young parishioners. During the sixties it made a conscious effort to change with the times: some young priests began to act like social workers among the underprivileged; they wore dog collars and trousers, grew out their tonsures and became less severe with women in the confessional, especially in matters related to sex. Saturday-afternoon Masses now 'counted' as Sunday Mass, so that young people could sleep in on Sunday mornings or go away for the weekend without missing their weekly service.

Over the years I watched Spanish women change, I saw them fight to become the individuals they would have been in the first place had they not been submitted to that unnaturally prudish upbringing, that long repression, that clipping of their wings. Unlike their mothers, who had a memory of the Republican days when women were encouraged to make a life for themselves and fight for sexual equality, Spanish women of my generation had no memory whatsoever of freedom. Nothing to call their own. When, in turn, they brought up their daughters, they often handed down their old fears and pious attitudes to men and marriage, for want of anything else to hand down.

What would I have to hand down to my children? Was I another *sueca* in the eyes of every Majorcan girl? Or was I, despite all my apparent freedom, subjected to some of the same limiting conventions that Spanish girls had to follow, just because my boyfriend was Spanish? Had the nuns and priests managed to leave a few patriarchal moral values inside me before I escaped from their clutches? If that were so, why did I feel emancipated and unclassifiable, and why was I con- vinced that my boyfriend's wordless language of music transcended nationalities and backgrounds and made him different from other Spanish men? But all such thoughts were cast aside when the summer came to an end, and Persephone was back in the dark book-lined Hades of the Taylorian Institute. Back among the illuminated parchments of the mediaeval world and the moving words of the poets and playwrights.

XI

A Musician's Wife

When I was exploring Barcelona after my five-year absence, I spent a while sitting on a bench in the gardens of Plaça Sagrada Família, under the shadow of Gaudí's famous unfinished church. No other corner of the city could have enabled me to recapture the atmosphere of the late sixties more vividly than this one, if 'vivid' can be applied to a time when Spain seemed to be permeated by drabness. For although an entire new façade with four more spires has been added to the temple since those days, and another, more elegant park — with a lake, and exotic plants — replaces the pell-mell of warehouses and open yards that used to fill the space opposite its Nativity Façade, the gardens still look much the same, and memories were easily invoked.

These gardens, which date back to 1928, two years after Gaudí was fatally run over by a tram, formed a green island in the grid of residential buildings, markets and small industries that made up the quarter where my husband had been born and raised. Here women sat chatting to one another while their children played on the swings or ran about shouting their heads off, and old men wandered slowly up and down the paths, passing the time. I used to go there with my daughter whenever I happened to be visiting my parents-in-law, who lived a few blocks away, down Carrer Provença. I would sit and read *La Vanguardia* while she filled her toy pots and pans with sand and bits of leaves and offered me endless salads and soups from her imaginary kitchen. There was something reassuring about this square and the way it performed its role in society. My mother-in-law had shown me a photograph of Ramon as a small boy, in short trousers and a white shirt, his hands resting on a low wooden fence that encircled parts of the gardens, and we had taken a photograph of our daughter holding on to the same fence, with the same bushes in the background. It was this small link with the past that made the gardens particularly attractive to me. There was life here, and continuity, and real stories were told among the people who came to the park, whereas on a more general level, the atmosphere that pervaded the country seemed artificial and stale, the result of long years of imposed silence.

After thirty years of Franco's regime, with official propaganda still dominating education and the media, the country had lost all collective memory of the past and seemed to be moving forward blindly, dazzled by the sparkle of new cars and new homes. The long ban on free expression had created a widespread apathy and it was only within the context of a family or a small community that one could experience any sense of immediacy, in the joys and sorrows of daily life, even in its dreariness. Outside those small circles nobody knew for sure what was going on, and the news reports of the government-controlled media seemed utterly phoney, with opinions dictated from above rather than reflecting any actuality or individual views. The pages of the newspapers I read in the park voiced only one aspect of Spanish thought, and showed only the official picture. Manuel Fraga's Press Law of 1966 had done little to change this, being both ambiguous and limiting, so that any attempts to reflect the social reality of the country, to report openly on university disturbances, on the dismissal of university professors, on strikes in the north of Spain, were either too timorous or had been suppressed.

But, then, in real life, behind the newspaper pages, it was much the same. At least, in my experience. Nothing controversial was ever discussed among the younger people who made up my new world: musicians, disc jockeys, sound engineers and their families. The men talked about their work and complained incessantly about how backward Spain was and how wonderful, in contrast, everything on the other side of the Pyrenees: musicians, recording technology, rock concerts. Spain, they all agreed, was *un país de pandereta*, a country of tambourines, and anything Spanish was an embarrassment. The women talked about their children, how much they slept and ate, and what medicines the doctor had given them to make them sleep more and eat more. In private, they discussed contraception and whether it was dangerous to go on the pill, and complained about their husbands and mothers-in-law, and how difficult they both were. 'She always has to put me down when she comes to lunch,' was the usual story, 'and tells me I don't know how to cook things the way her beloved son likes them. So the other day I said to her: "Mamá, why don't *you* cook for us next time you come?"'

From the bench where I sat and watched my daughter in 1968 or 1969, Gaudí's Expiatory Temple of the Sacred Family, the emblem of emblems for Barcelona, seemed to reflect the country's mood. The view I had from the gardens was of the rear of the Nativity Façade; it stood like an empty shell, or like a bombed-out building after an air raid, with the

sun pouring through its unglazed windows and the open-
work of its spires, its carved stone dulled and blackened by
pollution. Despite their Hansel and Gretel marzipan finials,
the four tall spires of the Nativity Façade loomed dark and
gloomy, resembling a row of gigantic candles that had been
blown out while wax was still falling down their sides to rest
at the base, or ghostly trees baring their roots on a riverbank.

Gaudí was both a strong Catalanist and a devout Catholic.
He was commissioned to work on the Temple in 1883 by a lay
association of ultra-conservative Catholics, whose idea of
propagating the cult of the Holy Family was part of a more
general reactionary movement against the atmosphere of liberalism, modernism, anarchism and other isms that at the
time threatened the stability and position of the Church. They
saw in Gaudí a man devout enough to express their Catholic
message. But despite his private religious views, Gaudí's
approach to architecture and form was anything but traditional, and this building is a feast of exuberance and freedom.
The Expiatory Temple of the Sacred Family was the over-
ambitious project of a genius, intended as a sublime
expression of Christianity, as a symbolic edifice in which
everything, from the general layout to the smallest ornament
or sculpture, was to represent either some religious concept,
or some event or personality of the New Testament. It
became Gaudí's obsession. But he died in 1926 without leaving any clear plans for this massive programme, and although
construction work continued on the first façade after his
death, the few sketches and notes he left for the rest of the
building were burned by anarchists just before the start of the
Civil War.

In the late sixties, when I used to visit the public gardens,
the controversial additions that are now in place had not yet
been built. The temple stood there awkwardly, roofless and

fabulous, unable to serve its purpose of inviting people in to pray. Only the crypt, where Gaudí lay buried, operated as a place of worship, a bizarre parish church, where weddings, christenings and funerals took place. Such was the way in which other things happened in Spain: only below ground, unseen and in secret, could there be any opposition to the government. The only voices of dissent that reached ordinary people like us were those of the increasingly popular songs of the *cantautores*, the poet-singers. These were fearless young musicians who sang with a guitar in their hands – Serrat, Raimon, Aute, Llach, Cecilia and many others – the men in black shirts, the women wearing simple dresses, with their hair long and straight, whose lyrics of shrouded metaphors and double meanings stirred the air a little.

Since my marriage to Ramon a few years earlier, in 1965, Spain had ceased to be the magical land of my childhood and school holidays. The disadvantages which as an outsider (of sorts) I had previously found almost charming – its exasperating bureaucracy, its overall backwardness, the open acceptance of bribes at all levels – now became an irritating reality. A Scottish friend of ours dubbed the Spanish political system of the sixties an *amigocracia*, since nothing could be achieved without influential friends – even getting a telephone installed within months instead of years was a question of whom you knew. None the less, there was a certain amount of novelty for me in this new life – quite apart from my first experience of maternity; there was the novelty of becoming a part of the Spanish social web, with neighbours who came round in curlers to borrow garlic or sugar, and aunts and uncles and cousins and parents-in-law who received me with open arms and took me into their back rooms to share their family secrets; and musicians' wives who told me about their marital problems while we pushed our babies round city parks like this one in Barcelona. ('I'm always having to say no. I just don't want another baby right now!') It was like seeing the circus tent with all its imperfections in the daylight, or getting to know the circus actors in the caravan and discovering the individuals under the layer of white makeup. It was also a time for my own self-exposure to them, when I was being judged by a set of people whose upbringing, education and values were often very different from mine.

In his book *Black Sea*, Neal Ascherson tells the story of Scyles, a Scythian prince who thought he could belong to two different cultures, and paid for this misconception with his life. He was so impressed by the Greek city of Olbia that he decided to become a part of it, but without renouncing his position in his society of origin. 'He became two people,' writes Ascherson. 'Outside the city walls he was a steppe ruler who commanded a complex traditional society with its wagons and herds and rituals. But within the city walls he became a Greek. Scyles kept a Greek wife in Olbia, and on entering the gates would change his nomad dress for loose Hellenic robes.' He became so much a Greek within the confines of Olbia, that he even took part in the Dionysian mysteries. But he had gone too far, and when his brother found out he usurped his throne and ordered his execution. 'The tale of Scyles,' Ascherson continues, 'is very much a Black Sea story. It is not only about the encounter with the new, but also about the distance between worlds. This distance may be cultural, a frontier in the mind, or it may be physical. The point is that a person cannot be two persons at once, but by traversing such a distance between cultures becomes at the end of the journey a different person.'

When I first entered the city gates of Spain to become a Spanish national, I did not think I was making any journey or crossing any frontier. After all, Europe is in many ways a cultural unit, in which myths, religion and social patterns have moved from north to south, from east to west and back again over the centuries, either peacefully or by force, but always influencing one another and creating a common pool of beliefs and attitudes to life, and I had always taken for granted the differences and similarities between the Mediterranean people and those from my original Anglo-Saxon background. I had loved them both and drawn nourishment from both as far back as I could remember, like so many millions of bicultural Europeans. I was convinced that I had achieved a cultural symbiosis. But the day I joined the long queue to have my *documento nacional de identidad* issued, shortly after my marriage, I began to think otherwise.

I had tried to take this step as an exclusively bureaucratic move with no emotional strings attached to it – all foreign women who married Spaniards were obliged to adopt Spanish nationality – but my natural distaste for the government to which I was submitting myself made me feel increasingly agitated as I inched my way up the queue in the stuffy hall of the police headquarters. It was as if I was losing something very precious, my position as a silent observer of Franco's Spain, the anonymity of belonging yet not belonging; as if that dual identity to which I had grown so accustomed was going to change shape, or lose its very essence, once I was down in their books as one of them. It became clear to me at that point that I was crossing a fine line and that to be on the other side of it was bound to change me in some way.

After about two hours I reached the counter. Perhaps I had been vaguely expecting some friendly remark from the policeman, some little welcoming phrase as he noticed my name and then the foreign-looking face that went with it. But he did not even smile as he took my index finger and pressed it first on the ink pad and then on the document; not even when he offered me a tin with some turpentine mixture in which to dip my finger and a tiny piece of non-absorbent paper with which to dry it, and told me to sign my name. Although married women do not change their names in Spain, but keep their birth names all their lives, Spaniards have two surnames, their father's and their mother's, so I now became Lucía Graves Pritchard, my civil status was 'married', and my profession was *sus labores* – a bureaucratic term for 'housewife', which literally means 'her chores'. When I left the police headquarters and stepped outside, the streets no longer looked Spanish, the geraniums in balconies no longer seemed colourful: they were just the streets and the flowers of my country.

The Catholic Church had also tried to lay its claim on me when I married a Spaniard, but in that area at least I had managed to maintain my independence. We were married in a Catholic Church, of course, although we would both have preferred a civil ceremony; but at the time Spain recognised only Catholic marriages and this was the only option for us if we wanted to have legitimate children and our papers in order.

A few months before the wedding, in 1965, Ramon and I had approached the priest in the mountain village to arrange our marriage – Spanish women traditionally marry in their home parish. We asked him to organise a mixed marriage, that is, a marriage between a Catholic and a non-Catholic. We knew that such a marriage could not be celebrated in the church itself within sight of the main altar – though I believe the rules have changed since then – and would have to take place in the vestry, or some other room or building within the church grounds. This pleased us both, and we knew it would please both sets of parents not to have to set foot in the church.

Ramon's family had been Republican sympathisers. His parents had married in a civil ceremony in 1938, so that, like Blanca, their marriage was no longer valid after the war. But his father, who was deeply anticlerical – partly because as a child he had been sent for a time to a seminary, which he loathed – and had been actively involved in the war as part of the Republican army, deferred the church ceremony as long as he could; nor did he have his children christened. Later on, Ramon needed a passport to go on tour with a band round Latin America, and no Spaniard could have a passport issued without first presenting a baptismal certificate. So he had to be christened. But before that could happen, his parents had to get married through the Catholic Church. My father-in-law had to give in: he had to remarry his wife in a church, then have his sixteen-year-old son and five-year-old daughter christened. It must have been an unpleasant experience for him and his whole family, which only increased the bitterness he already kept locked inside him. His resentment against the government was constantly being fuelled by the memory of his Civil War experiences and by reminders, such as these, of the prevailing repression.

When the subject of our mixed marriage was addressed, we discovered that there was a hitch. What we thought would be straightforward turned out to be very complicated. According to the village priest, mixed marriages could only take place between Christians, and I was not a Christian because I had never been baptised – not even as a Church of England Christian. Had I been Jewish the mixed marriage would have been totally impossible. My older brother, faced with the same problem when he married his Spanish girl-friend, solved it pragmatically by having an Anglican priest baptise him. But I did not want to belong to any form of Christianity. I just wanted to get married.

Don Miguel clasped his hands and looked at me beseech-
ingly with his watery brown eyes. I knew exactly what was
coming. 'Why don't you become a Catholic? After all, you
had a Catholic education. Think about it, dear daughter. It
would all be so much easier.'

'I've thought about it,' I answered quickly, 'and I don't
want to become a Catholic.' Memories of Father Velasco were
returning. I was not going to give in.

He sighed and mumbled and said he would see what could
be done. Then he rose and put out his hairy hand for us to
kiss. Ramon shook it and I managed a smile.

Some time later we saw him again, and he told us that he
had done all that was in his power to persuade the Bishop of
Majorca to have the papers ready in time for the wedding. But
the papal dispensation was proving very difficult to obtain; it
might take months, even years . . .

The invitations had already been printed and sent out –
what could we do? My Spanish sister-in-law came to the
rescue, pulled the necessary strings among the Palma bigwigs, and soon the papers were in order. The mixed marriage
between a Catholic and an agnostic was arranged. Don
Miguel gave me a booklet called *What Every Woman Must Know
Before Her Wedding*, recommending all sorts of totally unac-
ceptable sexist guidelines on how to be a good, submissive
and pious wife. This paragraph incensed me above all others:
'If you should have the great misfortune to miscarry a child,
you must examine your conscience with great care. Ask yourself: "What sin have I committed to deserve such a
punishment?"'

My wedding day – for all the happiness – remains fixed in my
mind more as a farewell to the past than as a celebration of the
future. Only a week before I had been taking my last exams in

Oxford. Only a few weeks before that I was punting down the Cherwell with my friends, past weeping willows and grassy banks and riverside brambles, thinking that my time at university had been too short, that I was still hungry for books and learning, and that apart from missing my boyfriend's company, this had been the best time of my life. Would I be able to preserve this treasure, remain as open-minded and independent as I had been encouraged to be here – and not allow anyone to change me, as my father advised me in my wartime birth poem? I often thought about that second verse:

> Outrageous company to be born into,
>   Lunatics of a royal age long dead.
> Then reckon time by what you are or do,
>   Not by the epochs of the war they spread.
>   Hark how they roar; but never turn your head.
> Nothing will change them, let them not change you.

Before setting off for the church, my mother insisted that I sit down with her and my father, in the shaded patio behind the kitchen. She brought out a bottle of whisky and some glasses. 'You must make him wait for you,' she said. 'Bridegrooms must always wait for the bride. Let's have a drink.'

She was wearing a yellow silk dress with a matching scarf. My father was in a grey suit; his hair was brushed back, and he had a carnation in his lapel. He tossed down the whisky and looked at me for a moment as if suddenly aware of my white dress and bouquet.

I held his arm as we walked up the hill to the church as if I was holding on to all the years of my childhood, and slowly we made our way through smiling faces to the little room on the side of the church where the wedding was going to take place, its round doorframe decorated by Elena, my sister-in-law, with palm leaves and flowers. A lot of people were standing around waiting, not only the friends and family who had come over for the occasion, but village people I had known all my life, the old postman, unrecognisable in a suit and white shirt, the fisherman and his family, the charcoal-burner and his family, Blanca, Jimena, and so many others. My father winked at me. I felt like a bride in one of the Majorcan *rondalles* about witches and dragons and enchanted castles, about magical gardens with rainbow water that produces multicoloured flowers, and trees that bear all kinds of fruit, who finally marries the prince of her choice with her father's blessing. 'And the wedding was celebrated with great feasts and banquets and they lived for many years in peace and happiness.'

In those symbolic gestures – being given away by my father to my husband, having the skin-lines of my index finger recorded by the Spanish police – had I been renouncing my original identity? Did I become a different person?

Married life began in Majorca, but it became increasingly difficult to sustain the jazz club as a profitable business – the tourists were far more interested in flamenco shows, and the Majorcan jazz fans were not numerous enough – so, during the next few years, until 1970, we lived a nomadic life moving first to Madrid, then to Barcelona, then back to Madrid, following Ramon's work contracts as producer for record companies and television programmes. Memories of Oxford faded fast as I took on my new role of musician's wife, ironing his work-shirts – though they never looked quite as white and smooth as the shirts ironed by other musicians' wives – doing all his paperwork, going along to recording studios and rehearsals, listening to his compositions.

Our first daughter was born in Madrid in 1967, where we were sharing a flat with a silent German pianist and a Surinamese guitarist who sang 'Georgia' at the kitchen sink. I have an almost surreal memory of driving through the deserted streets of Madrid that night on our way to the hospital, Ramon at the wheel, his foot hard on the accelerator of our Citroën 2CV. Empty of life and bustle, the streets seemed longer and wider, the red traffic lights interminable. I thought we would never get there in time. Later, in the delivery room, I remember that one nurse was standing with her back to me, complaining to another nurse about her neighbour in the flat above, and how she always waited to hang out her wet washing when the nurse's was already dry. Why can't they pay a bit more attention to me? I thought. When they did, it was to suggest that I call my baby Purificación, Purita for short, since that day, 2 February, was the feast of the Purification of the Virgin.

The atmosphere in Madrid did not seem to have changed much since I had lived there last, in 1961. Police still patrolled the streets, and there was a general feeling of being watched that seemed all the more real now, in my new Spanish situation. This was the centre of the spider's web, where all the government machinery was at work, generating control over the country. In December 1966 I had been to the polls with Ramon, to vote in a referendum for the new Ley Orgánica del Estado, a revised Francoist constitution that nobody knew very much about but which, it appears, enabled the government to continue as a one-party state and guarantee Franco's succession by Juan Carlos, the future monarch of his choice. The slogan in the referendum campaign was 'Vote YES for peace!' and the turnout was 90 per cent of which 95 per cent of us voted yes, the opposition having been duly intimidated. You just voted yes, without giving it much thought. Police watched you take the ballot paper – there were no envelopes or cubicles – and place it unfolded into a glass urn; they took your name and the details of your job. I had felt coerced and sheepish as I complied like everyone else; a thick, pasty taste, half fear, half anger, filled my mouth as I voted under the fixed gaze of a *guardia civil*. That same mixture of fear and anger was behind my decision to have our first daughter christened the following year. I did not want her to go through all the misery I had been through in my childhood and considered the christening as one more inoculation: smallpox, whooping cough, diphtheria, fear of eternal Hell.

Half the time I think I was in a daze, lost in the unfamiliarity of everything around me, sucked into the machinery of Spanish urban life. But maternity suited me: it allowed me to transcend that situation and recapture my childhood vision of the world, a simple world of seasons, elements and water-fairies, where the only scary policeman was Mr McGregor who chased Peter Rabbit round the cucumber frames.

During those years, in our various homes, I used to write the lyrics of the songs Ramon composed for various pop artists he produced. The words had to be catchy and banal – *muy comercial*, as the heads of record companies insisted – to make people forget their troubles. '*Lailolá*, pretty woman, *lailolá!*' I wrote. 'Life is a magical carousel', and '*Amigos*, there is nothing like true friendship!'; the words *felicidad* and *amor* were in almost every song. We were always hoping for a hit, and we did have one once, enough of a seller to pay for our house in the outskirts of Barcelona, when we finally settled there in 1970. I remember the exact moment when I realised that '*Fiesta*' was going to do well: I was walking down a street in Madrid with my young daughter (who, by the way, had not been called Purita but Natalia), when I heard a builder up on some scaffolding, whistling the tune. That night, we celebrated with a bottle of *cava*.

It seemed that we were always packing things into cardboard boxes, and with every move there was always a piano that had to be either lifted or lowered from a second- or third-floor flat – one crashed on to a pavement in Barcelona and that was the end of it. I longed for the day when we could stay in one place and I could anchor myself to its sights and sounds, and to its people. Whenever I saw a notice of '*Se vende*', stuck on to the window of an apartment building, I would try to imagine what it would be like to live there. The construction industry was booming in both cities, and everywhere you looked there seemed to be a building site with metal structures and piles of bricks ready to be turned into new homes – homes for young married couples like us who were looking for work in the metropolis. In the peripheral areas, where new flats were more affordable, many streets were still unpaved, with no history behind them. The day before there had been nothing there but open country, where perhaps families had once enjoyed a Sunday's excursion away from the city, and had sat eating picnics under the shade of a few solitary pine trees.

That is why, during the times when we lived in rented flats in Barcelona, I liked sitting in the gardens of Plaça Sagrada Família and then walking back along Carrer Provença to my in-laws' flat, past the market and the haberdashery shop, past the kiosk and the lottery stall, and finally past the *portera* who popped her face round the door when she saw me coming and squeezed my daughter's cheeks until she winced. There was history in every corner of that small flat, in every piece of furniture and crockery. Here my mother-in-law had sat up at

night, waiting for her musician husband to come home from
work, to offer him a plate of rice pudding with cinnamon.
Here Ramon had been born, in the middle of an air raid,
when Franco's forces were entering Barcelona in January
1939. 'The neighbours knocked on our door, insisting that we
go down to the shelter,' his mother would recount. 'Even my
mother and my husband wanted to carry me down there, but
I was not worried about the bombing. "Let them throw
bombs," I said, "as many as they like! I'm not moving from
here, I have my own private air raid to deal with!"'

When I sat on the park bench some thirty years ago, under
the ghostly shadow of Gaudí's Sagrada Família, I would look
through the extensive property pages of *La Vanguardia* and
dream of a permanent home. I hoped it would be in
Barcelona, where our children would learn to speak Catalan –
the language of their father – and have the same trilingual
upbringing as I had enjoyed. Besides, here we would be only
a ferry ride away from the island and my parents.

As I recall those days I can see myself doing just that, looking at a full-page advertisement for new apartment blocks in
some deserted area outside Barcelona that promises 'a paradise for your children'; it has pretty drawings of trees,
gardens and playgrounds between the blocks, but I wonder
what it will look like in ten years' time. Will it be lost among
dozens of other housing estates, or surrounded by unsightly
industrial constructions? Will the paint have peeled off the
swings in the playground, and will the gardens be strewn
with rubbish? Further on, there are ads for everything that
makes up a perfect home: television sets, washing machines,
furniture, all offered at bargain prices to be paid in instal-
ments, all presented by girls in short skirts and beehive
hairstyles. The advertising language goes something like this:
'Let me tell you: Mirasol floors are dazzling! What a delight

to walk on them! You can even run on them in complete
safety because they are slip-proof. Ah . . . I never tire of
looking at myself in them!'

I have seen some of these ideal homes – the spotless flats
owned by my new acquaintances, the impeccable ornaments
and curtains of the sitting rooms that are seldom sat in, the
neon lights of the kitchens where never a plate is left
unwashed, never a crumb forgotten in a corner, where shiny
pots and pans are stacked in perfect order and the coffee
machine is put back into its cardboard box after every use.
('Señora, for a delicious coffee that will never fail to please
your husband, Italian coffee-pots Nova Italia!') And the lack
of books – only a neat row of expensively bound classics that
came free with the sitting-room furniture and are never
opened, and the occasional art book on some second-rate
watercolour painter, a Christmas gift from the local bank.
The homes of my friends are barren homes, with nothing old
in them, and even the children's toys are placed out of the
reach of their little owners to keep them looking new. But
that is what everyone wants, a sparkling new home with no
history to it.

Spain was new then, and the population now entering adulthood and the work market was made up of a generation – my
generation – with no real sense of historical link with the
past. Their history books had spoken only of their country's
success, unity and undying patriotism, and they did not
understand or even want to understand the story of their
own parents. They had been trained to see the Civil War as
something that was almost a legend, a crusade of high religious ideals against a Red enemy – the colour of the devil –
who had nothing to do with reality, with *their* reality. All they
could see was the present, which they inevitably compared to

that of the more developed countries of the West. The famous phrase 'Africa begins in the Pyrenees' angered them because they felt it was true, and they wanted, above all, to be European.

Many of the people I knew had a mother or a father, or both, who had moved to the city from some poor rural area of Spain at the end of the war. I sometimes met these parents and they always seemed to me more real and interesting than their children: quiet, almost silent figures whose minds and bodies had been formed in the tough landscapes of Spain, who spoke little but always wisely, men with berets and skin like leather who came round to take their grandchildren for a walk, women in black who sat in a corner of the kitchen shelling peas or crocheting. They would have had as much to say as Jimena, I suppose, had I got to know them better. In our friends' spotless apartments there was always a cheese or a ham that some relative had brought back from the *pueblo*, but otherwise there was little connection with the home of their forefathers. The *pueblo* represented backwardness, poverty and boredom for a generation that had been born and raised in a city. For them the country was full of insects, a place where there was nothing to do, no running water and, what was far worse, no television.

It was a generation that had been told what to think and do, and what to want, and whose fast-growing economy was proof that the present one-party system of government was not such a bad thing. They made up the huge mass of in-between people who belonged neither to the right nor to the left. In-between people whose parents had probably never told them the truth about their past because they were either too afraid or too hurt, or too ashamed. The pain and suffering of those who had lived through the war on the losing side was expressed only in whispers over a glass of cheap brandy, behind closed doors, soothed sometimes by the success of their adult children, or dulled by the thrill of a Barcelona–Madrid football match or a bullfight with El Cordobés. When anyone did speak up and say something that accurately expressed the feelings of those who were most deeply affected by Franco's regime, their words became manifestos for the resistance, like the famous interview given by Escarré, abbot of the Catalan monastery of Montserrat, to the French paper *Le Monde*. This was in 1963, when the government had inundated Spain with posters announcing 'Twenty-five Years of Peace' to remind Spaniards how lucky they were with the present state of affairs. Escarré's words were not published in Spain, but spread quickly round the university halls, or so I am told today: 'Where there is no real freedom there is no justice, and this is what is happening in Spain. Spain is still divided into two parties. We don't have twenty-five years of peace behind us, but twenty-five years of victory.'

But all such efforts to voice an opposition to the government and to achieve freedom of speech were still very much a thing of minorities, and occurred underground, in the hidden crypts of Spain. The great neutral mass of the postwar generation – the people I knew at the time – was, if not unsympathetic, certainly uninterested. One of the most common phrases of those days was '*Yo no me meto en política*, I don't want to have anything to do with politics.'

There I am in 1968, reading *La Vanguardia* as I sit in the park. As usual, the front page is plastered with photographs of Franco, one wearing hunting gear in some marshy landscape with his daughter, the Marquise of Villaverde, another sitting in his palace talking to two Arab chiefs, another watching a military display. I turn the pages and come to the section on

foreign affairs, which includes references to the May '68
events in Paris, and the Russian tanks in Prague – these
reports are quite short and expressed in a language whose
subtext is very clearly 'These things don't happen in Spain
because we are a well-organised, well-governed, Catholic
country.' After a while I come to the *página de sucesos*, the
'events page' (my parents called them 'success pages'), with
the usual appalling stories – a human head has been found by
a gypsy in a cardboard box; a couple have murdered their four
children using four different poisons, a woman has leaped
under a train. It is more like reading through my father's
Greek Myths.

The sports section has the familiar football and bullfighting
coverage, and I think of what people say about football – particularly the older people – that it is 'the people's opium',
that Franco encourages it in order to keep Spaniards from
thinking about other things. Then comes the cultural section,
always the dullest, with reports on regional dances organised
by the Sección Femenina, and the blessing of a new monument to celebrate thirty years of the liberation of Lérida from
the Reds. All the Catalan place names are written in Spanish,
of course. Lérida for Lleida, Gerona for Girona, like the
names of streets and squares all around me: Plaza Sagrada
Familia, Calle Provenza, Calle Cerdeña. Last but not least, I
come to the two or three pages devoted to religion, with
tedious reports on new appointments. How grim everything
seems. I fold the newspaper and get up to take my daughter's
hand and walk back to the flat.

These were the years when I became acquainted with my
new family. The aunt and uncle who lived in Lleida, where we
always stopped on our way to Madrid – they were in the fruit
business, and would give us whole crates of apples and pears,
and large jars of bottled peaches, to take with us. The uncle

in Barcelona who had a successful second-hand car business where his three sons worked. The other uncle who was a cabinet-maker, and the one who worked in a tyre factory in Barcelona. And, of course, my in-laws. Meals and more meals followed by cakes and *cava*. Sunday afternoons with football on television, cigars and brandy. In the kitchen, while the men watched the football, the women told stories of pregnancies and births. And later, when each child grew old enough for storytelling, there was a whole repertoire of tales and songs. I remember Maria, my mother-in-law, bouncing my eldest daughter on her knee and singing:

> *Arri arri tatanet,*
> *anirem a Sant Benet,*
> *Comprarem un formatget,*
> *Per dinar, per sopar,*
> *Per a la . . . Natàlia no n'hi haurà!*

> Gee up little horse
> we'll go to Sant Benet
> To buy a little cheese
> for lunch, for supper,
> but there won't be any for . . . Natalia!

And from the sitting room came the voice of the men shouting, '*goooool!*', because Barcelona had just scored.

There were moments when I was aware that my mind was becoming idle under the influence of the widespread Spanish apathy, and the cosy smallness of domestic life, and then I longed to be alone, in libraries, among books again. Soon I would lose myself in the world of translation and dictionaries, to the point of not knowing where I began and where I ended, translating myself in and out of the different languages. It would become not only a way of keeping my mind busy, but a means of setting aside the question for which I still do not have an answer today. Why did everything seem so empty all around me? Was it my new role as a musician's wife and as a Spanish citizen that made it seem that way — was it, in fact, just a question of social atmosphere?

As I sat reliving my memories, I thought Plaça Sagrada Família had not changed very much — I noticed they had made room for a roller-skating area and built an outdoor ping-pong table for public use, but the bushes and the benches and the low green fence were still there, and so were the paths and the trees. In the new park on the other side of the church, with the pretty lake, the pine trees and the exotic vegetation, old men no longer have to walk aimlessly up and down, but can enjoy themselves in the bowling alley. The church has, of course, grown enormously, thanks in part to Japanese invest-ment (the Japanese are mad about Gaudí). Its new façade makes the place look more and more like a Disneyland fan-tasy. Inside, what was once an empty area is now filled with dense scaffolding, as they work on the columns. The girl at the information desk in the museum told me they were hoping to have the vaults over the central nave completed by 2008; but there are many protesters who believe Gaudí's work should have been left as it was, an unfulfilled dream. I myself prefer to remember it like that, and as I saw it, a mirror of my own feelings.

XII

The Valley of the Dogs

The morning my father died – in December 1985 – I was sitting at my desk in our house near Barcelona, staring out of the window at the hills on the opposite side of the valley. I had just finished translating the last sentence of his novel *Wife to Mr Milton*:

> The child, seeing how my husband stretched forth his hands
> to seize him, escaped and ran away from him shouting: '*Son
> Mun, Son Mun!*' and held out his arms to me to be kissed.

As I sat there for a moment, looking into the distance, I felt overwhelmed by the emotional power of that last scene in which John Milton the poet, now almost totally blind, is trying to make his two-year-old son John say the words 'my son John'. The little boy is finding it difficult, because 'J is a hard letter for a prattler's mouth', and he keeps saying 'Mun' for John. The narrator is Marie Powell, the young wife of John Milton and the child's mother, and Mun is coincidentally the name of her first and only love, the Royalist captain Edmund Verney. So much was compressed in the thirty-four

words of this sentence – irony, pity, humour, love, with the
added undercurrent of sadness for the reader who knows
what the narrator does not know: that Marie Powell will die
soon, when she gives birth to the child she is carrying.

I had translated many of my father's books by that date, and
with each work I felt I knew him more intimately, that I was
becoming more familiar with his thought patterns and the
preoccupations that motivated them; that even those dark
thoughts on man's innate brutality, which had at first shocked
me because they did not seem to belong to the amiable man
I knew, were part of the cohesive edifice of his work. But no
book had given me as much satisfaction as this one. Not only
had it always been my favourite of all his prose works, but it
had been a challenge for me to try to match the mid-seven-
teenth-century style of the original.

Every time I rendered one of my father's books into
Spanish or Catalan, I could hear his voice as clearly as if he
were talking to me over my shoulder, even in those last years,
when he had stopped speaking and lived in a world of bewil-
dering silence, having lost his grip on reality; and that
morning in 1985, without my knowing why, his voice
sounded even closer than usual. In the beginning it had been
different. My first translation, back in 1971, had been a novel
of my father's, and I had been able to discuss the text with him
as I went along. But by the time I was on my second book he
was already showing signs of being unable to concentrate for
long and I was forced to rely on myself for accuracy. That was
a good thing, of course: I admired him too much for his own
translations to feel I could work competently on my own, and
now I would have to find my own techniques and my own
style. I soon realised that when I translated his work all I had
to do was listen to his speaking voice in my head as I read for
all the nuances and layers of meaning to become clear.

The closer I came to my father through his books, the further apart he grew from me in real life. Two different forces were at work – one pulling him towards me, the other pulling him irretrievably away from me, from all his family. Every time I went over to the island I would sit by his wheelchair holding his hand, speaking to him about nothing in particular, and expecting no response from him; and every time I understood more and more what his life had been, because I could hear him speaking to me through his books. My mother would read to him, as she did when we were small. 'How do we know he is not bored and unable to tell us?' she would say. Her love for him could be felt all over the house, in the meals she prepared for him, in the clothes hanging on the line, in the letters she answered for him, in her untiring dedication. I envied her wifely love, her devotion; she became ill from exhaustion but never once complained.

It must have been about ten o'clock when I pulled the page out of the typewriter and left it on the translation pile. Minutes later, I was down in the town doing the weekend shopping; and because I had just finished a job that had taken me over six months to complete, I took my time over it, walking unhurriedly from shop to shop as I savoured my temporary release from dictionaries, notes and drafts, and enjoying the simple act of choosing and buying food without having to look at my watch. As always occurs when you have lived such a long time immersed in a textual world, every page of *Wife to Mr Milton* was so much a part of my thoughts that day that I could not help interpreting the world around me from the perspective it offered, even though there could be little in common between a suburban village of Catalonia in 1985 and England in the mid-seventeenth century. For despite the obvious differences between the two – social, historical, and of every other sort – it seemed to me that the clear, courageous voice of Marie Powell, whose unhappy marriage to John Milton was the main subject of the book, could be the voice of many of the women who queued with me in the bakery that morning. Spain had at long last recovered its democracy and women had become increasingly emancipated, but the changes had come too late for women of a certain age to whom the ancient subjection to male dominance was as natural as breathing. Even more so in a village, where everyone was under everyone else's scrutiny, and change was slower to take root than in the big cities.

The village where we had established our home since 1970 on the proceeds of 'Fiesta' lay fifteen miles south-west of Barcelona, past the factories and blocks of flats that made up the southern suburbs, and up the mountain road that runs parallel to the coast. It stretched along a valley enclosed by rocky mountains on one side and low pine-clad hills on the other, and when we first moved here a rural atmosphere still lingered in the community. Its main street was also the main N-340 road – a favourite route for lorry drivers bringing fruit and vegetables from Murcia and the south of Spain into Barcelona – but behind the buildings that lined the high street there was still plenty of farmland that had not yet been sold to the developers, and large areas of terraced land where the vines still grew, albeit wild and uncared-for and waiting for the cement mixers and caterpillars to move in. A small herd of goats still passed by our house every evening preceded by a bouncy dog and followed by a man who rallied them with ancient calm and a blade of straw in his mouth; and at the bottom of the small hill that led up to our house there was still a cow-shed with three black and white cows where we bought our milk every morning.

All these vestiges of rural life – now gone for ever – were being kept alive by a few old men whose children ran the village, the shops and services that were multiplying for the quickly expanding population. The children 'allowed' their fathers to keep up their quirky habits out of respect for their old age and as a concession to their senility. 'He's like a little boy with his cabbages,' they would say about the old man who walked into the glittering shop that sold domestic appliances, carrying a sack on his back, and sat down among the television sets and washing machines. His daughter, Angèlica, would shake her head as she showed her client the latest models of electric coffee machines and say, '*Pare*, go upstairs and get out of those dusty clothes. *Mare* is waiting for you with your glass of warm milk.' But the old man would always sit for a while longer, knowing he was still nominally the head of the family and could not be ordered about, and knowing too that none of this would now be here had he not worked his fingers to the bone for his children's sake when the shop was only a warehouse for coal, wood and cereals. In those days life was very hard, he once told me, there was rationing and illness and a lot of hardship, and none of these comforts we have now. He wore open espadrilles tied round his ankles with black ribbons, like ballet shoes; old grey trousers and an old grey shirt; and a thick black sash wound round his waist to keep away the lumbago.

In those early days, before the construction of hundreds of white villas ruined the natural geography of the place, there were many things here that reminded me of the mountain village in Majorca: the olive trees, the high crags above our house, the terraced slopes of the mountain, and the large remote farmhouses – called *masies* – that still belonged to the old rich families after which they were named. At one time these farmhouses had been small wine producers, but now all the wine production in this part of Catalonia was concentrated on the plain of Vilafranca del Penedès, some fifteen miles up the N-340, organised in large co-operatives, and the *masies* were only partially active, with just a few chickens and fruit trees guarded by enormous dogs. They were like curious archaeological remains of a former civilisation, but their presence contributed to perpetuate old stories of grander days, when this village had been a fashionable place for the Barcelona bourgeoisie to spend the summer, to breathe in the pure air of the pinewoods and drink the soft clean water that rose out of its many mountain springs. Where there was now a car park there had once been an artificial lake with rowing boats and weeping willows, and ladies sitting around in long white dresses holding parasols – the great-grandmothers of the present generation of women. And every year for carnival, so they said, there were fancy-dress parties at some of the farms with an orchestra and servants in livery to which the whole village was invited, like the masquerade in the first chapter of *Wife to Mr Milton*, which becomes a metaphor for the 'brave old days' about to be extinguished by Cromwell's Roundheads. Old people in this Catalan village still talked with nostalgia about the 'brave old days' which, as children, they had heard their grandparents describe.

Like so many other villages and small towns in the outskirts of Barcelona, this one had a number of modest factories. Some had been closed for decades, like the textile mill that stood ghostlike on the edge of the torrent, with its rows of darkened windows staring helplessly at the changing world; others were in full production – like the chocolate factory and the wood-processing plant that manufactured wooden planks and crates. The greatest industry, however, was the building of housing estates, the *urbanizaciones* that

were to grow extensively during the years I was there, putting
an end to what little rural life remained, and eventually turning the village into what it is today, a dormitory suburb of
Barcelona.

Our house was one of the first to be built in the housing
estate closest to the village. A cliff had to be dynamited to
level the ground for the foundations, and the raw white rocks
that loomed behind our kitchen never lost their wounded
look – even the ivy refused to climb over them. We threw
lorry-loads of earth over the flattened rocks round the house
and tried to create a lawn. We also threw compost on the dry
red earth of the surrounding flowerbeds and tried to create an
English garden, like the garden of my childhood; and every
time I went over to the island my mother gave me seeds of
sweet peas, love-in-a-mist and snapdragons to take back to
Barcelona. We planted cherry trees, apricot trees, fig trees
and lemon trees, quinces, a bay tree and a beautiful weeping
willow – and lots of roses. It was a constant battle against the
unyielding red earth that was not meant for British horticul-
ture, and each bunch of flowers from the garden was my
private victory. The children – there were two girls by now,
and there would soon be three – had a swing and a sandpit.
After five years of moving around in rented accommodation,
it was a relief to live in a real home. We even had cats. And a
dog.

In that land of neither this nor that, of neither town nor
country, there was one thing that was guaranteed: practically
everyone who owned a house in one of the housing estates
owned a dog. Not, like ours, a pet who jumped on the sofas,
stretched out in front of the television at night and scratched
at the door when he wanted to be let out or in. These were
strictly guard dogs, to guard the television sets, cameras and
stereo systems against the constant threat of burglars. They

were mostly huge Alsatians with bad tempers and loud barks, fed mainly on boiled rice and tied up to a post or a porch day and night. They were untrained and unloved.

The housing estates grew and grew, until the green hills I could once see from the sitting-room window became dotted all over with little white villas, and from every villa, this side and that side of the valley, a new dog would add its voice to the chorus. Some of them were visible, like the dog who lived tied up on a flat roof, with only a piece of corrugated iron to protect it from the elements, but most were hidden from view by trees or buildings. During the day they were quiet – perhaps the sound of the traffic through the main road, or the cement mixers, or even the flamenco singing of the builders drowned the barking – but in the evening they would begin their serenade, often started by León the roof-dog and followed by his neighbour Óscar, until all the dogs had joined in. The sound of the barks bounced back and forth from the top of the mountain to the other side of the valley, and in my mind it became the voice of a society tied irrationally and for no purpose to its homes, to its circumstances; it seemed to express the general unrest of the eighties, with growing unemployment despite all the promises of the socialists, growing crime and terrorism, growing problems of drug addiction. That restless barking seemed also to echo my own dissatisfactions, a new sense of imprisonment within my own home, a feeling of having reached the end of a journey only to discover I was in a station with no doors to the outer world, in a cul-de-sac.

The village community was a cross-section of Catalan society. On the one hand there were the locals: the shop- and factory-owners whose families were all connected in some way. The son of the man who owned the garage was married to the daughter of the man who ran the bus service to

Barcelona. The mother of the photographer was a sister of the
man whose daughter was married to the butcher, and so on.
Next came the people from Barcelona who had a holiday
home in one of the housing estates and came up for weekends
and school holidays, or those who, like us, lived in the housing estates all year round. We were known collectively as
estiuejants – summer residents – by the locals and always considered outsiders. Even after years of permanent residence, I
was always addressed with the more formal *vostè* or *senyora*.
Lastly there were the immigrants from Andalusia, Murcia or
Extremadura, who had come to Catalonia in search of work
after the war, and went on coming until the socialists under
Felipe González put some effort into revamping the south of
Spain. The locals made it clear that they alone belonged here,
and kept their distance. But, in my mind, the only inhabitants
who were a real part of this land were the old men in
espadrilles with their sacks of cabbages. All the rest of us
were in-between people, including the younger locals who
had sold their hills to the developers and knocked down their
old homes to build drab apartments where once stone walls
and cobbled floors had stood.

There were moments when I felt I had spent all my life as
an in-between person, like the families from Barcelona
whose base was not this village, like the Andalusians whose
roots were in the lands of the south, or like John Milton's
wife, Marie Powell, whose heart belonged to Captain
Edmund Verney. My work as a translator relieved me of that
feeling. Not only because I now had a world of books and dictionaries, which became as real and alive to me as the world
in which I ran my home, raised my children and interacted
with those close to me, but because in attempting to evalu-
ate and define the full meaning of a word in one language and
find its nearest equivalent in another, I was making the act of

being an in-between person a virtue, or at least a service. Besides, being engaged in a constant battle to eliminate linguistic ambiguities in my world of books and words, I learned the knack of dealing with the ambiguities and double meanings that abounded in my eclectic world in much the same manner as I dealt with language problems. In translation, I often had to reach compromises that involved sacrificing part of a word's meaning, and risk not getting the full message across. If I had to translate *una copa de vino* into English, I might say 'a glass of wine', but how could I be sure that the English reader would picture an elegant glass with a fine stem? I would just have to hope he would. On no account could I say 'a cup of wine', even if 'cup' and *copa* were originally the same word, and still are equivalents when they mean 'trophies'. And if I had to translate 'a glass of wine' into Spanish, how could I be sure, unless the English context was explicit, what the glass looked like? I would have to decide between *un vaso de vino*, which the Spaniard would immediately visualise as a glass with a flat bottom, and perhaps imagine a scene in a tavern or a humble home, and *una copa de vino*, which would make the glass a stemmed one, and create a different backdrop. The ambiguities of my daily life were much the same, and resulted from the old problem of attitudes and values, and the different ways in which I could relate or react to people, events or circumstances, depending on the culture in which they were lodged. Living in the Catalan village it was easy for me to adapt, to fall into the whole way of thinking and reacting that went with the Catalan and Spanish languages, even if that meant sacrificing a part of my English self, the untranslatable part, and risk giving the wrong image of myself. With neighbours, for example, I sometimes would agree with, or at least not contradict, opinions that I did not share – about social issues,

about women's rights, about education – just because to dis-
agree would have sounded to them like gibberish. My
attitude was that things did get lost in translation and that
there was little one could do about it. This now makes me
realise that by keeping that untranslatable part hidden, I was
becoming an exile again, a stranger among people I loved.
What had begun as a childhood game, this switching of gestures and attitudes depending on the nationality of the
person with whom I was speaking, had become a debilitating
activity. And during those years when, through no fault of
either of us, my husband and I began to drift apart, he into
his world of music, me into my world of words, unable to
work together on the unfinished dream of togetherness we
had conceived in the jazz-club days, this way of keeping one
part of myself hidden became a habit and estranged me from
him even more. Ramon was turning to more serious com-
position, to more abstract ideas, and the notes of his piano
floated down the stairs when the children were away at
school, but found no room in my heart; I was too busy with
my thoughts, trying to express in my own words the unstoppable crumbling of our youthful love:

> Without breaking the water's dark surface,
> a ghost,
> timeless,
> a woman,
> wades through slimy weeds
> that sometimes shine fluorescent.

Working as a translator affected my life in other ways too.
Translators often get to know the books they translate better
than their author. They have to stop and think about each
word, look at its shape, its history and associations, listen to

the sound of its vowels and consonants, something that the author does not necessarily have to do when writing because such things are simply part of the creative energy. For although the ultimate aim of any translator is to become invisible to the reader, and make him, or her, forget that the words in the translated book were originally written in another language, it is also every translator's duty to try to retain as much as possible of the original content, including its linguistic subtleties. In a novel or a play, the translator must understand the characters fully and choose the right linguistic costume to make them come to life. I threw myself into this task, often battling against frustration, other times enjoying the supreme satisfaction of finding the right word or expression. And in becoming so involved in each book, the book often coloured my whole perception of life. During the years when I was translating Anaïs Nin's diaries things did not look the same as when I was translating Katherine Mansfield's stories, or Christopher Columbus's letter on the New World, or a novel by Galdós's contemporary Emilia Pardo Bazán.

I was lost in thought about all this as I did the rounds of the shops that Saturday in December, with *Wife to Mr Milton* still claiming me, and my father's voice still ringing in my ears, as if I had just come out from watching a convincing play or film and had not yet adjusted to the outside world. Its characters seemed so real in my mind that they assumed the faces of the people I saw around me: there was the rigidly puritan John Milton, his spirited young wife Marie Powell, who had married him without love, in payment of her father's debt, Marie's outspoken mother Anne and her quiet father, Richard, her brothers, her sisters, her maid Trunco – they were all standing in the bakery queue with me.

I knew all the real people in that queue – locals and Andalusians, Barcelona weekenders and resident outsiders – and they knew me. They each held a spotless cotton bag folded over their arm, with the word *Pan* (Spanish) or *Pa* (Catalan) embroidered diagonally across it, and even perhaps a decorative ear of corn in a corner, and frills round the edge. When they reached the counter, they unfolded the bag and held it open for the baker to put the long baguettes in it. Some chatted, others waited silently, some looked happy, others unhappy, tense, or thoughtful. They were just going about their daily business in this small Catalan community. They were performing their routine chores, living their small-town lives. But they, too, could be characters in a book. They, too, could be written about in detail – if I highlighted their peculiarities, or exaggerated their emotional and psychological dispositions. I might even be able to translate them into English, giving them some regional accent, different clothes and hairstyles.

There was Anna, for example, a spinster in her mid-forties who retained a childish expression in her eyes and always looked as if she was about to be scolded. She wore her hair set in tight waves with a little bow clipped on to the side, and she was thin and nervous, and prone to worrying. Her father was the village watchmaker and, being an only child, she had been trained by him to help in the workshop so that she could take over the business when he retired. I often wondered why she had not married, and whether there was some sad love tale in her life. Anna adored her father and was afraid of her mother, a fierce-looking woman, always dressed in dark clothes, always sitting by the shop window to watch the world go by. She called her husband by his surname. 'Ferrer,' she would say sternly, 'here is the lady who has come to collect the silver chain.' And Ferrer, whose first name I never knew, came out in his slippers with a soft smile on his lips, always reassuring but never able to find the envelope he was looking for. 'Come back tomorrow,' he would say. 'I'll ask Anna when she comes in. She's sure to know where I left your chain. It's my memory, you know.'

There was Montse, who owned the *papereria*, the tiny stationer's where we bought newspapers and magazines, ballpoints and blank paper. As the seventies advanced, the newspaper headlines in her shop told the story of a changing country, of Franco's death and the re-establishment of democracy; but nothing made an impression on Montse. She did not care one way or another about anything, and whatever you asked her she always shrugged her shoulders for an answer. She sat on a high stool by the till, next to the door, and in winter wrapped a scarf round her neck to nurse her perpetual cold. When censorship was lifted and the market was invaded by pornographic magazines, she shrugged her shoulders again when mothers complained that she placed the publications within reach of children. 'That's your affair, not mine! If you have children you must look after them, not expect me to do your job!' She was fat, unusually badly dressed for a Catalan, and ill-humoured. Children were afraid of her. But I liked her. There was a refreshing honesty about Montse, a lack of pretence to which I warmed. She lived in a flat at the back of the shop, and kept forty cats, so people said. Every time the side door to her living quarters opened, a reek of cat pee filled the *papereria*.

Opposite Montse's shop, on the other side of the road, was another group of shops: the chemist, the butcher's, the elegant shop with washing machines and television sets – where the old man sat down with his sack of cabbages – and the main food store for the village. In this small supermarket every story was turned into a scandal, and every rumour into

a proven fact. As you queued up for your half-pound of ham –
the older generation of Catalans still weighed in *lliures*
(pounds) and *unces* (ounces) – or your quarter-pound of
grated cheese, the tongues of all the women were set free,
while Antònia, and her mother, *Senyora* Matilde, sharpened
their knives and made appropriate comments to encourage
and prolong the gossip. It was there one found out about the
lesbians in the block of flats who had been discovered by one
of their daughters in her lunchbreak from school (in the most
scandalous positions!). Or about the carpenter's wife, the
one with the mentally deficient child, who ran off with a successful café owner and abandoned her baby. Or the poor old
man who hanged himself in the terrace of his council flat,
only to be followed by his friend, the next-door neighbour,
who could not conceive of living without playing dominoes
with his companion every afternoon. Accidents, dramas, the
breakdown of human relationships. There was no mercy for
anyone.

Gossip of another kind was what you heard at the doctor's
surgery. Here, sitting in one of the chairs that lined the walls
of the waiting room, you could listen to detailed accounts of
operations, accidents and illnesses. One day, I even heard
how to cast a white-magic spell on your husband if you think
he has stopped loving you. This was at the family-planning
clinic that was available to all villagers once a week, courtesy
of our new Communist local government – how things had
changed since the sixties! – and it was Carmen, a girl from
Seville, who was telling a lady sitting next to her about the
spell. She had heard this, she said, from her Galician sister-in-
law – Galicia, in the north-west corner of Spain, is well
known for village witches and ancient Celtic lore. 'You take
a pair of your husband's underpants and cut them into very
fine shreds,' she explained, giggling as she spoke. 'Then you

mix lots of different herbs with the shreds and tie the whole
thing into a bundle, which you place at the very back of your
husband's underwear drawer.'

'And what herbs do you use?' asked the incredulous lady.

'Oh, that I cannot tell you,' she answered, giggling again.
'My sister-in-law says it's a secret that can only be passed
from mother to daughter. But I'll try to find out for you.'

'Goodness, no, I'm very happy with my husband, thank
you very much!'

The most talkative were always the Andalusian women,
who livened up the waiting room with their linguistic grace
and their unbounded sense of humour. The Catalans, on the
contrary, usually sighed and shook their heads as they listened
to each other's misfortunes with a glum expression. Children
sat quietly on the chairs, their long legs, usually bruised and
grazed, dangling in the air.

We were having lunch at my in-laws' the following day, so
I went into the *pastisseria*, the cake shop, to buy a cake and a
bottle of champagne for the dessert. My in-laws lived next
door to us. Soon after we moved, they had bought the land
next to ours and they became our neighbours and baby-sit-
ters. From my house I could hear my father-in-law playing the
trumpet – long mournful notes that had once encouraged
couples to hold each other closely in an elegant dance hall
now drifted over in the breeze. At other times, especially
after a downpour, I would see him wandering about the
garden in his dark mackintosh and wellington boots, turning
up leaves and stones with a long stick he carried with him,
looking for snails. The best time for snail catching is at night,
and then we would see his torch shining in the dark, and my
youngest daughter would rush out to join him.

My mother-in-law cooked the snails for him, though she
hated the very thought of them herself, leaving them first to

starve overnight in a covered pot. More than once the hungry animals had managed to push open the pot and were found the next morning wandering all over the kitchen ceiling. She was a quiet, intelligent, good-looking woman who had been brought up to think more about her family than about herself. She cooked and mended clothes, and went about the house remembering the good old days during the Republic when she was young and worked in a factory in Barcelona and had just met the dashing young trumpet player who would become her husband. Sometimes I could hear her sing Spanish operetta songs as she pottered around in the kitchen – she had a beautiful voice. My children lived in and out of their house, which was a blessing for me at times but not easy at others – culture clashes creating more problems of translation.

One of my children's favourite tales was a true story told by their grandfather, which they called '*El conte de la lluna, The Moon Story*'. It went something like this:

When I was a little boy I lived in a village near Lleida with lots of fields all around it and an old broken-down castle on the top of the hill. My father, your great-grandfather, was the village *calderer*; he made big boilers and metal urns and was always busy in his workshop. We had our home above the workshop, and one evening, when I was very tiny – about one and a half years old – I was sitting in my little wooden chair on the balcony with our nanny, a young girl from the village who came to look after me and my brothers and sisters while my mother cooked the dinner. Well, I was sitting in my little chair when I saw the moon. It was a huge round moon, like a yellow balloon. It looked so close, so very close, that I was sure I could catch it if only I got a little bit closer. The girl who was meant to be watching us was not doing her job properly because she didn't notice how I stood up on my chair and raised my hands, like this, up and up, trying to catch the moon. Then I put one little foot in a flower pot to get a bit higher, and every time I thought, I'm nearly reaching now, nearly, nearly . . .

Meanwhile, my father, who was closing his workshop for the evening, was talking to a neighbour who was passing by on his way home from the fields, carrying a large sack full of grass for his rabbits. They were talking away about this and that when suddenly, *pam!*, just when I thought I had got the moon in my hands, down I went! And where do you think I landed? On top of the sack of grass! And if my father hadn't been talking to the farmer, and if the farmer hadn't been carrying a sack, I wouldn't be here to tell you this story, and you wouldn't be here to listen to it!

It occurred to me that this tale could be used as a metaphor for all Catalan people who, like my father-in-law, had lived through the Civil War. Here was a man who had embraced the ideals of the revolution, who had fought for his nation in attempting to achieve them and had managed to get back on his feet again, even if it had meant living the rest of his life with the bitterness of defeat.

Another war had marked my own father – my childhood hero Captain Graves, who had been left for dead among the wounded soldiers in the Somme. I thought of him again now, as I waited for the cake to be wrapped up into a neat parcel. On my way out of the cake shop, I bumped into Juanita, the lady who came to do the cleaning once a week. Juanita and I always talked when she came to my house, but although I tried to offer her coffee or fruit juices, or tea, all she ever accepted from me in those twenty years was water from the tap. Her favourite expression was one of her own invention: '*Las casas son lo peor*, houses — that's the worst thing there is.' She did not blame men, or humanity, or governments, or even God for her misfortunes — and there were plenty of them — but only the houses she had to clean to make a living.

Juanita came from Almería, in Andalusia, and once or twice a year, she went down to her *pueblo* in a special coach chartered by a group of Andalusians in the area. When she came back, there were always fresh reports on her father's health and her sister's strange behaviour. One day she told me her father had died, and she was going to the *pueblo* to sort out the family papers and try to persuade her older sister to come back with her to Catalonia. But her sister could not be persuaded. 'My sister is very special,' said Juanita. 'Very special. She refuses to leave the *pueblo* now that my father has died, because she thinks her *novio* might come back one day. Imagine: he left her thirty years ago, and she still waits for him. He's probably dead, and if he's not dead he's married someone else. But there is no way of reasoning with her. She exasperates me. Sometimes I say to her, "Why wait for him anyhow? What do you want a husband for? Men add nothing but complications to one's life!" But she just looks at me and says, "I must wait for Juan. I promised."'

I met Juanita's sister once, after she had finally been dragged out of the damp old house in the Andalusian village — it was practically falling on top of her — and had been brought to Catalonia. The change must have worsened her mental state, because she refused to share the house with her sister; instead, she had made herself a room in the garage. She did not speak to anyone, and when I met her she stood hovering by the garage door, with a large bunch of keys in her hands, which she kept putting in her apron pocket and taking out again.

'How is your sister?' I asked Juanita that Saturday morning.

'Just the same,' she answered. 'She goes out every evening and starts calling her *novio*. "Juan! Juan!" Luckily, the neighbours have got used to her and don't complain. We'll just have to keep going somehow.'

We all kept going. All the characters in that unwritten book, we were all prisoners of our own circumstances. For me, the years had gone by almost unnoticed, time had slipped in and out of our house until suddenly the place was full of teenage girls playing the same rock and roll hits I used to hear in Geneva, and there were boys on motorbikes waiting for them on the road.

I went into a small boutique that had opened a few weeks earlier and bought myself an emerald-green jumper. My father liked green and had once given me an old Majorcan necklace with bright green glass beads. He told me the colour suited me, just as it suited my mother. He had given me many other bits of jewellery over the years: a Greek carnelian signet ring with a delicate carving of Eros mounted on a horse with a dolphin's tail; a silver drachma, with the goddess Athena on one side and her owl on the other, set in a band of gold that followed the uneven shape of the coin; a gold necklace from Ibiza; gold and garnet buttons from an old Majorcan folk costume. My mother had similar jewels that lived in a wooden box on her dressing table when she was not wearing them, among her bottles of perfume, her softly scented compact and her lipsticks.

I kept thinking of my father that morning, and about *Wife to Mr Milton*. It occurred to me that the voice of Marie Powell was the voice of yet another unknown woman whose strength had allowed her to make the most of adversity. She had the same courage I admired in Jimena, in Juanita, and in so many other women I had encountered during my life. My father had wanted to make Marie Powell's life shine through time, he had wanted her truth known, because her truth could help other women. Hers was the story of a civil war, of an unhappy marriage, of growing blindness. Of the persistent crushing of women by men.

I still had the problem of the title to resolve. How could I translate *Wife to Mr Milton* into Spanish? *La mujer de Mr Milton*, *La esposa de Mr Milton*, *La señora Milton*, *La mujer del señor Milton* – they all seemed inadequate. None conveyed the 'to', which held so much meaning in its apparent insignificance. Marie Powell never belonged to John Milton, she was not Mr Milton's Wife, and that was the whole point of the book. The word 'to' gave the phrase a legal or contractual tone, it stressed the fact that she held back, that she agreed to marry but never gave herself to her husband. There was only one solution, to use the subtitle 'The Story of Marie Powell' and make it the title. I decided on *La historia de Marie Powell*.

When I arrived back home with my purchases, my husband was standing on the terrace outside our front door with one of the children, waiting for me. There had been a phone call from my mother, he said, to say that my father had passed away at ten o'clock. I understood then that those thirty-four last words of the book had been his way of saying goodbye to me. A few hours later, when Ramon and I flew over the Mediterranean for the funeral, everything looked as timeless as the story of Marie Powell: the Majorcan coast with its promontories like giant lizards asleep in the sea, the fisherman's cove, the windmills of the plain, the rows of almond trees. And, later, the funeral rites. The ever-repeated patterns of life. That evening, as I walked up the hill to the village church with my mother, behind my father's coffin, I became aware of how much wisdom is contained in these old habits, in these plays staged at the end of every life – the unhurried walking, the gathering of people, the dark clothes, the outward expression of grief and respect for death, inseparable sister of life. Here was a community bidding farewell to an old man whose natural time had come. '*Es ley de vida,*' they all said, it is the law of life. Next to me was his widow. Outliving the men also seems to be *ley de vida*; having to learn to live with an absence.

XIII

Sepharad

Six weeks after my father's death, I had a dream about him. I dreamed that I was alone with him in his study and that he was dead. He lay stretched out on the low couch, between the desk and the fireplace, which had been set up for the night nurses during his illness. In my dream I knew that the reason he was lying in his workroom and not in the room next door, where he had actually died, was that this was where all his books were kept – all his knowledge was contained in this room. The odd thing was that, although he was formally dead, his body was warm and he was breathing, and I knew, the way one knows in dreams, that there were three days to go before he would be taken away for burial. Outside the room, in the small patio where we had downed the whisky on my wedding day and where we drank tea every summer, photographers and television crews waited for the coffin to appear.

Suddenly I became aware that he was speaking. He spoke so softly that I had to crouch down and put my ear close to his mouth to hear what he was saying. His eyes were closed, but the words came out uninterruptedly, in a controlled, even tone. I knew I could not speak to him, because he was dead, and yet his words kept flowing, like the words of an oracle. I could listen only for a while at a time, because the emotion of hearing my father's voice was too much for me to bear, and every time I stood up to recover from the experience and make a note of the things he had said, I knew that I was probably missing great revelations, wise advice, beautiful words that would be lost for ever.

When I woke up the next morning, I did not at first remember the dream, but began to think, for no reason whatsoever, about Girona, a town north-east of Barcelona, and its old Jewish quarter, known among Catalans as the *call*. Joana, a teacher at my children's school and a good friend of mine, had often spoken to me about it. 'You must go to the *call* of Girona,' she once said. 'It's a good place for meditation. Wander around the streets and visit the house of Isaac the Blind. It used to be an important centre of Jewish mysticism, and its stones are still charged with ancient harmony.'

When I first met Joana she lived in the next village to ours along the main road to Barcelona, but a few years later, in the late seventies, she and her husband moved to a house in our *urbanización*. She was an energetic and imaginative teacher, sincerely committed to the whole question of Catalan nationalism, and to the Catalan educational programmes which since Franco's death have been recovered and put back into circulation. As a private person, Joana was deeply spiritual; her preoccupations went beyond the questions of Catalan independence, to a more general interest in human behaviour and psychology. She was always expressing the need to re-establish the natural harmonies between the masculine and feminine elements of life, and knew my father's *White Goddess* well. We communicated in Catalan, but her open-mindedness and the nature of our conversations made me forget what language I was using. I did not need to translate myself into my Catalan persona for her.

Logically or not, a few moments later when my dream resurfaced, I immediately linked it to my thoughts about Girona and to Joana's suggestion of visiting the *call*. I felt – or perhaps it would be more honest to say I *wanted* to feel – that there was some sort of connection between the two; the biblical symbolism of the three death-in-life days seemed to indicate that there could be. I knew that it was quite common for one's subconscious to find ways of coming to terms with the death of a loved one, either in dreams or in daydream apparitions, and whether I really believed that the dream was a posthumous message from my father, or knew deep down that I was inventing such a message as a way of coping with his loss, made little difference. What mattered to me was that the link existed in my mind, and that it had given me something different on which to focus my attention, something outside my reclusive world of words and translation, and the blind alley into which my marriage seemed to have entered. My knowledge of Jewish culture and civilisation in Spain had already provided me with an insight into Spanish and Catalan history, and Joana's advice, 'You must go to the *call*', seemed like an augury. Would I make some sort of discovery? One day, I decided, I would go on a pilgrimage to Girona.

I first learned about the Jews of Spain at university, and I remember finding it hard to believe then, in 1962, that Spanish rulers had not only tolerated them in the past but had actually maintained a friendly and productive relationship with them. Jews had lived in the Iberian Peninsula since Roman times, I was told, enjoying periods of peaceful co-existence with both Arabs and Christians. Hebrew science and letters had flourished under the Moors between the eighth and the eleventh centuries, and from then on the superior education and scholarship of the Jews had also been put to good use in the Christian realms of the north, where the kings granted them special privileges. They had excelled as physicians and financial advisers, as cartographers and as men of letters. Spanish Jews played a key role as translators in the transmission to Europe of Arabic-Greek learning during the Middle Ages, and as map-makers they made possible the discovery of America. Under the Crown of Aragon (the Catalan-Aragonese federation ruled by the count-kings of Catalonia) the Jews were considered royal property and owed allegiance and taxes directly to the king, who in exchange protected them.

By the thirteenth century, however, popular anti-Semitism, encouraged by the Dominican friars and fuelled by social and political tensions, began to spread, in much the same way as had occurred in other European countries, where the devastating effects of the Black Death were interpreted as a punishment from God for man's sins. The Jews of Spain were accused of financial extortion, of the ritual murder of Christian children, of the profanation of Eucharistic wafers, of spreading the plague, of poisoning wells. They became scapegoats for Spanish society and were held responsible for all its misfortunes. This anti-Semitic fever culminated in 1391 with extensive waves of killings and pogroms against Jewish communities across the Iberian Peninsula. Thousands of Jews died, and of the survivors, some left the Peninsula, others converted to Christianity; the Jewish population was decimated and impoverished. A century later, Ferdinand of Aragon and Isabella of Castile – the Catholic Kings – who had created a unified Spain through their marriage, ordered an edict of expulsion whereby all

Jews were forced to choose between leaving the country or converting to Christianity. Those who left then, or had left earlier and were now unable to return, were known as Sephardic Jews. Those who stayed and converted became New Christians, or *conversos*, and would be persecuted by the Inquisition for centuries to come.

In one of our first philology classes – held in a tiny room at the top of a building in St Giles from which one could see the roofs of St John's College across the street – I discovered the existence of the Sephardic Jews. Only then, in 1962, did I realise that my Turkish friend from Geneva was himself a Sephardic Jew and that his odd-sounding Spanish was in many ways purer than mine. I now learned that Ladino, the Spanish they still speak today, can inform us about the phonetics and grammar of Old Castilian, rather like discovering an audio tape recorded in the fifteenth century. Despite the influences of other local languages on Ladino over the centuries, its isolation from the Spanish spoken in Spain meant not only that it has preserved forms of words that are no longer in current use, like *agora*, instead of the modern Spanish *ahora* (now), but that it has also kept certain phonetic features that have disappeared altogether from modern Spanish – both in Spain and in Latin America – such as the soft *s* (as in the English *rose*) and a sound corresponding to the English *s* in *pleasure*, which has been replaced by the harsher laryngeal *j*. Unfortunately, the Catalan spoken by the exiled Jews was lost, because the Catalans were completely outnumbered by the more numerous communities of Castilian-Spanish speakers; but many Catalan words and expressions were also absorbed into Ladino.

It was not just the question of the language that I found interesting. It also amazed me how, after their expulsion from Spain, these people had managed to survive, in different

countries of Eastern Europe and North Africa, as communities
with a strong Spanish identity for almost five centuries. How
did they keep it up? What was there so strong about Spain that
could survive in foreign lands? And why would they want to be
loyal to a country that had banished them for ever? I began to
see the story of the Sephardim as an illustration of the complex
feelings about identity and belonging that I had been carrying
about with me since my adolescent days in Geneva. The more
I learned about these people, who for five centuries – since
their total expulsion from Spain by the Catholic Kings in
1492 – have kept their Spanish language and culture alive, the
more their history seemed to illustrate my own situation.
During the cold grey English winters it comforted me to
realise that I was not alone in feeling the enormous pull that
Spain can have on its inhabitants when they are far from their
country, the passion its memory can produce. In wedding
songs and lullabies, in stories and ballads that have been
handed down from one generation to another, Sephardic families all over the world celebrated the same faraway land of
lemons and pomegranates that I myself missed. I could even
take the comparison with my own experience of 'exile' one
step further because, just as I had two countries to which I was
emotionally attached, namely Spain and England, the
Sephardim also had two countries to which they felt strongly
connected: the land of Israel, their original home, and
Spain,which they called Sepharad, their second home.

In his autobiography *The Tongue Set Free*, Elias Canetti, born
into a Sephardic family in northern Bulgaria in 1905, writes
about these double loyalties:

> The loyalties of the Sephardim were fairly complicated. They
> were pious Jews, for whom the life of their religious
> community was rather important. But they considered

themselves a special brand of Jews, and that was because of their Spanish background. Through the centuries since their expulsion from Spain, the Spanish they spoke with one another had changed little. [. . .] The first children's songs I heard were Spanish, I heard old Spanish *romances*; but the thing that was most powerful, and irresistible for a child, was a Spanish attitude. With naïve arrogance, the Sephardim looked down on other Jews; a word always charged with scorn was *Todesco*, meaning a German or Ashkenazi Jew.

Parallel to the story of the Sephardic Diaspora was that of the *conversos*, or New Christians, the large numbers of Jews who decided to convert to Christianity in order to be allowed to remain in Spain. With the memory of Father Velasco still haunting me at times, their fate at the hands of the Inquisition made my heart go out to them, and revived all my anticlerical and anti-Franco feelings. It seemed to me that there was a clear analogy between the performance of the Spanish Inquisition throughout the sixteenth and seventeenth centuries and Franco's regime of religious and political intolerance. The Inquisition's obsession with heresy went hand in hand with the country's pursuit of *limpieza de sangre*, purity of blood – written proof of non-Jewish and non-Moorish racial purity – which became an indispensable prerequisite for any post in the government, the Church or the army, as well as for many professions, and lingered on well into the nineteenth century. This provided me with a further analogy with twentieth-century Fascism and Nazism.

Eventually the *conversos* were absorbed into the non-Jewish Spanish society, their surnames modified or changed, or their origin forgotten, so that few Spanish people today are able to tell whether any Jewish blood runs through their veins. This, however, is not the case in Majorca, where *conversos* never

integrated with the local Christian population. They were
known as *xuetes*, a name that probably comes from *jueuet,* a
diminutive of 'Jew', or perhaps from *xulla*, pork fat, because
of their habit of standing by the door of their homes or shops,
chewing bits of pork fat in an attempt to prove that they had
truly renounced their Jewish faith. But despite these shows of
adhesion and their strict observance of all Catholic rituals
and laws – *xuetes* are, if anything, more Catholic than the old
Catholics – they were never accepted by the rest of Majorcan
citizens. They remained in a sort of self-imposed ghetto and
intermarried, working mainly as silversmiths and money-
lenders. Even today, if one walks down Carrer Argenteria, in
the heart of what was once Palma's Jewish quarter, one can
see *xuetes* standing at the door of their little jewellery shops,
in a way that no non-Jewish Majorcan shopkeeper will do,
welcoming you into their tiny shops, and bringing down the
prices if you politely reject an offer.

At the school of the Dominican sisters there were a few
girls with *xueta* surnames in our class, names like Fortesa,
Miró, Aguiló and Bonnín, and although I had no idea what
xueta meant, nor, I feel sure, did my peers or even the *xueta*
girls themselves, I did know that having a *xueta* name was in
some way degrading. It was the sort of thing that was mentioned in private as the ultimate insult: 'And anyhow, she's a
xueta, didn't you know?' It was an inherited, barely understood anti-Semitism, like the custom of banging pots and
pans, or hitting the ground with sticks by Catalan children
during Holy Week, called '*Matar jueus*', Killing Jews. This was
a game that even my husband played as a child, quite innocently and quite understandably, when he was allowed to step
out on to the balcony of his flat with a wooden spoon and a
pan at three o'clock on Good Friday afternoon, and join all
the other children of the neighbourhood in a rowdy

drumming session. Those two words, *Matar jueus*, had lost their original meaning centuries before – they were just sounds, banging and clanging sounds, to relieve the gloom of Holy Week.

Although there were practically no Jews living in Spain in the 1940s – most of the six thousand Jews who had settled in the country since the nineteenth century had left by the time the Civil War was over – Franco was fiercely anti-Semitic. As a schoolgirl I had been indoctrinated with Fascist anti-Jewish ideas during history and religion lessons, and the picture of these evil people who, because they were considered responsible for Jesus's death, had to be thrown out of Spain, contrasted with all the interesting talk about Judaism that went on during our meals at home; and I was well aware of the warm relationship between my father and Joshua Podro, with whom he wrote *The Nazarene Gospel Restored*, the rewriting of the Gospels in the light of historical and apocryphal documents. The word *judío* (with its rasping *j* sound) and the word *xueta* or *xuetó* were insults in my childhood, whereas the English word 'Jew' had very different connotations for me – I had the good fortune never to have heard it used in any pejorative sense.

When university came to an end and I moved back to Spain, to Sepharad, the story of the Spanish Jews took on yet another significance for me, in particular after we settled in Catalonia in 1970. By then, the fight for the restoration of democracy was becoming more open and popular. From our village outside Barcelona we began to hear about demonstrations in the capital and in the larger industrial towns of the periphery. The lyrics of the *cantautores* became more daring. In his immensely popular '*L'Estaca*', Lluís Llach sang 'Can't you see the stake to which we are all tied? If we don't get rid of it, we'll never be able to walk! But if we all pull it will fall . . .' And the chorus went, 'If I pull from one side, and you pull from the other, it is sure to fall, fall, fall, it must be quite rotten by now!'

> *Segur que tomba, tomba, tomba*
> *ben corcada deu ser ja!*

Everyone, including us, bought a few yards of Catalan flag material to hang out on the balcony on 11 September, the day in which Catalans commemorate the suppression of their ancient privileges by the Bourbon King Philip V.

What may have contributed towards this growing confidence and sense of purpose was the impact of Salvador Espriu's poem '*La pell de brau*, The Bullskin' – its title referring to the shape of the Iberian Peninsula – among literary, artistic and student circles. Published in 1960, it had become, for those people, the manifesto of Catalan opposition. The long poem uses the story of the Spanish Jews repeatedly as a powerful image through which to convey the bitter resignation of Catalans, and of Spanish democrats in general, and the curse of a fraternal quarrel that would remain unresolved as long as the oppressive attitude of the victors persisted. The term Sepharad is used to express the notion of a repressed Spain, and a repressed Catalonia:

> *Ni una gota d'aigua cau*
> *als llavis secs de Sepharad*

> Not a drop of water falls
> on the dry lips of Sepharad

'The Bullskin' also paved the way for the Catalans' present interest in their Jewish heritage, which began in the wake of the dictator's death. It seemed that with the return of Catalan culture and language from internal repression and exile, the return of Jewish culture was also necessary and natural. In the late seventies, guidebooks started to include sections on the remains of Jewish buildings, baths or tombstones in Catalan towns, and I began to see books about the Catalan Jews – and in particular about the Cabalistic circle of the Girona Jews during the twelfth and thirteenth centuries. The Cabala was a Jewish mystical and theosophical movement which had originated in the Languedoc and then spread through Catalonia and the rest of Spain. Cabalists had many things in common with Ramon Llull, the Majorcan Christian mystic; both shared the idea that creation was only a tenuous reflection of God's divinity and that everything on earth and in the skies has a hidden meaning, a small part of which can be deciphered after years of study and meditation. The Cabala appealed to the spiritual side of the Catalans, and their interest in esoteric religions, secret wisdom, alchemy and magic seemed to complement their more practical nature.

Perhaps the spirituality displayed by some Catalans is in part inherited from their Jewish ancestors. Being married to a Catalan and living in Catalonia, I soon became aware of how much Jewish blood in fact ran through the Catalans' veins – I saw it in their intellectual and artistic genius, in their strong sense of racial identity and in their aptitude for business and finance. I saw it, too, in their tendency to dejection – a dejection often accompanied by cutting irony – which counterbalances the loud firecracker outbursts of their emotions, their *rauxa*, as they call it. If you ask a Catalan how he or she is, the answer will never be, 'Fine', but '*Anem tirant*, we're getting along somehow', as if it were bad luck to admit that all is well. And they have a curious way of telling the time: a quarter past eleven becomes a quarter of twelve, a quarter to twelve becomes three-quarters of twelve, so that they are always thinking ahead and reminding themselves of the inexorable passing of time and the shortness of life. How often, waiting in those eternal queues at the village shop, someone would suddenly cry, '*Déu meu*, it's a quarter of eleven already (10.15), and I haven't put the stew on yet!' and a shared feeling of doom would spread round all the housewives in the shop who knew that an *escudella* had to boil at least three hours if it was to taste of anything at all.

Catalans easily become crestfallen and anxious, and Salvador Espriu himself was well known for his pessimistic temperament. I remember once watching him being interviewed on television. This must have been in 1981 or 1982, when he received a series of public honours, when the Catalan autonomy had been reinstated, and Catalonia was recovering from its wounds. In fact, there was a lot for Espriu to be happy about. But the poet sat in the studio looking glum and did not smile once. When his interviewer asked him whether, in view of all these changes, he was not happy, he answered impatiently, 'And how can you expect me to be happy seeing how the world is rapidly advancing towards its own self-destruction?'

A few weeks after having the strange dream about my father, one day in February 1986, I paid my first visit to the *call* of Girona. As I was leaving the village I saw Juanita walking up the hill of our *urbanización* and I waved at her from the car. I felt as if I was going on a long journey into the unknown, and after crossing the murky Llobregat, instead of making my usual right-hand turn into Barcelona I headed north along the motorway that circles round the city, past sprawling industrial areas, past hypermarkets and the University of

Bellaterra, until I found myself in open country, in a picture-postcard landscape of green fields and low hills covered in dark trees, dotted here and there with solitary *masies*. The car radio played a Schubert sonata as I passed the Montseny mountains on my left, and not long after I was entering the province of Girona. Far in the distance, the Pyrenean foothills came into view, and I remember thinking, why don't I do this sort of thing more often?

When I reached Girona I parked the car in a large municipal car park, crossed the bridge over the river Onyar, and began walking up the old streets that led into what had once been the Jewish quarter. Unlike Jewish quarters in other Spanish towns – Barcelona, for example, where what was once a ghetto has been totally absorbed into the rest of the old town and is filled with bars, boutiques and antique shops – the Jewish quarter of Girona developed as a separate part of the city, in an area situated above the commercial centre of town. As a result it has remained unchanged for centuries. I soon found myself in a dense labyrinth of steep, narrow streets, some partially covered to form dark archways, at the end of which the sun lit up the stones again, exposing the details of their textures, their shades of grey and brown. The place was deserted and silent; I did not meet anybody else walking about, although the houses showed signs of being inhabited by their present owners – a brass nameplate on a door, a well-fed cat lying in the sun – and despite the occasional pools of sunlight, the air was cooler here: you could feel a chill seeping out through the walls, passing through layer upon layer of fingerprints and history. When I touched one of the buildings, and felt its damp, rough stone, I thought how these same walls had been seen and felt by the Catalan Jews who had lived here for centuries until they were forced to leave; and suddenly, standing there on my own, with nothing in sight to bring me back to the present, it seemed I had travelled back in time. It was a very powerful feeling, which set my mind in a sort of trance, making me receptive, I felt, to the reality of a life that had taken place five, six or seven hundred years before mine; as if the streets and houses were filled with the ghosts of the Jewish Catalans who had once lived there.

I walked up and down the steep cobbled streets, many of them patterned with the geometric lines of the mule steps; between tall buildings that almost touched at roof level, with lichen softening the edges of the tiles, and weeds pushing through cracks, and ivy growing rank on the shaded walls. Above some of the walls the tops of trees gave away the secret of hidden gardens. I came across mysterious squares at the meeting of various streets; I turned round sharp corners that led into more arched alleyways. Some houses had tiny latticed windows and large front doors, others still had a hole chiselled into the stone lintel where the *mezuzá* was once kept, the holy text that blessed every Jewish home and began, 'Hear, O Israel: the Lord our God is one Lord.' The past was here, nothing had changed for five hundred years. Even the ivy looked as if it had been clinging to the walls for centuries. There was order and proportion in the architecture.

Through a half-open door I saw a patio with potted plants and a stone well in one corner surrounded by a semicircle of low steps, spreading out like ripples. A small staircase led from the patio to the main door of the house. Here, in this very place, I thought, a family would have been preparing for exile in July 1492. A few days before the thirty-first of that month, the last day they could remain on Spanish soil, groups of people in long tunics locked up their homes and carried heavy bundles down the mule steps and out of town, watched silently by the Christians who had been their friends and neighbours – and by their *converso* relatives. It must have been a small crowd: only about twenty practising Jewish families were left in Girona by that time. They stopped outside the town walls, where their cemetery was, to bid a last farewell to their dead and say a last prayer. The women crying and wailing; the men hanging their heads.

Halfway up Carrer Sant Llorenç I found the house of Isaac the Blind that Joana had told me about. It was named after the famous Cabalist whose disciples formed the Girona school, and had recently been set up as a cultural centre. After paying my entrance fee I was free to wander around, and here again, there seemed to be nobody else but me. The silence was complete and created an extraordinary sense of calm and peace as I walked down a spiral staircase to the large kitchen, with its mediaeval cooking oven and its well, and further down still, to the basement, where a large oval stone and an ancient spring are supposedly the remnants of a pre-Christian religious centre. The upper floors had rooms at different levels, with sloping ceilings and small windows, with alcoves in dark corners and uneven steps, all sparsely decorated, as I remember, with Hebrew motifs and items reminiscent of Catalan mediaeval life; I came to a terrace with a wooden balustrade and looked down at the bare patio below, framed by the tall, ivy-clad walls of the neighbouring buildings. This had been the site where the synagogue and the community buildings had stood at the time of the expulsion, and in a tower that rises to the left of this building, the most famous of Girona Cabalists, Nachmanides, is thought to have spent much of his time, mapping out the spheres into which he saw the universe divided; or gazing at the constellations in the night sky; or meditating on how God manifests his hidden essence throughout the harmonious order of creation; on how the words and letters of the Hebrew language contain the very essence of God. And I thought of Ramon Llull on the rocky coast of Majorca, transported to a similar plane of thought; and of St John of the Cross and St Teresa also climbing up the ladder of meditation towards a closer contemplation of God.

Jewish women came into my daydreaming too, working in the kitchens, hanging out the washing, making bread for the Sabbath; I saw them chatting to one another as they looked down from the top of their houses at the town of Girona, at the river Onyar and the marketplace; women called Preciosa, Gracia, Stelina, Meliosa – Catalan women who knew no other land but this. There was so much peace all around me that it was easy to imagine quiet domestic scenes, ordinary lives in ordinary times. Joana had been right, this place was charged with harmony.

But grief and despair had also filled these rooms. I thought of the horror of pogroms and persecutions, of the difficulties suffered by the Jews when the *call* had become a closed ghetto and harsh measures had been taken to enforce the separation between Jews and Christians, in particular between practising Jews and those who had converted to Christianity. I had read an account of a Jewish woman from Girona called Tolrana, who had been separated from her husband because she had refused to follow his example and become a Christian. He was obliged to live outside the *call* and wanted his wife to join him; but despite his efforts to persuade her, she had flatly refused to convert. 'I refuse to cohabit with my husband,' she said, before the court of justice, 'and even less do I wish to become a Christian. Never, for any reason, will I stop being Jewish.' Had she lived in one of the houses I could see from this balcony? Or perhaps in the building across the street?

It was beginning to get dark. The lights went on in the patio revealing the pattern of the tiles, which formed a large star of David. I looked at my watch, and at the same time heard the voice of the doorman shouting up the wooden staircase, '*Senyora, que ja tanquem!* We're about to close!'

When I left the house of Isaac the Blind I felt as if I was stepping out of a dream, and I knew that, like the dream that had originally sent me here, its message could be interpreted in many ways. Perhaps I had gained a new understanding of Catalonia; perhaps a new understanding of myself, and of my tendency to escape into the past – into a past remote enough to border on legend and fable, where I could impose an order and a structure that my own life seemed to lack. Or maybe this had been my way of letting go of my father: I had come here still clinging to him, led by a dream that I had interpreted as his message to me, but now, as I was leaving, the sadness for his loss felt lighter, easier to carry around.

I made my way down a steep alley, went under an archway and then emerged, as if from a tunnel, into the busy streets of the Girona shopping centre. Suddenly there were lights everywhere and cars passing by and people strolling along the pavements; there were televisions blaring out of small bars, competing with the music from jukeboxes and the bleeps of fruit machines. On the street leading down from the Jewish quarter I noticed a Catalan-Jewish surname over a shop door: Astruc, which means Star, the Star of David. Soon I came to a square with arches on either side and I noticed a bookshop on one corner. Its lights were still on, so I went in, and walked up some wooden steps to the area marked *Història i Religió*, where I found a section on Catalan Jews and on Jewish mysticism, next to books on horoscopes, alchemy and astrology. Below me, near the front door, a man wearing a white shirt and a grey cardigan was sitting at a table, busy with paperwork.

'Are you looking for anything in particular?' he asked, glancing up.

'I wanted a good history of the Jews of Girona,' I answered.

'Yes, yes, there are few. You'll find them there.'

I chose a book and took it down to the man at the desk. By now it was quite dark outside – I must have been his last customer that day.

'Is this any good?' I asked.

He looked at the book and nodded approvingly. 'Yes, this is the most complete history that has been published so far. We also have more general books on Catalan Judaism in English, French and German, because we get a lot of Jewish visitors from all over the world,' he said. 'They come from America, Israel, Turkey, Bulgaria. . . Are you Jewish?'

I shook my head. 'I'm English by birth,' I explained, 'but there is no Jewish blood in our family – as far as I know. *I vostè?* What about you?' I asked.

'I somehow thought you looked *estrangera*, but you speak Catalan so well that . . . *Un servidor,* myself, I have a name that may well have been Jewish originally. But I don't know for sure. And I have to say, living here, and reading all these books, makes me feel . . . I don't know . . . a strange connection.'

'It's funny,' I said, 'I've just spent the afternoon in the *call* and I feel, like you, a strange connection, as if I had touched their past. What it is about the Jews, about the ghosts of the Jews, that reaches so deep?' I asked him.

'Ah, that's very simple,' he answered. 'Of course, you need pay no attention to me, but I've thought about this a lot, and I believe very strongly that we Catalans have had a lot in

common with the Jews – especially in recent history. We
have had to keep quiet for many years, and even now it is not
always wise to talk about the past. But you're an *estrangera* so
I can tell you things I cannot tell my own people. Here is an
example. When the Jews were thrown out of this town,
where do you think they went? To France, that is obvious.
The people of Girona have always crossed the Pyrenees when
they have needed to get out of Spain in a hurry, unless they
have had the time and money to arrange for a sea voyage to
Italy or some other destination. And in 1939, after the Civil
War, Catalan Republicans followed the same route as the
Girona Jews had taken, towards Figueres and La Jonquera
and across into French territory. History was repeated. I was
a boy of twelve at the end of the war, and I remember as if it
were today what Girona was like in the last days of January
1939, when Franco's forces were pushing into Barcelona and
the Republican army was retreating towards the French
border. Not just the army, but whole families of civilians who
were afraid of staying in Catalonia poured into Girona on
their way to France – people travelling on foot, carrying children, suitcases, bundles of all shapes and sizes, mattresses,
cages with chickens and rabbits . . . Girona was one great
mass of people filling the streets, the squares, the bridges.
Every archway and staircase was packed at night with people
who could not find anywhere else to sleep – up in the Jewish
quarter and on the cathedral steps, even out here, under the
arches of this bookshop, there were people sleeping in the
freezing cold. In the daytime rumours spread from street to
street and up the long queues of people trying to get passports and safe-conducts to cross the border. "They say the
Republican government and the army chiefs have moved to
Figueres," or "They say it is still safe to take a train – the bor-
ders are not controlled by Franco yet . . ." But it was all

confusion and disorder. I remember the sirens, and the bombs falling on Girona, and all the families from here who were also packing their things and leaving and joining the exodus. I was just a spectator, watching all this from behind our balcony window, because my father had died before the war and my mother decided to stay here with her children and hope for the best. I also saw lorries filling up with people, all fighting to get in. You will say to me, "Yes, but the Jews had three months in which to prepare for exile, and there were not that many of them." I agree. But I have read these books on the Jews and what I am saying is that the anguish, the fear of the unknown, and the pain of having to leave their home, all that must have been the same for them. And you know,' he went on, 'the Jews who left Spain, just like the Republicans who went into exile, went on loving the country that had treated them so badly. I know that from what I read in these books, and from the way the Sephardim who come to Girona talk to me about their "Motherland".'

I handed him some money and he opened the till.

'*Miri*, look,' he continued. 'Here's another example of our connection with the Jews. Here, in Girona, there were a lot of *franquistes* in the forties, all those bigwigs, very powerful people, but there were also a lot of secret Republicans who had decided to stay, just like the *conversos* who went on practising their Jewish religion in secret. At the end of the war people were encouraged to denounce their friends and neighbours, even members of their own families, for Republicanism, just as the Christians and New Christians had been encouraged by the Inquisition to denounce the secret practice of Judaism. In those days any *converso* could be accused of secretly returning to his old faith. It was enough to say that no smoke came out of his chimney on Saturdays, or that too much cooking was done on Fridays, or that a scrap of parchment with Hebrew characters had been seen lining his shoes for the man – or woman – to be arrested, thrown into prison or burned at the stake. Much the same happened with the Republicans in this century. I remember a family who lived opposite our house – very Republican, you know, I think they were Communists too, they were all the things you were not supposed to be in those days. I used to play with their son, he was my age. Then one day he told me that his mother had gone away. In fact she had been arrested and put into prison in Figueres. When she came back home, two years later, she was not the same person. She had tuberculosis or something, and died soon after. Well, you tell me, isn't that the sort of thing that happened to the Jews? That is what I say, *Senyora*: what difference is there between this and the stories of the Jews? It is all one and the same story. The *conversos* were told to stop speaking Hebrew; we were told to stop speaking Catalan. That is why their story reaches so deep, as you say. Because it is our story, because they were a part of our culture. But I'm sorry, you are probably in a hurry. I talk too much.'

He gave me my change and handed me the book.

'I must go home. It's a two-hour drive from here,' I said. 'But I'll come back one day.'

'Oh dear. And I suppose you still have your dinner to cook . . .?'

'Don't worry,' I reassured him. 'I made a big pot of *escudella* yesterday, so all I have to do is heat it up.'

XIV

The Queen Who
Never Was

One day it was Catalan *escudella* and the next Irish stew, or shepherd's pie – or perhaps grilled peppers in olive oil: even through my cooking I seemed to be perpetuating my mixed background, feeding it to my children.

I had watched them learn to speak – English with me, Catalan with their father and grandparents, Spanish, the television language, with many of their friends – mixing their three languages, disentangling them, playing with them as they translated them, and I had seen my own childhood repeated in these games. Their first phonetic attempts at English spelling – 'I lav mami', 'Remember to weik me ap' – I found both amusing and touching, as I suppose mine must have seemed to my parents. But they sometimes spoke a strange language in their sleep, made up of incomprehensible words and meaningless sounds; to me it sounded like a Tower of Babel nightmare, and I knew how important it was to anchor them firmly on one of the three they knew.

We decided to send them to a Catalan school, where my friend Joana was a teacher. It was one of the few in the private sector to teach in Catalan even before the end of the

dictatorship, and to follow the progressive educational programmes for which the Catalans had been pioneers in Spain
during the brief years of the Second Republic, much in keeping with other European educational movements of the
thirties. A school where art and music, meteorology and
chess were all important subjects on their curriculum, and
where religion was glaringly absent – a dramatic contrast to
the secondary education I had received. Our children were
therefore among the first to be learning how to write cor-
rectly in Catalan since the end of the Spanish Civil War and to
learn their times tables in their parent tongue, whereas the
whole of my husband's generation had been deprived of that
basic human right, as a result of the educational policies of the
dictatorship. They were also among the first for whom history
class meant Catalan history as opposed to Spanish history, the
emphasis being on Catalonia and its relation to central Spain,
and not the other way round. They knew the names of all the
Catalan rulers, made relief maps of Catalonia out of
Plasticine, and when we drove back home in the afternoons,
after school, they sometimes sang '*Els Segadors*', the Catalan
national anthem, at the top of their voices:

> *Catalunya triomfant,*
> *tornarà a ser rica i plena!*

> Triumphant Catalonia
> will once again be rich and full!

At home, their cheerfully coloured crayon drawings decorated our walls: pictures of men and women in mediaeval
costume, or of St George, patron saint of Catalonia, killing
the dragon, or of the fireworks and bonfires that light up
villages and cities on St John's Eve. In fact, although religion

was not taught as a subject, it governed the calendar of traditional activities. For Lent they would make a *Vella de Quaresma* (the Old Woman of Lent) – a cardboard figure of an old crone with a wide skirt and seven legs, one for each week of Lent, who held a salted cod in one hand; she was pinned up on the wall and one leg was torn off every Sunday until Easter. They learned how to prepare *panellets* for All Souls' – dainty pastries made of almonds and sweet potatoes, and decorated with pine-nuts – and how to make Nativity scenes for Christmas. In their satchels there were always clay horses and dragons made during art class, with tails and ears missing.

Behind everything the children did, one could sense the enthusiasm of their educators for the reintroduction of a culture that had been buried by forty years of dictatorship, and their elementary history books were proof that history was being rewritten in a new light – and in a new style, devoid of the sentimental rhetoric and hyperboles which had marked Franco's indoctrination programmes. By now – late seventies and early eighties – we lived in a democracy; Catalonia had recovered its prewar autonomy within Spain, with its own parliament and president. But it was through the children's education that the reality of these political changes was first brought home to me. There was no more learning by rote now; no more long lists of sins and articles of the Catholic Faith, no more Fascist ideas tinting the whole of Spanish history in retrospect. The same was occurring in all corners of the Spanish state.

Since my Oxford days I had not given much thought to the episodes of Catalan history I had read about while studying its literature. And even then, in the sixties, what I had learned about the Catalans' ancient democratic institutions and principles seemed remote and completely unrelated to the

Catalonia I knew. But now that Franco's long historical parenthesis had been closed and a new generation of Spaniards was being told openly about its past, and now that my children were happily engrossed in young detective's books or comic strips, unaware that they were reading them in Catalan because they were able to take for granted what had once been lost in a war, I began to see that the link was still there. The Catalans among whom I lived were becoming easily recognisable to me as the descendants of those other Catalans whose pragmatism and industriousness had once managed a great Mediterranean empire; who had later linked their fate to the fate of Spain through the marriage of Ferdinand and Isabella, and whose sense of identity had clearly survived the recent dictatorship, as it had survived other periods of repression.

I would sometimes look at my daughters and see them as a living testimony of all that history; and when they dressed up in Catalan folk costume, their hair tied back in a black net, their hands and arms covered in black lace gloves, I wondered where their British genes were hiding; even my fair-haired youngest daughter looked the part. Through them, I saw modern Catalonia emerging naturally from the past, something that would have seemed impossible only ten or fifteen years earlier when I sat on the bench in Plaça Sagrada Família looking at Gaudí's church; and I came very close to feeling at ease with my circumstances, at one with my surroundings – for the first time since I had moved to Barcelona.

Among the cooking pots and the piles of ironing, and in between thinking about whatever translation I had in hand, my own opinion of the Catalan people was changing, enhanced by this new sense of historical perspective that gave me a greater insight into their minds. Whereas before I had seen the reserve and bitterness of some of the older generation only as a reaction to the Fascist victory and everything that came with it, I now saw how a much bigger picture also encompassed the present. I understood the relevance of the fact that their country can boast the oldest constitution in Europe, and the oldest flag, that as a nation they have always formed a bridge between Northern Europe and the Iberian Peninsula, open to foreign influences and to the transmission of culture and ideas, that throughout their history they have shown a certain attitude to life which makes them both very rational and Northern and also very impassioned and Latin. And then one day, when I chanced to read about a certain Margarida de Prades, a noblewoman who had lived in Barcelona at the turn of the fifteenth century, I realised that this sense of continuity worked both ways – that it could be projected from the present to the past as well as the other way around.

I had come across Margarida de Prades by chance, when reading a collection of poems by Jordi de Sant Jordi, as the woman who inspired some of his poems, and from the start she had seemed very real to me, someone I might have met, or read about, or even seen taking part in some current affairs or literary programme on the Catalan television channel. She could have been one of the elegant mothers I sometimes chatted to outside the school building while we waited for the children to appear – women in leather trousers and shoulder-padded Loewe blouses, who had their own interior-decorating business or some high-powered job in a bank. She was, in fact, the beautiful widow of Martí the Humane, the Catalan king whose death without issue in 1410 brought an end to the five-hundred-year-old dynasty of the House of Barcelona, creating an unprecedented situation which would become one of the great turning points in Catalan history. Margarida herself achieves little more than a passing mention in most history books, but the more I learned about her, the more I liked her, and the more I saw her as an apt forerunner of all the educated and spirited Catalan women I had come to know. Not because her life was an exemplary one – in many ways it was not exemplary at all – but for something that I recognised as intrinsically Catalan, a mixture perhaps of energy, originality, determination and audacity, with a strong dose of practical common sense. Small coincidences kept leading me back to her in one way or another, always revealing some new fact about her life and circumstances, which I found increasingly intriguing. I felt sorry for her. I admired her. At times I was puzzled by her. Whenever I felt trapped by the circumstances of my own life, and failed to find my true self amid the different roles into which I had been cast – my husband's wife, my children's mother, my father's daughter – Margarida de Prades would often wander in and out of my thoughts. She became an imaginary friend.

The book where I had first learned about her existence focused on her role as muse and patroness of a literary circle that gathered in Barcelona over five hundred years ago. The poets who formed this small literary court were among the last to use the archaic style of the troubadours of Provence, speaking about love in the courtly, measured, almost ritualistic manner that had characterised this first European literary renaissance. But behind the old stylistic conventions there was a freshness and vitality that belonged much more to the new Italy than to the old Provence, and Margarida no doubt encouraged these new tendencies. Her short-lived influence captured a defining moment of energy and enlightenment in Catalan literature, which by the end of the century would fall silent as a result of the centralisation of Spain and the establishment of Castilian as the language of the court in all the kingdoms of the Crown of Aragon. Like Eleanor of Aquitaine in the twelfth century, Margarida was seen by her courtiers as the embodiment of the ideal woman of her day: intelligent, educated, gracious and beautiful. She inspired young Catalan poets to write in praise of her, not just because she was King Martí's attractive young widow – 'one of the most beautiful ladies ever known in the world', according to a contemporary chronicler – but because of her intellectual qualities and the vitality she irradiated. Jordi de Sant Jordi, a Renaissance man in every sense – courtier, soldier and poet – wrote these words to her:

> *Sovint sospir, dona, per vos, de luny,*
> *e sospirant va crexent ma follia*
> *de vostr'amor . . .*

> I often sigh for you, lady, when I am far away,
> And my sighs only increase the folly
> of the love I feel for you . . .

When these words were written, Catalonia was still a very powerful nation, despite showing some symptoms of economic decline. It had originated in the ninth century as the County of Barcelona, and by the twelfth century was strong and successful enough to form a confederation of the so-called Levantine states, which included the kingdom of Aragon – hence the name 'Crown of Aragon' by which it was known. From then on, the confederation had enjoyed a vast Mediterranean expansion through conquest and maritime trade which reached its peak in the fourteenth century.

After further reading I was able to piece together the strange events that made up Margarida's life, how she came to marry the king, and what happened to her after his death. Born in 1387, she was the great-granddaughter of the Catalan King Jaume II, and as a young girl became lady-in-waiting to Queen Maria de Luna, the wife of King Martí. The intellectual and refined atmosphere of the royal court opened Margarida's mind. She loved reading and had access to the royal library which held almost four hundred volumes, including a large number of Greek and Latin classics – an impressive library in the days before printing, when each book was individually hand-produced. Among her favourites, I discovered, were the works of Titus Livy, the Bible, chivalry romances and the poems of the troubadours. In the large halls of the royal palace, Margarida saw the king arrive from his travels or set off on new expeditions to Italy or Provence; she met noblemen from Castile, Italy and France, listened to conversations about political intrigues and wars, or the latest translations of Italian poetry. Once a year she attended the Jocs Florals, the Floral Games, a contest of troubadour poetry held in the Catalan court, which were modelled on the original Provençal competitions of the early fourteenth century. The third prize was a violet made of silver, the second a rose made of gold, but the first prize was a natural rose, since nothing made by man could outdo the beauty of nature.

For the Catalans of today, the rose is still a symbol of man's intellectual awareness of nature, and on 23 April, St George's day, our children would each choose a rose from the garden, wrap it in tin foil or Cellophane and take it with them to school. It was El Dia de la Rosa, the Day of the Rose, and competitions were held in the classroom for the most perfect specimen to celebrate the fact that when St George killed the dragon to free the distressed damsel, she offered him a rose in gratitude. It was also El Dia del Llibre, the Day of the Book, when book fairs were held in every town of Catalonia, and lovers of all ages exchanged gifts of books and roses. St George's day always makes me think of Margarida.

The details of Margarida's life flooded back to my mind the other day, while I wandered round the pedestrianised Gothic quarter of Barcelona, still under the spell of the colourful procession I had watched from the hotel balcony, with its gigantic kings and queens and its fiery dragon. There were no children to collect from school, no urgent errands to do while I was in town, no anxiety. But still I thought of those days, of the children's history books and my own story of Margarida de Prades. These were the streets she had known, many of these buildings were already standing when she lived here. A busking musician sat by a fountain playing the guitar, like some mediaeval lute player, and his pleasant music followed me as I walked round the back of the cathedral cloisters towards the Royal Palace.

Large sections of the palace still stand – spacious halls and courtyards and the lovely chapel of Santa Àgata. I ascended the stairs to the higher levels of the palace and as I looked out from one of the balconies I tried to imagine what Margarida could see from this very spot at the start of the fifteenth century. Looking one way the view was of a vast expanse of fields and woods which then stretched all the way up to the hills that surround the city. In the opposite direction lay the densely populated Burgada de Mar, the *barri* that had developed outside the Roman walls during the Middle Ages, presided over by the tall new church of Santa Maria del Mar; and beyond that, the sea and a profusion of masts and sails from the vessels that traded with all parts of the known world. Although the port was the heart of the city's activities, it was still only a sandy beach then, so that ships anchored at a distance from the shore and skiffs were used to fetch and

carry crew and wares from morning to dusk. Watching all
that bustle, proof that her country was still an important maritime power in the Mediterranean, how much was Margarida
aware of the general impoverishment of Catalonia? No doubt
she had heard these matters discussed in court – how the
country had been suffering a prolonged economic crisis
during the last half of the fourteenth century, as indeed had
much of Europe, due to famines and plagues and the consequent drop in the population, how there were added causes in
the case of Catalonia: the expenses of wars against Italy and
Castile, the disruption of sea trade as a result of the rise of the
Ottoman Turks in the eastern Mediterranean and the constant
attacks by Berber pirates, how banks had collapsed and social
unrest prevailed. Was she still too young to fear for her
country's future?

A young Japanese couple walked past me. This must be
their honeymoon, I thought, a journey to Europe. My
fifteenth-century image of Barcelona disappeared immediately, and in its place was the bright new city I had encountered after my five-year absence. As I watched the buildings
change colour in the afternoon light, my Catalan past suddenly seemed as remote as Margarida's. It came back to me
only in snatches, in unconnected images, like the sudden
recollection of my occasional visits to Castelldefels in the
winter, whenever I went shopping in the large hypermarket
near the airport. On the way I would pass fields smelling of
artificial fertilisers, and always, on the corners of the fields,
even in broad daylight, there would be girls in miniskirts
and heavy make-up waiting for customers. They looked like
scarecrows, or like peasant women gone mad. Out of
season, the holiday resort was like a ghost town, with
notices clanging in the wind and boarded-up bars on the
waterfront, but the beach was beautiful in its solitude. I

wondered whether Margarida had come here too, when she was older, to try to make sense of her life, as I was trying to make sense of mine.

Margarida would probably have married one of the young noblemen who frequented the royal palace, had King Martí's only surviving son not died in 1409. By then, the king was a widower. Courtiers and governing institutions all pressed him to take a new wife who would give him another child to per-petuate the dynasty of the House of Barcelona. He was presented with two candidates, carefully selected from the Catalan nobility, one of whom was Margarida de Prades. The king chose Margarida, perhaps because he knew her well and thought she would make a good queen, perhaps because she was beautiful and had a strong body that promised healthy children. Whatever his reasons, this was a marriage of con-venience, if ever there was one – and Margarida must have had little say in the matter. They were married by Pope Benedict XIII (this was Pope Luna, the antipope, and a rela-tive of King Martí's first wife) on 17 September 1409 – Margarida was twenty-two, the king fifty, Margarida tall and slender, the king short and fat. The wedding took place in the chapel of the little palace of Bellesguard, which the king had recently built as a refuge against the plague that was con-stantly hitting the city.

Bellesguard – which means Beautiful Sight – stood high above Barcelona, at the foot of the hill called Collserola. The journey must have been a pleasant one for Margarida, leaving the rather sombre buildings of the walled city and riding her horse along country lanes with a group of courtiers, passing farmhouses and fields, until she reached the village of Sarrià and the church of Sant Gervasi. From there the steep hill to Bellesguard was hard on the horses. Margarida dismounted

and walked up that last stretch, with her ladies-in-waiting
fussing about her, smoothing down her bridal gown, while
she turned her head every now and then to look down at the
distant port and listen to the church bells ringing for her.

Sometime in the early eighties I followed the same route
Margarida took on her wedding day, except that my journey
was in a car, with no restful views of fields or farmhouses, no
neighing of horses, no stops for refreshments. On the pas-
senger seat was a piece of paper with an address, where I was
going to collect my daughter from a birthday party, and a
street-map of Barcelona. I reached the square of Sarrià, and
then drove past the grand houses built by the rich
industrialists of the turn of the century – where the upper-
middle-class Catalans still like to reside today, with Filipino
maids who take their poodles out for walks in the early
morning.

Sadly, however, nothing remains of the original fifteenth-
century building. Today's Palau de Bellesguard was built by
Gaudí in 1907 over the ruins of the original house. As
usual, he has left us an architectural extravaganza, an
extraordinary castle-like building with buttresses and battlements, arches and balconies, surrounded by luscious
gardens and quiet vaulted patios. Only the pale mountains
that rise behind the house, on the other side of a motorway,
are still relatively bare and probably look the same as they
did in 1409; and close to the site there are a few empty
areas of yellow earth in which pine trees and cactus plants
have rooted.

As we drove home, Natalia told me more about it.

'That house is full of mysteries, Mummy,' she said. 'Enric
took us into the garage and showed us a hole in the wall. He
told us there was a secret passage that started here and led all

the way down to the centre of Barcelona. And then he showed us a room below the kitchen which is full of arches – he says it was once the dungeon of the King of Catalonia. It was a bit scary.'

The royal couple settled in Bellesguard, but eight months later the king became ill and died – he appears to have suffered from diabetes – without Margarida having conceived the heir they had hoped for. Margarida's role had come to an end, and so she stood aside and watched as an electoral college was formed to choose the next king and six different claimants were nominated. It was a time for political pacts – Catalans are still great believers in settling differences at all levels through deals and agreements – but it also brought about bitter fights between factions.

The final choice of Fernando de Antequera did not prove a wise one. The new Castilian-speaking dynasty had a different political mentality and no real understanding of the constitutional laws and institutions that held the country together; neither did the courtiers who came with them, and gradually the traditional harmony between the monarchy and the governing classes was lost. Later in the century, with the marriage of Ferdinand (Ferran, as he is known in Catalonia, grandson of Fernando de Antequera) to Isabella, and the consequent union of the two kingdoms, Castile would become the dominant power, and in 1492 the discovery of America would shift European sea trade from the Mediterranean to the Atlantic. Castile held the trade monopoly and barred the Catalans, who faced the Mediterranean, from participating in any commercial ventures with the New World of the Atlantic. Catalonia entered a dark age and virtually disappeared as a country in its own right.

During the two-year interregnum between the death of her husband and the election of the new king, Margarida was the only person who symbolised some sort of regal authority in her country, and this was brought home to me by yet another of those small coincidences that always seemed to link her to my life. After my visit to Girona, I discovered that the book I had bought there contained a reference to a letter dated 21 April 1411, from the councillors of Girona to a certain Berenguer de Gálvez, secretary of Queen Margarida. In it, the councillors beg Gálvez to plead with her in favour of the Jews of Girona, whose homes had been lying in a state of ruin since the terrible incidents of 1391, and who were being subjected to extortions and ill-treatment by 'so-called' Crown officials posted in Girona. Although it remains unclear whether Queen Margarida did anything to remedy the situation, this unexpected connection between my widowed queen and the Jews of Girona – the Jews of my dream – was an exciting one for me and added a new dimension to the picture I had already formed of her life and time.

Margarida had other worries. King Martí had bequeathed her the beautiful house of Bellesguard and one of the royal palaces in Barcelona, known as the Palau Reial Menor. He had also left her his entire library and other valuable goods, and had made provisions for a pension to be passed to her as long as she remained his widow. But – a reflection of the times – the houses had to be mortgaged to pay for the king's funeral, the books and jewels had been pawned to pay for the wedding expenses, and the pension proved difficult to collect. There exists a great deal of documentation concerning her financial problems – letters to creditors, inventories, pleas for the payment of her dues. With all, she managed to build herself a life in the old style of the Catalan monarchy, surrounding

herself with the intellectuals and artists of her day and creating a literary circle which became central to her life. She was
an emancipated woman in an emancipated country, shackled
only by the inherited financial situation, defying the threat-
ening winds of change.

In 1415 her life took another unexpected turn. Margarida
fell deeply in love with a nobleman from Valencia called Joan
de Vilaragut, and married him. But he was penniless, and the
couple decided to keep the marriage secret so that she could
continue to receive her royal widow's pension, keep her title
with all its privileges, and go on living as she had until then.
During the interregnum her husband had been actively sup-
portive of prince Fernando's main rival. Could there have
been a streak of revenge against the new Castilian court in her
decision to hold on unlawfully to her royal title? The priest
who married her, and the two witnesses who slipped in unobserved through one of the back doors of the royal palace of
Valencia, then crept up a disused staircase to the room where
the wedding took place, promised not to reveal the secret;
and they kept their word. Margarida named Joan her cham-
berlain so that he could reside with her openly in her palace –
the bedroom arrangements are said to have been just as discreet – and he always called her *Senyora reyna* in public.

When she realised she was with child she arranged to
spend the last months of her pregnancy in Perpignan where
people did not know her; after the birth of her baby, a boy
called Joan Jeroni, she returned to Barcelona and handed him
over to a wet nurse to be cared for. This was quite a common
procedure among the nobles of those days – she herself had
been brought up by her wet nurse until she was three or four.
But when the boy was older, Margarida continued to hide
him from the world, for although her financial situation
seemed to worsen every year, she never lost hope of a change

of fortune as she struggled to keep her properties and her situation. The boy was eventually sent to the monastery of Santes Creus to be personally educated by the abbot, who was a friend of hers.

Like most Catalan women of today, Margarida was fiercely possessive of her estate, and spent years trying to hold on to what she believed was hers by right. The fact that the Catalan word *dona* means both 'woman' and 'wife' is no coincidence. *Dona*, which in its Spanish version *doña* is now used only as a courtesy title before Christian names, comes from the Latin *domina*, meaning mistress, and for Catalan women, the sense of property and ownership is indivisible from the sense of womanhood and sexuality. This awareness of personal ownership within marriage is so much a part of their tradition, of their collective subconscious, that it is quite common to hear Catalan men specifying, '*És de la dona* – it belongs to the wife,' during a conversation among friends, when referring to a building, a car, or even a business.

In the old days when a woman was given a dowry by her father, that dowry remained the property of the woman, although administered by her husband, until her death, when it passed to her children; or it was returned to her if her husband died and she was left a widow with no children. This was a practical means of ensuring that family fortunes did not end up in the wrong hands. But with the gradual disappearance of the dowry system, Catalan women were left with the simpler, underlying concept, known as the law of Separation of Property – a marriage law which is directly derived from the old feudal *Usatges*, and is still in force today in Catalonia and the Balearic Islands. It means that when Catalans or Balearics marry, each of the spouses retains the property of what is his or hers at the time, and of what each

may acquire individually during the marriage, unless otherwise arranged in a marriage settlement. In the rest of Spain
the law is different: man and wife jointly own everything they
may acquire individually during the marriage as well as the
rents or interests of any properties which belonged to them
separately when they were single. Again, this can be changed
by a pre-marriage settlement, and today these *capitulaciones*
are becoming more and more frequent outside Catalonia and
the Balearics. The Catalan law has been criticised by people
who have seen it as benefiting only women from wealthy families, whereas a woman who owns nothing before marriage
and is tied to the house bringing up the children, cooking and
washing, never has anything to show for her work if the husband decides to keep his property to himself. Perhaps. But it
has also made Catalan women want to become independent
and go out to work, and it has made them strong. Besides,
Catalans have by nature a deeply rooted sense of social justice,
a belief in equal rights for all classes, and this has made it
much easier for Catalan men to accept the feminist developments of the twentieth century.

In 1421, Margarida's financial situation became so desperate
that she had to give up the Palau Reial Menor, where she had
spent most of her time and entertained her literary friends.
But she still owned Bellesguard, the little palace above Sarrià
where she had married King Martí, and now she left the city
and travelled up there with her husband, only to find that
her old friend Violant de Bar, to whom she owed a substantial
amount of money, had taken possession of this house as well.
With nowhere left to go, the couple moved into the convent
of Valldonzella, run by an aunt of hers. There her husband
became ill and died, in June 1422. Heartbroken, and tired of
fighting, Margarida retired from public life and turned her

mind to religion. She never saw her son again. Two years later she took the veil at her aunt's convent and in 1428 she became abbess of the monastery of Bonrepòs, a convent in her own lands of Prades, where she died the following year. She was forty-two.

In the poem he wrote on the occasion of her death, the Marquis of Santillana curses fortune, '*porque tan gentil figura de este siglo se apartava*, because such a graceful figure was leaving this century'. But much more was leaving Catalonia, and neither the Marquis, who, in his day, admired Margarida's country for its modernity and literary prestige, nor even Margarida could have foreseen the extent of the dire changes to come. Catalonia entered into a decline when it ceased to be an independent kingdom; those Jews whose fate had been in Margarida's hands for a short while became part of a mass-exile from all Spanish kingdoms; Catalan culture, flourishing in her lifetime, went out like a candle for almost three centuries. Its art and literature, its very being, lay dormant all that time. It was only in the nineteenth century that a literary revival known as the Renaixença turned people's attention again to the late mediaeval society, proclaiming it the most resplendent era of Catalonia, rather like the Pre-Raphaelites looking back with nostalgia at Arthurian legends and mediaeval history. The Renaixença even reinstated the Jocs Florals to stir the Catalans' sense of nationalism and collective identity. Language became the centre of attention, and Catalan was put back on the map, rescued from the fireside and the marketplace. With the reinstatement of the Catalan autonomy during the Second Republic, the long process of re-Catalanisation seemed complete. Then came the Civil War, and once again language and culture were banished to the shadows.

Today, after twenty years of Catalan autonomy, the
Catalans are just as impassioned in these matters as they have
always been, and their continued insistence on the widespread
use of their language has been the subject of some criticism
from other Spaniards. Having been so close to the fight, I can
understand this insistence. And yet, during these days I am
spending in Barcelona, I sense that opinions are beginning to
divide, that objectives are not as focused as when all Catalans
were waving their flags and fighting on a common front for
the re-establishment of democracy and their culture. The
rotten stake Lluís Llach sang about in '*L'Estaca*' has fallen, the
old oppressor no longer exists and people can walk and talk
freely; but now they are beginning to feel that their sense of
purpose has been diluted. All the more so in this new age of
global communications, when centralisation means much less
than it did even ten years ago. Some see the fight for Catalan
language and culture as a battle that has already been won,
while others fear that, despite all that has been achieved, the
Catalan language is doomed to disappear, because the issue of
its preservation has come to be dismissed as irrelevant in the
booming market economy.

I looked at my watch and made my way down the palace
steps, through the chapel of Santa Àgata, past the large hall
where Columbus was received by Ferdinand and Isabella on
his first return from America, and down the wide fan of semi-
circular stairs that lead into the square. Soon I will meet my
mother for dinner, I thought, in a small Cuban restaurant
near the hotel; and tomorrow we will move into the hospital.
But now I am still alone with my Catalan past. I can see myself
again. I am waiting outside the house of my daughter's piano
teacher who lives in an *urbanización* close to ours. I have
arrived too early so I am wandering about aimlessly, not

wishing to ring the bell and go into the premises yet, because the teacher's two dogs, Pluto and Black, will start barking their heads off if I do. I am on the top of a hill, in a wood of pine trees, and from here there is a view of the valley below, of the village with its small factories, of the main road leading to Barcelona. I do not know why I am crying. Perhaps I can already foresee the end of my stay in this country, as Margarida may have foreseen the end of her country's well-being. The light is fading. My life seems to be fading. I wish things were otherwise, but I know they are not. Margarida has told me so.

XV

Objective Burma!

Since I left London a few days ago I have been carrying a letter around in my handbag. It is an old letter from Joana – dated 6 December 1991 – which for some reason was never filed away but assumed an erratic existence in one of my drawers, among restaurant bills, photographs and postcards, turning up every once in a while when I was looking for something else. I came across it again the other day, just before leaving for the airport; taking this to be some sort of omen, I thrust it in my bag as a safeguard against the growing apprehension I was feeling about my return. It says:

> My dear friend,
>
> I was overjoyed to find your letter in my letter-box. But when I read it, I was saddened to hear of all the difficulties you have been through. Changes are always hard, one way or another, and we tend to grieve for what we have left behind. Perhaps, now that you are in London, the distance will help you understand these changes better. I do feel, however, that until more time has passed – months, or even years – you will not be able to review your past with the serenity it requires

and deserves. I speak from experience. I do believe that life has its cycles and that if we just wait, if we don't give up, what now may look to us like a meaningless end, will become a meaningful beginning. Truth will eventually fall off the tree of life like a ripe fruit, and its seed will bury itself and germinate; from it a new tree will grow, resisting winds and rain and snow. But we must be patient, we must learn to wait; that is something I have to keep repeating to myself. It's not easy.

The same applies to history – its wheels turn and turn. We ourselves have lived through one of the darkest eras and watched it come to an end, and then give way to one of the brightest and long-lasting in many centuries. Not just for Catalonia, but for the whole of Spain. When I look back now and think of those days, almost twenty years ago, I see far more clearly than I did at the time how certain events stand out among the rest. They have become part of history books, of the so-called 'transition'; but at the time, how were we to know where they would lead, or who would write the history books of today? . . .

I, too, look back now, as if I were watching a documentary on the end of Franco's life, and remember a day in 1973, the day Carrero was killed. This was Admiral Luís Carrero Blanco, Franco's prime minister since 1969 and one of his oldest collaborators, the man chosen by the Generalissimo to ensure the continuity of his policies after his death. He was on his way home from his daily Mass that morning when a mine placed by the Basque terrorist group ETA exploded and sent him flying in his Dodge Dart over a Jesuit hall of residence in the centre of Madrid. We spent all day listening to the radio to catch the latest on what at first was reported to have been an accidental gas explosion. In Madrid the streets were deserted all day. There were police everywhere, even in

Catalonia, with checkpoints on the roads, in the airport and stations. In our village, the older women were stuffing their shopping bags with two or three extra packets of rice, sugar and flour. Just in case.

But Glòria, the butcher, seemed unperturbed. I remember that she was talking to a client that morning about how to make the Christmas broth. 'My mother always added two small cups of white wine a few minutes before serving it.'

'I've never heard of such a thing!'

'It's the recipe from her village. She came from Tarragona. Well, every village has its traditions.' She used the word *poble*, which means both village and people.

I started to think about *my* people, about the turkey, the Brussels sprouts, the stuffing and bread sauce that would appear on the dining-room table in my parents' house on Christmas Day. My father would hide an old silver three-penny bit in the Christmas pudding; it was always the same coin, kept in a box in his study, and whoever found it in their helping had to hand it back so that it could be used again the following year – keeping the good luck, of course. Then there would be mince pies, crackers and champagne, and the toast, 'To absent friends!' followed by a moment's hush. I was standing in the butcher's, hoping that this terrorist attack would not lead to anything worse and that we would be able to travel, as planned, to the island. The children were already counting the days.

'Yes, all right, they're all a bit different, but let's face it, a Catalan Christmas broth is a Catalan Christmas broth. Now, if you go to Valencia, or Madrid . . .'

'We'd better leave Madrid out of this, especially today. Pretty fireworks they've sent off for Christmas, eh?' said a male voice. It was Glòria's husband Jordi, coming into the shop with a sheep's carcass.

With her blond hair neatly lacquered, her face carefully made-up, and wearing an impeccably white frilly overall over an elegant blouse, Glòria always exuded self-confidence and stability. On a corner of the counter there was a tiny Nativity scene; on the wall, the Black Virgin of Montserrat in a gold frame, with the Catalan flag – nine yellow and red horizontal stripes – decorating the base. You got the feeling that every-thing was under control when you stood waiting in that shop, even if prime ministers were being blown up. Nothing could be allowed to perturb the smooth flow of life.

'There's a lot of police out there,' said Jordi that day.

'We were going down to Barcelona to the cinema,' said someone in the queue. 'But I'm not in the mood any more.'

'It's a day for staying at home, close to the fire, and letting them get on with it,' said Jordi as he left.

Every one of us, including the self-confident Glòria, felt uneasy as we stood in the shop and talked about broth. What had happened in Madrid a few hours earlier, the murder of the man with thick eyebrows and an impenetrable expression whom we often saw on television and in the newspapers standing next to Franco, was something with unforeseeable consequences: further terrorism, further repression, wide-spread protest – anything could happen. For optimists – and these were proved wrong – it could mean the election of one of the more progressive members of Franco's cabinet to take Carrero's place. Now that these events have their proper place in history, they are commonly interpreted as the first open sign of *la transición,* the transitional period between the end of the dictatorship and the first democratic elections in 1977. Franco, we now learn, was shattered by Carrero's death: he is reported to have moaned, 'They have snapped the last thread that connected me with the world!' and to have been unable to eat or sleep for days.

The last years of the dictatorship bring another date to my mind – 2 March 1974. For days there had been talk of the possible execution of the young Catalan student Salvador Puig Antich, accused of killing a policeman during a rally and of belonging to the Anarchist Party. News trickled in about efforts that were being made to secure his pardon – even the Pope intervened. With the whole world watching these developments, nobody believed he would be executed. Besides, despite the repressive instincts of the new prime minister, Arias Navarro, whom the older generation silently remembered as the 'butcher of Málaga' for his part in the horrific wartime executions, it seemed that he was intent on giving the government a softer and more open image. But Franco refused to commute the death penalty. Was this his revenge on the assassination of his old friend Carrero Blanco? A spurious show of authority to cover the government's weakness?

The news of the execution was announced on the radio, but missed the papers that day. The following morning, Sunday 3 March, when I went down to the *papereria*, I saw this headline on one of the inside pages of *La Vanguardia*: 'Salvador Puig Antich was executed yesterday by means of the garrotte.' Montse sat on her stool by the till and when I mentioned the news, instead of shrugging her shoulders as usual, she answered, 'Yes, what bad luck, *pobret* – poor boy – what bad luck!' Back home, we read the detailed but dispassionate account of his last twelve hours – after his sentence had been announced in the evening – and I felt sick in my stomach. Until the very last moment, the article said, he had been convinced that his sentence would be commuted. According to one of his lawyers, he had spent the last hours speaking to him about the recent British elections, and about subjects of national interest. He had been allowed a visit from

three of his sisters, and from a Salesian priest, who was a
friend of the family. At eight o'clock in the morning, the sisters had been ordered to leave the prison. An hour later his
lawyers were also told to go, and only the priest remained by
his side, until two minutes before the execution. Puig Antich
did not lose hope until that moment, when he was hand-
cuffed and led off to the execution room, to have his neck
placed in an iron collar that would be tightened until stran-
gulation occurred. Later, the priest gave the news of the
execution to the group of people waiting outside the prison.
I remember another detail: among the prisoner's personal
belongings, recovered by the family, were two rings; but the
letters he had written to his family and to his lawyers were
withheld by the prison authorities.

On the same page there was news of another execution,
one that had no political motive, but that was probably
intended to make light of the first, in some macabre way.
This unfortunate person was Heinz Chez – a thirty-three-
year-old Pole who had killed a Civil Guard one night when he
was drunk. He was garrotted in Tarragona, some sixty miles
or so down the coast, at exactly the same time as Puig Antich.
In the paper, his lawyer reported: 'Mr Heinz Chez behaved at
all times in a most admirable manner, speaking with us ami-
cably and with great serenity. Mr Chez, whose family have not
been present, spent the night playing Parcheesi with his
guards and took his leave of various people, asking them to
forgive him if he had ever offended them in any way.'

I can remember exactly how I felt that Sunday in March,
reading the accounts of the two deaths, and I recognise in
those feelings the same mixture of fear and revulsion I had
once felt in the presence of Father Velasco or Sister Valentina,
or the police who took my thumbprints; and the same anger
I felt over the years against the Fascist victory that had

changed the fate of people like Blanca or Jimena, against a political system that had managed to affect the very way people around me thought, and expressed themselves, and lived. For despite an increasingly open opposition to the government, particularly in Barcelona and Madrid, the vast majority of people simply got on with their lives and kept quiet. As for the more general significance of the executions – and of the five that followed in September 1975, this time by firing squad – time and history have encapsulated them in the final black chapter of Franco's life. They will always mark the grim end of his rule over the Spanish people.

The end came. On 20 November of that year, when we turned on the radio in the early morning and heard classical music being played on all the stations, we knew that Franco had died. We had been expecting it. For weeks now there had been talk of his illness. The night before, there had been a change in the television programmes. Instead of a new musical show, starring Julio Iglesias and featuring comedians, foreign singers and a group of dancers in high heels and feathers, we were shown *Objective Burma!*, an old film on the Second World War. The lead was played by Errol Flynn and it described the exploits of an American platoon in the Burma campaign. There was no suggestion in the film that British forces were even involved in the campaign – I read somewhere later that this had created a minor diplomatic incident at the time – and I thought of my half-brother David. I thought of him in the sticky pre-monsoon weather, marching with his battalion towards the Japanese positions in the Arakan peninsula, in north-west Burma, passing through jungles of flowering bushes and leafy trees, with the hills in the distance covered in an eerie mist, his eyes squinting against the sun, against death. The attack took place on 18 March 1943, the objective being to secure several Japanese strongholds in the area. I thought of him bombing his way across open ground under enemy fire, trying to regain the offensive when the British companies found themselves unable to move forward, taking one Japanese post and continuing to advance alone with a fresh supply of grenades; and then being shot in the head and falling into a trench, from which his companions were unable to retrieve him.

My birth and David's death have always been connected in my mind. And now the half-brother I never knew was returning to my thoughts because Franco was dying and this film was being shown on television.

'Franco must be worse,' Ramon had said. He was right.

That morning in November we kept turning the dial on the radio, but all we got was classical music. Then we heard the news. 'His Excellency Don Francisco Franco has died. At the moment of his death, five twenty-five a.m., four of his grand-children were at his bedside, as well as his daughter and her husband . . .' It felt strange. Had it really happened? It had taken so long!

That really was an end, a big 'The End' in Technicolor, with sentimental rhetoric covering the pages of all the news-papers, and the television showing the crowds filing past Franco's body in the palace of El Pardo; a month's public mourning and no school for the children for the next few days. Later came his burial under a thick marble slab behind the main altar in the basilica of the Valle de los Caídos, the Valley of the Fallen. This is a vast Fascist monument to the *nacionales* fallen during the Civil War, built by the forced labour of Republican prisoners. They say that shops ran out of champagne, that people were celebrating in bars and in the streets. Perhaps they were, in the anonymity of the large cities, but in small towns like ours nobody dared raise a voice;

not yet. And although a huge wave of relief had swept over
Spain with the announcement of the old man's death, in the
papereria Montse shrugged her shoulders all day long. There
was still a great deal of expectation and uncertainty, and
nobody was quite sure which way things would go.

Only now, as I sit in this hospital waiting for my mother to
return, do I begin to understand how difficult I have found it
to try to move forward within my own self during the twenty
years of my life as a Spanish married woman. How contagious
the atmosphere of passivity could be, sucking me into its stillness from where I escaped into unreal worlds of thoughts.
How hard it was to reconcile the different voices I heard
inside me – the voice of freedom and the voice of conformity.
There was always a part of me, the freedom-loving part, that
I held back and was reluctant to show. Joana always encouraged me to step out, as she had encouraged me to visit
Girona, or to read Salvador Espriu, or to accompany her on
long walks, during which we would visit Romanesque
churches lost in remote valleys. It is becoming clear to me
only now, as I reread her letter, that my story is partly the
story of Spain; that all these ends and changes in Spanish life
reflected ends and changes that also occurred within me. The
reinstatement of democracy after Franco's death broadened
viewpoints, uncovered layers of forgotten culture and created
new possibilities of human interaction. At the same time my
own life was changing: with the screening of *I, Claudius* on
Spanish television, Spaniards discovered my father and wanted
not only to read all his books, which meant a lot of translation
work for me, but also to get to know him, to interview him,
to fuss over him. By then he was not well enough to take this
on, and the media began to approach me as his spokesperson.
I started to give interviews and write articles about his work

and gave talks at universities in Spain, Britain and the US. Travelling suited me, and having to face an audience, which meant having to battle with stage fright, was a small price to pay for the freedom and mobility the lectures offered. Then, in 1984, my eldest daughter went to England to complete her further education; she was followed by our second daughter in 1987; and by the youngest in 1989. Ramon travelled back and forth to Madrid for his work. The house in the Catalan village was losing its inhabitants, we were all dispersing, and Ramon and I were growing further apart.

I miss our conversations in your kitchen or in mine – what better place for women's talk than the ancient 'hearth'? – when we sat and talked and turned things over and over. We spoke about how to reconcile freedom with responsibility, and I always said to you that responsibility begins with oneself. I remember you once quoted these words of Hillel 'If I cannot be for myself how can I be for others? If not now, when?' But I believe there is a time for everything. We each have a pattern, full of cycles, full of ends and beginnings, and we must be try to be aware of where we stand in that pattern. Mary Stuart's motto: '*En ma fin git mon commencement*', 'In my end is my beginning', can be applied not only to her tragic execution but to the smaller ends and beginnings that make up our lives . . .

Eliot used that motto in 'East Coker':

Dawn points, and another day
Prepares for heat and silence. Out at sea the dawn wind
Wrinkles and slides. I am here
Or there, or elsewhere. In my beginning.
From the moment I stepped out of the timeless context of

my childhood, where death was a coffin on the sand and birth a large shiny nipple in a dark room, I lost that first vision of reality, pure and unadulterated, free of the layers of history that colour the world, of the layers of meanings imposed on things by languages. Later, in my years of Spanish schooling, everything in life became subjected to the opinion of the Church and the state, holders of the only truth, paragons of justice and kindness. There was nothing that could simply be itself, freely, and I tried in vain to reconcile my first appreciation of the world and the truth I felt prevailed in my home with the new truth I was being handed by my superiors. I was too innocent to believe in falseness. Later, in the years spent away from Spain, I shook myself free of all that oppression, but returned to find its trail still haunting me, still powerful enough to lay traps for me.

> Home is where one starts from. As we grow older
> The world becomes stranger, the pattern more complicated
> Of dead and living.

Long before his death, Franco had arranged for the monarchy to be reinstated after his lifetime – adjusting the Spanish laws of succession to suit his convenience, since he preferred Juan Carlos to his father, Don Juan, who was the rightful heir. Juan Carlos was proclaimed king the day after Franco's death, and *la transición* began in earnest. The man with the thin moustache, Arias Navarro, who had filled Carrero Blanco's post, continued at the head of the government until June 1976, when Adolfo Suárez, one of Franco's youngest ex-ministers, was chosen by the king as his new prime minister. No one was quite sure what was going to happen next, but to everyone's surprise Suárez initiated a comprehensive programme of political reform. Religious freedom was proclaimed. Political parties were legalised, clandestine opposition leaders surfaced, and one poor man who had been hiding in a garret for almost forty years at last dared to come out into the open. Capital punishment was removed from the penal code. Well-known exiles began to come home; figures like La Pasionaria, who returned after the legalisation of the Communist Party, and President Tarradellas, the Catalan president-in-exile, who in October 1977 greeted the crowds from the balcony in the Plaça de Sant Jaume in Barcelona with the words '*Ja sóc aquí! Here I am!*'

Everything happened very fast. The first democratic elections since 1936 were held that year; a constitution was drafted by an all-party commission and approved by referendum in 1978. Suárez's centrist UCD (Centre-Democratic Union) had won the nationwide elections, but the local elections in 1979 showed a major shift to the left. In our little town we had a Communist local government for the next four years, and saw many improvements in community services – a well-run infants' school, which my youngest daughter attended, and a family planning clinic once a week, which helped to get rid of old taboos, even if Galician witchcraft was still discussed in the waiting room. There was also a change in colour, which immediately altered the outward image of the country. All the silver-grey postboxes were painted a bright yellow, and the steel-grey uniforms of the policemen were changed to a soft brown. The black patent-leather three-cornered hats of the *guardias civiles* were largely replaced by more friendly-looking caps.

With the arrival of democracy, the word *Libertad!* was on everybody's lips, as it was in dozens of pop songs – like the one that repeated: '*¡Libertad, libertad, sin ira libertad!* Freedom, freedom, without anger, freedom!' People were out in the streets in huge rallies, demanding amnesty for political pris-

oners, shouting, '¡*Amnistía, libertad!*' insistently, like the
chorus in a Greek drama. Amnesty, freedom! And all this
was reported by the media. The fear had lifted from people's
faces, and one thing followed another. Freedom of press was
restored, and in Catalonia publications in Catalan multiplied
and the first Catalan television channel was inaugurated.
Every change soon became a matter of course. Middle-class
Catalans no longer had to travel across the border to
Perpignan to see films like *The Last Tango in Paris*, but had X-
rated films shown in their local cinema. All over Spain the
masses woke up from their inertia to look at erotic magazines
and shows; to watch sex chat shows on television; to witness
the surfacing of the gay society from its underworld of perse-
cution. The new generation, the generation of my own
children, was not oppressed.

Old and new Spain lived side by side, and I have a memory
that illustrates that coexistence. I was on a beach near
Barcelona. Close to me two children were playing on the
edge of the water, splashing about, laughing and shouting.
Their mother was sitting on a rock, topless, her eyes closed,
her chin raised, her naked body, shining with suntan lotion,
asserting her emancipation. On another rock sat an old
woman in black – presumably the children's grandmother –
crocheting a little white table-mat, her grey hair tied in a bun
at the back of her head. She had removed her shoes and her
stockings, and every now and then she would look up and cry,
'*Niñaaaaa!* Don't splash water all over your brother. You'll
give him a stomach cramp!'

Here were three generations of women: mother, daughter,
granddaughter, each doing what she thought was right,
women whose names mattered as little to the world as that of
the unnamed woman in a divorce petition, the 'woman
unknown' of legal documents. And yet, because of the way

they were able to project their personal convictions in the new Spain of freedom, their existence and their example, if not their names, were for me a cause of celebration.

So the darkness shall be the light, and the stillness the
    dancing.

Apart from the failed attempt at a military coup on 23 February 1981, nothing perturbed the new Spain, or the popularity of the socialists, who won the elections in 1982 and stayed in power for fourteen years. Jimena was overjoyed, and like many people of her generation and background, has stood by her hero Felipe González, even when his party became bogged down with scandals and accusations of corruption. 'Felipe is clean! I can assure you,' she always says.

Like many people who lived through the Civil War and the terrible early days of the dictatorship, she believed that the only alternative to the socialists was another Franco. For fourteen years, this provided the bedrock of the socialists' unquestioning right to govern, despite blatant acts of dishonesty and greed that were being denounced by the media – the only real opposition to the government. But those fourteen years also supplied a long breathing space, a time when Spaniards could learn to think for themselves. With the election in 1996 of a right-of-centre democratic party, Spain has finally overcome its terror of losing its newly recovered liberties. The two Spains – for there will always be two Spains – can now exist together in a democratic state.

At the time of the wondrous events following the end of the dictatorship, the most noticeable changes in our little town were those related to the recovery of the Catalan language. Shops began to change their notices from Spanish into

Catalan – the reverse of what had happened at the end of the war. In 1939, following the victory of the Fascists, all shop-keepers in Catalonia hurriedly obeyed the order to delete all Catalan wording from their shop-fronts. My father-in-law once told me how one poor shopkeeper called Joan Raspall was so confused and frightened by the order that he thought it best to translate his surname as well as everything else. The word *raspall* is Catalan for 'brush', which in Spanish is *cepillo*. So he painted *Comestibles Juan Cepillo* – 'John Brush: Grocer' – over the old notice. But now people were changing only because they wanted to. *Papelería Montse* became *Papereria Montse*, *Panadería* changed to *Forn de Pa*, the *Carnicería* was the *Carnisseria*, and so on. Children's names changed as well. During the dictatorship no Spaniard had been able to be reg-istered under any name that was not in Spanish and did not figure in the calendar of saints' days. Now Catalan names became popular among the new generation – names like Dídac, Bernat, Jordi, Oriol, Laia or Joana, became fashion-able – just as among the immigrant population from the south of Spain Anglo-Saxon names proliferated: Jonathan, Vanessa, Gwendolyn, Pamela and even Sue Ellen (the TV series *Dallas* was an enormous hit) were now quite common in the infants' school.

Church and state formally separated. This meant that civil weddings were permitted once again. The divorce law, passed in July 1981 as a result of the new Spanish constitution, came too late for many – too late for Blanca, sitting in the home for the elderly, whose 1933 divorce and second marriage could now have been legalised; too late for many couples, who had separated and started a new relationship during the dictator-ship despite the social stigma that such a move brought with it – by now they had grown so used to their irregular situation that they could not be bothered to go through the upheaval of a divorce. In their pro-divorce campaign, the Socialist Party spoke of 300,000 marriages on the brink of breakdown, but in fact the number of cases filed in the first four years following the divorce law was much lower, more like 70,000, and mostly took place in large cities like Madrid and Barcelona. Even today the figures show that divorce is still not a socially acceptable move, despite the growing secularisation of Catholic Spain – perhaps in part because families are large and close-knit, and the older, more conservative generation still exerts a great influence on their children. Had I lived in England instead of Spain, my own divorce would probably have taken place earlier than it did. I, too, was influenced by the Spanish atmosphere and the tight network of extended families.

> . . . I think of you, in London, walking through that quiet park on the edge of the river, living in that ordered society that you speak of in your letter, and what I say must seem so remote . . . My wish for this coming year is that all the worries you harbour in your mind and in your heart may turn into strength, that the mist that for so long has covered your sky may lift, giving way to the brightness of day, and at night, to the maternal guidance of the full moon . . .

I think the mist began to lift with the end of an era that was outside me – but also inside me, without my knowing. It is something I did not understand at the time – that the end of that oppression was also the beginning of a new cycle within me, of a new understanding of myself.

As I put the letter back into my bag, the door of the hospital room is flung open and two orderlies wheel my mother back in from the operating theatre. It all happens very fast and their swift movements stir the air that has been so still. The nurse has come in behind the trolley and now she is settling my mother in her bed, arranging her pillows, fixing a drip into her arm, and giving me instructions, all at the same time.

'It all went very well,' she says, when I ask her, and then leaves the room.

The silence that follows radiates a new sense of peace.

XVI

Departure

The hospital room where my mother and I have been staying is one of a row of small rooms that open on to a spacious hall, furnished with black leather armchairs arranged in groups round glass coffee tables. We have packed our cases and are waiting in the hall for the nurse to bring my mother some eye drops and prescriptions. Then we will leave, as will most of the patients in this small section of the hospital, whose operations took place on the same day. Every now and then one of the doors opens a fraction and someone looks out – just for something to do, and says, '*Hola, ¿cómo estamos?*' just for something to say. We are all rather subdued this morning; each of us is thinking of our journey home and the return to our normal life. But last night this hall was as animated as a village square.

At six o'clock the head nurse had knocked on all the doors.

'Get dressed and follow me. The specialist will see you now and remove your bandages.'

Two hours later, back in the room, my mother was testing

her newly recovered eyesight, picking up newspapers and books, looking around the room, examining the frieze with the Egyptian figures behind her bed.

'I wonder how the others are,' she said.

We walked out into the hall to see if any of the people we knew were there, and saw Doña Carmen with her husband sitting in the leather armchairs. Next to her was Luisa, who was here looking after her niece. Don José was wrapped up in his brown satin dressing gown, his white and brown striped pyjamas buttoned right up to his neck.

'How are you?' asked Doña Carmen, the moment she saw my mother. 'Are the doctors happy with the results? Sit down, sit down,' she added, pointing to one of the armchairs.

'I've gained forty per cent vision,' replied my mother. 'How about your husband?'

'He's like a boy with new shoes,' said Doña Carmen. Then she turned to him and raised her voice: 'I said to this lady that you're as happy as a boy with new shoes, now that you can see again!'

Don José beamed. 'It's true,' he said. 'I never thought I would feel like this at eighty-eight. There were moments when I didn't think it was worth going through all this business, you know, having to come to Barcelona and have the operation, it's all such an upheaval at my age. We came by train from Valencia, you know. I don't really like flying, nor does my wife. ¿*Verdad, Carmen*? And the trains are tiresome too. But it's wonderful. I can't hear a thing, but I can see again. How shall I say it? It's like being reborn.'

A lively conversation began between people who, three days earlier, had been complete strangers to one another. The shared experience of hospital life had brought them together, at first tentatively, in timid smiles and salutations, while the fears of surgery still troubled their minds; but now shared risk had become shared relief; it had loosened their tongues and made them eager to talk. With the bandages, all barriers had come down. The conversation was easy – an unconstrained exchange of personal feelings, memories and opinions, which I could not imagine ever taking place in a British hospital. There was no hurry. Things were said and silences fell between sentences, more to savour what had been expressed than for lack of new words. As if the village square had suddenly become quiet, and we sat listening to the sound of running water that flowed from the fountain.

It emerged that Luisa came from the same village as Don José, a small town near Madrid, and when his wife had repeated this for him to hear, he became very excited.

'Ah, really? Do you remember the village school? Now, what was the name of the priest who ran the school? Don . . . Don . . . you know, he was tall and thin, and we boys were always making fun of him—'

Doña Carmen interrupted him: 'José, can't you see this lady is far too young to have been even alive when you were a schoolboy?'

'Yes, of course, of course. I keep forgetting how old I am! You must excuse me. But I wish I could remember his name. Of course, later, during the Republic, they changed the school. There was a lady teacher then, I think she came from Valencia. But you are also too young to remember those days . . . By then I was studying chemistry in Madrid, where I lived with an aunt – one of my father's sisters – a real miser.'

Don José was silent for a moment and smiled. 'She was always "making economies", as she put it, by adding water to the soup. And my poor mother was always sending me parcels of food and woollen jumpers to keep me warm through the winter . . .'

'Mothers! What do you expect?'

Doña Carmen speaks with that beautiful clear accent of her native Madrid. She wears a silver chain round her neck, with a large collection of medals.

Last night, at the gathering, she was showing them to the lady from her husband's village. 'Look, here is St Rita, and this is Our Lady of Guadalupe – my mother was born in Cáceres and had great devotion for this Virgin. My own personal favourite is this one, see? Our Lady of Almudena, patroness of Madrid. I always pray to her. If I'd had a daughter I would have called her Almudena. The other day, when I was getting ready to leave I thought to myself, Which one shall I wear to help José with his operation? And as I couldn't make up my mind, I decided to wear them all.'

'What about St Lucia? You should have her round your neck too,' I said.

Doña Carmen smiled triumphantly and fingered through her medals until she found St Lucia holding the salver with two eyes. 'Here she is, see? How could I forget her? Patron saint of dressmakers, protector of eyesight!'

'Oh, I can do even better than that,' said Àngela. Àngela had wandered over from another corner of the sitting room to join the group, and was now sitting next to Doña Carmen, with her crochet work. She had come to the hospital to look after her granddaughter, a teenager with dark curly hair who wandered around in white silk pyjamas, listening to her Walkman. 'You see,' she explained, 'God is my son-in-law, so I have a lot of influence up there.' She paused to enjoy the effect the words had caused on her audience and added, 'My daughter is married to him!'

'Ah,' said Luisa. 'You mean she's a nun!'

Àngela must be in her mid-sixties, tall, with hair tinted a reddish brown. She smiled and looked at us defiantly, her manicured hands busy again with her crochet, knowing that the mother of a nun should be more discreet, especially when talking in the presence of someone as devout as Doña Carmen. But Doña Carmen was as amused as everyone else, and we all relaxed.

'Where is she?' she asked.

'In Angola. She's been there for four years now . . .' Àngela shook her head slowly as she spoke. 'She's a doctor, too. She works as a doctor in the mission.'

'How long has she been a nun?' asked Luisa.

'About seven years, I suppose. She took her vows a few months after she finished her medical studies. I was hoping, when she started studying medicine, that she would meet someone, that perhaps she would fall in love with a medical student – or that something else would make her change her mind. But her mind was made up . . .' She shook her head again and sighed. 'What I think is that the nuns turned her head. They brainwashed her, you know? She's my only daughter, and this has cost me many tears, may God forgive.' She tugged at her white skein and continued making neat little loops with her crochet hook, linking one to the other, one to the next, as she went on with her story.

'We lived in a village in the mountains near Tarragona, and moved to the capital when my daughter was ten or so. She was my last child, the only girl after a string of boys, and when we moved to Tarragona we sent her to the convent school of St Teresa. We wanted to give her a good education, and I remember having to persuade my husband to send her there – he didn't want her to go. He wasn't much in favour of nuns and priests – the war, you know – I wish I'd listened to him. I remember that one afternoon, soon after she had started there, when I was waiting in the hall with all the other mothers for the girls to come out of their classrooms, the Mother Superior suddenly walked in and asked to speak to me. I couldn't imagine what my daughter had done, and thought, How strange, as I followed her into the office. And then she started telling me what a good girl my daughter was, what a wonderful student, what a joy to have in the school. I didn't like the sound of all that, somehow, I felt something was wrong; and later my suspicions turned out to be correct, because one of the nuns started writing to her during the holidays, and she would never come with us to the beach – she just never seemed to want to enjoy herself.'

She stopped speaking for a few moments and went back to her crochet, but nobody said anything. We all knew this was only a pause.

Then she continued, 'I kept on asking her, "What's the matter? Something is the matter, you're acting strangely." But she only answered, "*Nada*, Mamá, nothing is wrong." When the term started I asked to speak to the Mother Superior myself. *I* knew what the matter was, it was pretty clear to me. I said, "Listen, I know what's going on, and you may mean well. But she's been in a village all her life, we've only just moved here, what can she know about becoming a nun, about vocation? She's only twelve years old!" It made me very sad, my only daughter – the others are all boys. When she finished school and went to university to study medicine she had already committed herself to the order.

'First they sent her off to Portugal for a year, to learn Portuguese; there she worked in a hospital for drug addicts and people with Aids. After that she went to Angola. She loves it there, but I miss her a lot. I only see her once every two years, when she comes over for a medical check-up . . . *Resignación*, that's all there is for it.'

'I'll pray for her,' said Doña Carmen.

*

Now that my mother and I are about to leave these people, the circle will close. But I know we will both remember them – Carmen and José, Àngela, Luisa, and the young couple from Seville, María and Juan; Juan lost the sight of one eye through medical negligence in Seville, but has now regained full vision in the other eye and is hoping to go back to his job – he hates sitting around at home while his wife is out at work all day; and, of course, we'll always remember Agustí, the ten-year-old boy who was born with severe brain damage and cannot speak, or walk, or see, and is the focus of everyone's attention. Everyone fusses over him – nurses, patients, doctors. His beautiful mother pushes him up and down the corridor in his large push-chair to keep him quiet, to keep him from moaning. It seems that she had three miscarriages and then had Agustí, who is her only child and now is having his third eye operation. We hear the nurses saying, '*Hola*, Agustí!' as they pass him in the corridor. I remember that booklet given to me by the village priest when I married Ramon, and the paragraph about miscarriages: 'If you should have the great misfortune to miscarry a child, you must examine your conscience with great care . . .' I hope she is free of those cruel threats.

My mother and I have parted in Barcelona airport. She is flying back to the island with my youngest brother Tomás, who has travelled over this afternoon from Majorca, where he lives, to accompany her on the journey home. And I am flying back to Heathrow, to my other island. On the plane a young Spaniard sits next to me. We start talking. He tells me he comes from León but has lived in Catalonia for five years now, working as a waiter in a hotel on the Costa Brava. He is going to London to brush up his English. His name is Virgilio.

When I tell him he's the first Virgil I've ever met, he explains that all his family have rather unusual names. 'You see, my grandfather was *un idealista*,' he says, 'an idealist Republican general, and he gave unusual names to his children. One of my uncles was called Napoleón, another Sócrates, and my father was called Virgilio. So I was called after him. At the end of the war he left Spain – he would have been shot if he'd stayed. My grandmother was left behind with all his children and never saw him again.'

'Surely those names would not have been allowed after the war. Everyone had to be given the name of a Catholic saint. How did your grandmother manage to keep them?'

'Well, I don't know. Maybe they had some other name on their official papers, but that's what everyone called them. With my name there wasn't a problem, because there is a St Virgil.'

'Oh, really?'

'Yes, I think he was a French bishop or something. I celebrate my *santo* on March the fifth.'

'Mine is on December the thirteenth.'

'Ah, Santa Lucía. I had an aunt called Lucía. So, are you Spanish or English?'

'A bit of both, I think. I used to live in Barcelona. I was married to a Catalan for twenty-six years. But now I live in London.'

'Oh . . . so now . . . But I'm asking you too many questions. I don't mean to be impolite.'

'Oh, no, don't worry. Yes, my husband and I divorced a few years ago and I have started a new life. Life is full of beginnings and ends. One cycle ends and another begins. Don't you agree?'

'Yes. And you have to take life as it comes and make the most of it, that's my philosophy.'

I look out of the window and say farewell to Barcelona; to the hills south of the city where I spent twenty years, raising my children, translating, living but not living, battling against a feeling of emptiness and futility – but no, that was before. I no longer see those years as futile or empty. I have recovered them now, together with all the happiness they also held, moments that made them worthwhile and good. Now we are crossing the Pyrenees, mysterious and white in the evening light, with their deep green valleys that form corridors between Spain and France. It all looks so peaceful down there, unperturbed by the tragic events that have marked its history: the mass exile of Republicans at the end of the Spanish Civil War, the exile of Jews in the summer of 1492, trudging through the dusty roads to an unknown destiny, and further back in time, the destruction in 1244 of the heroic Cathars who were holding out in the mountain stronghold of Montsegur. This part of the world was the cradle of courtly love, of chivalry and troubadours, the meeting-point of Arab, Jewish and Christian ideas that turned the history of European thought. And the cradle of Catalonia.

Not far from Montsegur, on the French side of the Pyrenean foothills, lives my ex-husband's uncle, who makes gravestones for the local cemetery. The youngest of the family, he left Spain in the fifties in search of a job and settled in France where he worked as a builder and also became a skilled stonecutter. Once, when we were visiting, he showed us round the cemetery and pointed out all the marble figures and stones he had made. It was a tiny graveyard, in the outskirts of a small village, with fields of vineyards swooping down into the valley below. The vines were a soft midsummer green, beautiful to gaze upon. Here and there a withered bouquet, its lilac ribbon still full of colour, and photographs in round frames, and *Chère Maman* written in gold or silver on a few stones. He stopped by a large slab of marble, flanked by two praying angels. It had his family name on it: 'This is the best house I have ever built. There's room for you here, if you like. You're one of the family.'

It is getting dark. All I see now is the little light on the wing of the Boeing. My mother will be home by now, the dogs barking their heads off with excitement as she walks up the drive to the house of my childhood, where she still lives since my father's death, with the books and the garden and the view of sunsets in the sea. And Doña Carmen and Don José will be back in Valencia, perhaps being greeted by the *portero* at this very moment with '*Hombre*, Don José, good to see you back again!', and Juan and his wife are on the night train to Seville, and Àngela is driving back to Tarragona with her son and daughter-in-law who have come to fetch the teenager with the Walkman. Àngela will be looking out of the car window and thinking about her daughter in Angola, and the dangers of the mission, and the fact that she will never have any grandchildren she can feel really close to. And Agustí . . . he will be leaning on his mother's bosom . . . and thinking who knows what beautiful thoughts.

From the cab window I now see the tidy rows of English houses with their inner lives showing through net curtains. In one there is a red lamp on a table and a man talking to a boy. In another the only light is the light of a television screen. I cross Kew Bridge. The Thames looks both serene and powerful, and I think of Jorge Manrique's famous lines, and of the times you and I discussed them in tutorials when we first met, before life took us in different directions:

Nuestras vidas son los ríos
que van a dar en el mar

Our lives are the rivers
that end in the sea

But soon I will be home, and then I will tell you, my dearest,
of the long journey I have made.